# Criminal Appeals

Scottish Criminal Law and Practice Series

*Series Editor*

The Rt Hon The Lord McCluskey

# Criminal Appeals

**Lord McCluskey**, Senator of the College of Justice

Edinburgh
Butterworths
1992

| | |
|---|---|
| United Kingdom | Butterworth & Co (Publishers) Ltd, 4 Hill Street, EDINBURGH EH2 3LZ and 88 Kingsway, LONDON WC2B 6AB |
| Australia | Butterworths Pty Ltd, SYDNEY, MELBOURNE, BRISBANE, ADELAIDE, PERTH, CANBERRA and HOBART |
| Belgium | Butterworth & Co (Publishers) Ltd, BRUSSELS |
| Canada | Butterworths Canada Ltd, TORONTO and VANCOUVER |
| Ireland | Butterworth (Ireland) Ltd, DUBLIN |
| Malaysia | Malayan Law Journal Sdn Bhd, KUALA LUMPUR |
| New Zealand | Butterworths of New Zealand Ltd, WELLINGTON and AUCKLAND |
| Puerto Rico | Equity de Puerto Rico, Inc, HATO REY |
| Singapore | Butterworth & Co (Asia) Pte Ltd, SINGAPORE |
| USA | Butterworth Legal Publishers, ST PAUL, Minnesota, SEATTLE, Washington, BOSTON, Massachusetts; AUSTIN, Texas and D & S Publishers, CLEARWATER, Florida |



A CIP Catalogue record for this book is available from the British Library.

ISBN 0 406 12135 4

Typeset by Kerrypress Ltd, Luton
Printed and bound by Thomson Litho Ltd, East Kilbride, Scotland

'An appellate court is a group of people who, in the cool of the evening, undo what a better man did in the heat of the day'.

Ian Richard Scott
*Barber Professor of Law*
*The University of Birmingham*

# Preface

This book is intended to be used by practitioners at all levels. No one practising in the courts, in whatever capacity, needs to know — still less to remember — all the details of procedure. What is needed is a manual of practice giving swift access to the necessary details or pointing to where they may be found. Accordingly a book such as this partakes of the character of a railway timetable rather than that of a collection of essays. It is meant to be used to find ways and means, forms, styles, timetables and techniques for taking an appeal and carrying it through. As rapid access to the information is essential, a 'how to' book of this kind needs a usable index, and the author, even at the risk of repetition, has sought to construct one which should enable the necessary information to be found by anyone who has a passable knowledge of the vocabulary and jargon of criminal procedure. But, even for whose come fresh to this branch of practice or are returning after a long absence, the book seeks to explain as well as to tabulate; and where possible, especially in chapters 1 (Introduction), 5 (*Nobile Officium*, European Questions, Fundamental Nullity etc), 7 (Miscarriage of Justice and Grounds of Appeal), the author has tried to use language which is not impenetrably technical. At some points in the text, and also by providing some styles, assistance is offered to help the practitioner draft or prepare whatever appeal documents the circumstances may require.

The book could not have been written about the unstinting help of others. No fewer than five of the current Depute Clerks, Alan Hogg, Norman Dowie, Tom Cruickshank, Bob Sinclair and Tom Thomson suggested and later revised material for chapters 2, 3 and 5. Ian Dean, CB, formerly the Crown Agent and Bill Howard, ISO, sometime Deputy Principal Clerk of Justiciary, helped with chapter 4. My own knowledge of the criminal legal aid system was minimal, but Sheriff Charles N Stoddart, LLB, LLM, PhD, SSC, who knows exactly how it works, kindly wrote the whole of chapter 8. My colleagues Lord Morton of Shuna and Lord MacLean read some parts of the text where I was straying from the known facts and speculating about the law. The doyen of criminal law authors, Sheriff

Gordon, QC, LLD, was generous enough to read and comment upon part of the text concerning references to the European Court. Indeed so generous was all the help given that I was tempted to depart from the author's customary acceptance of responsibility for mistakes and to say, If you find any errors, don't blame me, blame them. But that would be churlish and ungrateful. All remaining errors are mine; fortunately, with such help, I have been spared many more. I should be grateful to anyone who drew my attention to any remaining errors or suggested how the index could be improved.

Mrs Marlene Olsen, working in her own time, converted my appalling manuscript into a convincingly presented text; and my wife, Ruth, patiently read it to help ensure that even the non-lawyer could understand most of it. I am immensely grateful to them, and to my publishers Butterworths whose assistance was invaluable.

When he heard I was writing this book, Professor Ian Scott volunteered the dictum attributed to him; it is perhaps a trifle cynical, but then he is an Australian.

The law is stated as at 1 May 1992.

# Contents

# Table of statutes

# Table of Cases

# 1. Introduction

## 1.01 How to use this book

This book is intended to be of use to practitioners at all levels in the criminal courts. It is designed to provide answers to the principal questions the practitioner has to ask when preparting a criminal appeal:

(1) Is there a right to appeal at this stage?
(2) What is the first step to be taken?
(3) Is there a style or form I should use?
(4) What should I be saying in the form?
(5) What other documents do I have to submit?
(6) To whom do I send the completed appeal documents?
(7) When am I supposed to take the next step?
(8) What is the next step?
(9) How can I seek relief for procedural errors and omissions?
(10) How and when can legal aid be obtained?
(11) What about bail?
(12) Can the penalties be suspended meantime?

The answers to these and most other questions are to be found in the legislation: the problem in practice is to find the quickest way to the governing enactment, and then to understand it and operate it. So this book aims to make the statutory provisions more swiftly accessible and, both by illustrating how they have been applied in reported cases, and, where necessary, by rephrasing them, to help make them more readily understood. As no practitioner acts for the accused and the prosecutor at the same time, the ordinary appeal procedures for accused and convicted persons (chapters 2 and 3) are kept separate from those used by the Crown (chapter 4). The special procedures dealt with in chapter 5 (*nobile officium* petitions, References to Europe, References by the Secretary of State and fundamental nullity) are of interest to both sides, as are powers of the court (chapter 6). Chapter 6 also discusses additional evidence separately because it is a fairly new, special and distinct ground of appeal for convicted persons. The whole basis of appeals after conviction (or acquittal) is miscarriage of justice. This developing concept is sufficiently important to merit fuller consideration (in chapter 7) along with a discussion of the related topic of grounds of appeal. Chapter 8 (legal aid) is essentially a 'how to' chapter. Chapter 9 (bail appeals and interim relief) seeks to explain how accused clients can be assisted to avoid being incarcerated or disqualified while the case - including the appeal - is still live. The appendix contains styles for use in certain appeals whose form is not prescribed by statute. The author's hope is that much of chapters 5, 6, and 7 may be read in full, and the rest of the book consulted in much the same way that a railway timetable is consulted. Chapter 1, however, is there to assist the beginner, the student, or the practitioner who has not practised in this field for some years.

Each paragraph in the book has been given a separate heading; but the heading is not designed to be a precis of the paragraph itself. It is there merely to help the busy practitioner to find his way quickly to the text he seeks. Information is sometimes repeated and is sometimes referred to as being in another paragraph; this is done in order to ease the practitioner's access to what he needs to know.

Finally, it is hoped that those who have to draft grounds of appeal, stated cases (and especially the questions therein), judges' reports and any other such material intended to place the issues clearly before the appeal court will find, throughout the book, examples of how it has been successfully done in the reported cases.

## 1.02 Courts of first instance

Proceedings in a court may be proceedings at first instance or proceedings on appeal. Criminal proceedings at first instance may be described broadly as those proceedings which are brought by a prosecutor against an accused person in order to place that person before a trial court on a criminal charge or charges, including any proceedings incidental thereto. The steps taken at first instance may include incidental steps such as obtaining warrants to detain persons in custody, or to search premises, vessels or persons to obtain material which might be presented as evidence. The prosecutor may obtain a warrant to cite witnesses for precognition even if no person has been charged: cf the Criminal Procedure (Scotland) Act 1975 (c 21), s 315(3), as amended (referred to as 'the 1975 Act'). In ordinary procedure the steps taken will include formal steps such as the serving upon the accused person, usually in a tightly prescribed format and within a statutorily regulated timetable, of a formal intimation and statement of the criminal offences which he is alleged to have committed, often accompanied by other incidental information as to the intended place and time for trial and notices as to penalties or previous convictions; in some instances there may also be served notice of the witnesses who may be adduced for the prosecution and of productions that may be referred to in evidence. If the criminal proceedings are not abandoned they will normally lead to a trial (at a 'trial diet') before a court which determines all questions of fact and law and pronounces a verdict of guilt or an acquittal. The defence has rights both at common law and under statute to take certain incidental steps in proceedings at first instance, eg to challenge the relevancy or competency of the indictment, complaint or proceedings: see also the Criminal Justice (Scotland) Act 1980, s 9 (citation of defence witnesses for precognition). In some cases the court of first instance may end the proceedings, in whole or in part, before evidence of fact is adduced, by holding as a matter of law that the case, or part of it, should not proceed further. In relation to a limited number of relatively incidental matters the court of first instance has a right to review, that is to say, to reconsider, its own decisions (eg on bail; s 30(2) of the 1975 Act), but such reconsideration is not an appeal properly so called.

The courts of first instance are the district courts, the sheriff court and the High Court of Justiciary. The district courts exercise summary jurisdiction within district or island areas created by the Local Government (Scotland) Act 1973. They consist of one stipendiary magistrate or of one or more justices,[1] and each such court has a legally-qualified clerk/assessor.[2] They exercise an original but fairly limited jurisdiction. In the sheriff court, the sheriff, or sheriff principal, sits alone to exercise summary criminal jurisdiction at first instance. Accordingly criminal summary jurisdiction at first instance is that exercised by a judge, a justice or justices, sitting without a jury, whether in the district court or in the sheriff court, in proceedings instituted by summary complaint. Solemn jurisdiction at first instance is exercised by a judge alone in the preliminary stages and by a judge and jury at the final, or trial, stage, such proceedings being raised by petition. The sheriff, or sheriff principal, exercises solemn jurisdiction at first instance. The High Court of Justiciary also exercises solemn jurisdiction at first instance when a Lord Commissioner of Justiciary in Scotland[3] sits with a jury for a trial (there may be a trial with two or more judges presiding), or, before the trial, deals with preliminary matters. Any judge exercising solemn jurisdiction sits without a jury in order to determine preliminary matters under the preliminary diet procedure[4] or to consider European questions.[5] Furthermore, a jury which has delivered a verdict after trial is *functus* in relation to any charges determined by the verdict once the verdict has been recorded in the minute of proceedings. Accordingly the trial judge in dealing with sentence is effectively, and sometimes actually, sitting without a jury.

1 District Courts (Scotland) Act 1975.
2 Ibid, s 7.
3 s 113(1).
4 See para 2.03 *et seq.*
5 See para 5.10 *et seq.*

## 1.03 The appeal court

Almost all decisions made by a court of first instance can be brought under review in the High Court of Justiciary, sitting as an appeal court. There is no appeal to the Court of Session in criminal matters: *Reynolds v Christie.*[1] There is no appeal to the House of Lords in criminal matters. Accordingly, in criminal appeal procedure in Scotland all appeals from courts of first instance are taken to the High Court of Justiciary, and there is no further appeal from the High Court of Justiciary sitting as an appeal court. Exceptions to the general rule that decisions are appealable include the provision that there is no appeal against a sentence fixed by law;[2] and certain decisions may not be immediately appealable, for example a refusal of bail at an early stage,[3] or decisions as to admissibility of evidence in the course of trial. Other examples are considered in their context. Some appeals may proceed only if leave is granted. The right of the Crown to appeal is much more limited than that of an accused or convicted person and may have to be exercised differently. However, in almost all instances where an appeal is competent, both the time for taking an appeal and the method of appealing are strictly regulated by statute, by Act of Adjournal or by law and practice; and the right to appeal, or the right to advance a particular ground of appeal, may be lost if the prescribed procedural steps are not taken properly and timeously. If the right to appeal or the procedure for appealing are not expressly regulated by law, or some extraordinary circumstance has arisen in which the interests of justice appear to warrant a review, it may be possible to petition the High Court of Justiciary to exercise its *nobile officium* to bring proceedings under review.[4]

The main purpose of this book is to describe the various methods of appeal and the relevant rules, including rules as to the time for taking certain necessary steps, governing appeal procedure. As is noted elsewhere in the text, where the procedure is prescribed by statute, including by Act of Adjournal,[5] it is always necessary to consult the relevant statutory provisions, not just as originally enacted but in their current form after any amendment. The statutes are readily accessible, though problems are sometimes caused by the insertion of Scottish provisions into UK, or even what are truly English, Acts of Parliament. It is unlikely that rules governing appeal procedure would be altered by Parliament in such a way but there can be, and there sometimes are, indirect effects resulting from UK-wide legislation, particularly, for example, that affecting road traffic or trafficking in drugs scheduled in the Misuse of Drugs Act 1971 (c 38).

1 1988 SLT 68, OH.
2 s 228(1), proviso.
3 ss 26(3) and 27.
4 See 5.01 *et seq* below.
5 See 1.05.
6 Cf 1.04 and 1.05 below.

## 1.04 Private prosecutions

The overwhelming majority of prosecutions are public prosecutions;[1] but private prosecutions are competent. A complaint at the instance of a private prosecutor for an offence at common law, or for a statutory offence where imprisonment without the option of a fine is competent, requires the concurrence of the public prosecutor of the court in which the complaint is brought, unless some relevant statutory provision renders such concurrence unnecessary.[2] Private prosecutions, though rare, do occur. A private citizen has the right to apply to the High Court for criminal letters authorising a private prosecution on indictment in the High Court: *X v Sweeney*.[3] The private prosecutor has effectively the same role in the appeal process as the public prosecutor: cf for example, *Sweeney v X*,[4] the appeal following the prosecution authorised by the grant of criminal letters in *X v Sweeney* above. Not all statutory procedures and forms expressly recognise the possibility that the prosecutor may not be the Crown[5] but most do, and the appeal forms can be adapted easily, if necessary.[6]

1 Cf *Renton and Brown*, chapter 4.
2 s 311(4): see generally *Renton and Brown* paras 13–19 *et seq*, and 4.04 to 4.06 below.
3 1982 SCCR 161.
4 1982 SCCR 509.
5 Cf. Act of Adjournal (Consolidation) 1988, SI 1988/110, r 68.
6 Cf ibid, r 127, Forms 70–76.

## 1.05 Legislation governing appeal procedure

Scots practitioners in the 1990s are extremely fortunate in that in 1975 virtually all the legislation governing appeal procedure was consolidated in the Criminal Procedure (Scotland) Act 1975. The subsequent legislation, although effecting very substantial alterations to the law and procedure, has employed the technique of amending the 1975 Act by alteration, addition, repeal or wholesale substitution. Thus almost everything that matters in the way of primary legislation regulating appeal procedure is now to be found within the four corners of an updated copy of the 1975 Act. Such may be found in the most up-to-date releases of the Parliament House Book [Division E], and, from time to time, the Stationery Office publishes an updated copy of the Act as amended, in *Statutes in Force*. In the present book, the Criminal Procedure (Scotland) Act 1975, as amended by any legislation since 1975, is referred to simply as 'the 1975 Act'; and, because that is virtually the only statute that matters in this field, it has been decided in most instances, unless the context renders it desirable to do otherwise, to refer simply to section N (or to s N, in footnotes) without the need to repeat that the reference is to a section of the 1975 Act. Any other statutes are referred to as fully as is necessary.

Finally, it has not been thought necessary to repeat in this text the lengthy footnotes that explain when and how any section in the 1975 Act came to be amended. Thus, for example, some texts[1] will give the full reference, namely 'section 102(1) of the Criminal Procedure (Scotland) Act 1975, as substituted by s 16 of the Criminal Justice (Scotland) Act 1980'. In the present work the reference would simply be to 'section 102(1)' or, in a footnote, to 's 102(1)'. Similarly, instead of setting forth the full historical description of a section, eg section 179(1), as in *HM Advocate v Clegg*[2] viz. 'Section 179(1) of the Criminal Procedure (Scotland) Act 1975, as amended by s 5(a) of the Bail etc (Scotland) Act 1980 and para 36 of Sch 7 to the Criminal Justice (Scotland) Act 1980', the present work uses the more modest description, 'section 179(1)'.

There are times when it is essential or at least desirable to check the legislative history of a particular provision, especially, for example, if a nice point of interpretation arises or if the decision in an earlier reported case may have turned upon the previous wording. When it is necessary to study the history (or even the archaeology) of the provision in force the practitioner should go to the *Chronological Table of the Statutes*, Part II (1951–1989) (published annually by HMSO) where that information is recorded to within a year or two of the present. So far as criminal appeal procedure is concerned, the principal reforming statute was the Criminal Justice (Scotland) Act 1980 (c 62) which effected the reforms by amendments of and additions to the 1975 Act.[3] The history of the 1980 Act is given by Sheriff Gordon in the introduction to *The Criminal Justice (Scotland) Act 1980*.[4] This essay and the third report of the Thomson Committee, Cmnd 7005 (December 1977), provide a complete guide to the reforms in criminal appeal procedure up to 1980.

Other minor alterations bearing upon criminal appeal procedure in the 1975 Act have been effected by the following statutes: Bail etc (Scotland) Act 1980 (c 4); Mental Health (Amendment) (Scotland) Act 1983 (c 39); Law Reform (Miscellaneous Provisions) (Scotland) Act 1985 (c 73); Telecommunications Act 1984 (c 12); Criminal Justice (Scotland) Act 1987 (c 41); Consumer Protection Act 1987 (c 43); Road Traffic Offenders Act 1988 (c 53); Extradition Act 1989 (c 33); Law Reform (Miscellaneous Provisions (Scotland) Act 1990 (c 40). The effects of these statutes are where necessary noted in the text but, in general, they effect changes to the text of the 1975 Act. Section 4 of the Criminal Appeal (Scotland) Act 1926 (c 15) has been amended but not repealed. It empowers the court (ie the High Court of Justiciary) to extend the time within which notice of appeal or of application for leave to appeal may be given. It also contains provisions anent appeals against sentence of death (still competent for treason and certain types of piracy, but not under the 1975 Act; cf s 220), and postponement of execution of such a sentence. A few other parts of the pre-1975 legislation survive but have no significant bearing upon appeal procedure. They are best found in the *Parliament House Book*.

1 *McKnight v HM Advocate* 1991 SCCR 751.
2 1990 SCCR 293.
3 Cf ss 12 and 33–37 of the 1980 Act and Schs 2, 3 and 4 to that Act.
4 G H Gordon, W Green & Son Ltd, 1981.

## 1.06 Acts of Adjournal

The High Court may by Act of Adjournal regulate the practice and procedure of the courts in relation to solemn criminal procedure under any enactment by virtue of section 282 of the 1975 Act. Section 282(2) also empowers the High Court by Act of Adjournal to modify, amend or repel any enactment, including any enactment contained in Part I of the 1975 Act itself in so far as that enactment relates to matters with respect to which an Act of Adjournal may be made under section 282(1).[1] Similar powers in respect of summary criminal jurisdiction and procedure are conferred on the High Court by section 457. Clearly, having regard to the limits placed upon the High Court's power by sections 282(2) and 457(d), an Act of Adjournal may be *ultra vires*.[2] Today's practitioner is fortunate because the Act of Adjournal (Consolidation) 1988[3] of 21 January 1988 revoked all the previous Acts of Adjournal having effect in this branch of the law.[4] Acts of Adjournal enacted since then have amended the Act of Adjournal (Consolidation) 1988. The amendments are incorporated in the *Parliament House Book* text of the Act of Adjournal [Division E].[5] New amending Acts of Adjournal are well publicised in the Parliament House Book itself, in the Scots Law Times, and in the Journal of the Law Society of Scotland; they are also printed in the final volume of each year's Scottish Current Law Statutes. The Acts of Adjournal enacted in 1991 are:

Act of Adjournal (Consolidation Amendment) (Extradition Rules and Backing of Irish Warrants) 1991 (SI 1991/19).

Act of Adjournal (Consolidation Amendment No 1) 1991 (SI 1991/847).

Act of Adjournal (Consolidation Amendment No 2) (Evidence of Children) 1991 (SI 1991/1916).

Act of Adjournal (Consolidation Amendment No 3) 1991 (SI 1991/2676.)

Act of Adjournal (Consolidation Amendment No 4) (Supervised Attendance Orders) 1991 (SI 1991/2677)

Only the No 3 Consolidation Amendment bears directly upon appeals. *Inter alia* it empowers solicitors who do not practise in Edinburgh to carry on the duties of a solicitor in relation to an appeal in summary proceedings. High Court of Justiciary practice notes are occasionally issued and may be found in the same periodicals as well as in Division E of the *Parliament House Book*. The numbered forms referred to in this book are those contained in Schedule 1 to the Act of Adjournal (Consolidation) 1988, as amended.

1 Cf also the Criminal Justice (Scotland) Act 1980, s 65.
2 Cf *Wither v Cowie*; *Wither v Wood* 1990 SCCR 741 at 754A/B.
3 SI 1988/110.
4 Schedule 2.
5 At the date of going to press the PHB is updated to 1 November 1991.

## 1.07 Reports of cases

As noted earlier, the Criminal Justice (Scotland) Act 1980 reformed almost completely the existing law and practice of criminal procedure in Scotland. Almost coinciding with the coming into force of the various provisions of that Act[1] the Law Society of Scotland began to publish the excellent *Scottish Criminal Case Reports*, edited by Sheriff Gerald H Gordon, QC, LLD. These reports are an indispensable tool for the serious practitioner. They are published within a few weeks of the judgments reported and contain full background material, and critical, informative commentary. A supplement for 1950 to 1980 of cases decided by the High Court but not reported is also published in the SCCR series; and the separately published *SCCR 1981–90 Index* includes cases reported in the supplement and also in Justiciary Cases and Scots Law Times. In this book it has been decided to give in the text the reference to SCCR in respect of any case reported there. If the case is reported elsewhere, and many are not, the reference to the other reports can be obtained from the table of cases at the front of the book. In the oral hearing in the appeal court, the court expects to be referred to the report in Justiciary Cases, if there is one. References to pre-1981 cases are seldom necessary on points of procedure because of the comprehensiveness of the 1980 reforms of the law relating to criminal appeals. Some of the pre-1980 cases, however, relate to forms of procedure (suspension, advocation, petitions to *nobile officium*) which pre-date the recent legislative reforms. Others relating to fundamental nullity are commonly referred to.

1 On various dates in 1981.

## 1.08 The role of advocacy in appeals

The principal aim of the advocate is to persuade the judge to see the issue from the perspective which is most favourable to the client. As Dr Johnson put it, 'A lawyer is to do for his client all that his client might fairly do for himself if he could'; adding – in support of the view that the advocate should advance any argument that may succeed, even if he himself would not necessarily be persuaded by it – 'An argument which does not convince yourself may convince the judge to whom you urge it; and if it does convince him, why, then ... you are wrong and he is right ...'.[1] It is clear, and is now widely understood, that a significant proportion of the cases that come before appeal courts raise issues that could be resolved either way. Judges make law: Lord Reid said, 'The jurist may ask what I mean by law ... the practical answer is that the law is what the judge says it is .... There was a time when it was thought almost indecent to suggest that judges make law – they only declare it ... But we do not believe in fairy tales any more'.[2] In the second Reith Lecture,[3] the present author gave many examples to illustrate how evenly balanced the arguments could be.[4] In 'The Law Lords'[5]

Alan Paterson quotes the opinions of many senior judges as to the proportion of appeals in the House of Lords that could be decided either way: their estimates range from 10 per cent to 'almost every case'. No one would estimate that so many of the cases heard on appeal by the High Court of Justiciary were evenly balanced. But some are; and the court can be persuaded to change its collective mind. We need go no further back than *Morrison v HM Advocate*[6] and *Leggate v HM Advocate*[7] in both of which benches of seven judges unanimously overruled unanimous decisions by benches of five judges pronounced within the preceding three years. In *Ross v HM Advocate*[8] a bench of five judges overruled (at least in part) a decision which for nearly thirty years had effectively excluded the defence that an accused who at the material time was acting under the influence of drugs, administered to him without his knowledge, lacked the necessary *mens rea*. The truth is that judicial perspectives do change. Experience and reflection and different sets of circumstances cast new light onto old problems and traditional solutions. Advocacy in the appeal court is the act of persuading the court by the skilful presentation of relevant principle and precedent, to adopt a favourable perspective on the case before it and, if necessary, to change its collective mind and alter the law.

1 Quoted by Alan Paterson, 'The Law Lords' from Boswell: *A Journal of a Tour of the Hebrides*.
2 The Judge as Law Maker, 12 Journal of the Society of Public Teachers of Law (1972) p 22.
3 'The Clanking of Medieval Chains'.
4 Cf 'Law, Justice and Domocracy' by Lord McCluskey, Sweet and Maxwell, BBC Books, 1987.
5 Chapter 8.
6 1990 SCCR 235.
7 1988 SCCR 391.
8 1991 SCCR 823.

## 1.09 Advocacy and preparation

It is bordering on tautology to speak of advocacy *and* preparation. Good advocacy is nine-tenths preparation. In our tradition the basis of the oral debate that takes place in court is trust. The court trusts the advocates appearing before it to have prepared thoroughly and to present the fruits of their labours ethically. The court of criminal appeal invariably consists of three experienced judges and they face a formidably large calendar of cases on most days when the appeal court sits. They depend to a very high degree upon the quality of the advocacy of those who appear before them. In his memorandum to HM Government commenting upon Government proposals to extend rights of audience in the higher courts, the then Lord Justice General, Lord Emslie, stated, 'I cannot emphasise too strongly in particular the very great extent to which, in the adversarial systems of the so-called common law countries, the higher courts are dependent upon the quality of professional performance exhibited by those who practise before them'. Speaking in the House of Lords debate on the second reading of the Law Reform (Miscellaneous Provisions) (Scotland) Bill 1989 (enacted with amendments in 1990) he said:[1]

> 'The strength of any court is not merely a reflection of the quality of its judges. It is, to a very significant extent, also a reflection of the quality of those who plead before it. The Court of Session in particular – I can speak of that from long experience – is heavily dependent on the quality of its advocates and furthermore upon the mutual respect which exists between Bench and Bar and in the relationships of advocates to each other, relationships which involve a high degree of trust.
>
> Of course, I do not suggest for one moment – and only a fool would – that all advocates measure up to the exacting standards required of them by the Court of Session and the High Court. . .. However, the great majority, by their training, discipline and full-time devotion to the art of advocacy contrive to display a high standard of professional skill, competence and integrity; and (dare I say it?) the best can stand favourable comparison with the outstanding advocates in the common law jurisdiction'.

These observations point to the qualities that an advocate (whether a member of the Faculty of Advocates or not) in the High Court should try to display. Above all, he must prepare his case thoroughly. That involves mastering the facts of the case and its procedural history. It is of the utmost importance that the advocate has a good knowledge of criminal procedure. A vital part of the process of preparation, however, is the selection of those arguments which are stateable and the discarding of those which are not. The whole balance of an appeal submission can be destroyed by the inclusion in it of an unstateable argument which serves only to irritate the court. Judges are only human. Brevity is another goal in the preparation process. The papers that go to the judges are voluminous. They contain all the written material that has had some bearing upon the presentation and decision of the case, as well as judge's reports, minutes of proceedings and the like. It is seldom that all such material needs to be referred to by the advocate. In preparing his submissions the advocate should identify such parts of any documentation to which it is necessary or helpful to draw attention and select the logical order for such reference. This process of selection must be fair in the sense that anything that is material must be included even if it is adverse to the submission. Ideally, the advocate ought to prepare so that when he comes to present his submissions they contain a logical and comprehensive narrative of the relevant circumstances such that the court could adopt it as the basis of its written judgment. If one needs a style for a submission, particularly for the introductory part, it may be found in any of the recent opinions delivered by the Lord Justice General or the Lord Justice Clerk; they are self-contained in the sense that they refer concisely to all the relevant facts and history and summarise all the arguments and authorities referred to. A submission modelled on such an opinion would be likely to be well received. Research into the relevant law must be thorough. It is the duty of the advocate to draw the court's attention to any relevant authority, including any adverse to the submission he is advancing; and the advocate in preparing the submission must ensure that he does not miss any case that is, or may be, in point. The court has ready access to the usual Scottish textbooks and case reports; but if it is intended to refer to any book or report not usually cited it is helpful to prepare photocopies for the use of the court. In any event, a list of the books likely to be referred to should be prepared to allow the court staff to ensure that the judges have the necessary books to hand. It is good practice, if the circumstances warrant it, to consider approaching the Crown before the hearing to see if agreement can be reached, or if any concessions are to be made, which can help to focus the submission at the hearing itself onto the real issues. It is essential to ensure that any submission which it is proposed to advance is adequately covered by the grounds of appeal – in whatever form they are placed before the court. The court is likely to refuse to entertain submissions on any ground of which due notice has not been given; and while, even without notice, the court may deal with matters that suggest that the case is vitiated by some fundamental irregularity,[2] it is proper practice to give notice of any such point when it comes to light; in at least some such cases further inquiry, by the Crown or by the court, into the circumstances might be necessary.

1 HL Official Report 30 January 1990, cols 183, 184.
2 See 5.26 *et seq* below.

## 1.10 Advocacy in court

If the submission has been properly prepared the presentation of the argument should be relatively straightforward. The advocate

can assume that the judges will have read the papers and can offer to confine his summary of the facts and circumstances to the salient, material facts. In some cases it will be sensible to ask the court if it would like particular documents or passages in them to be read or merely summarised or referred to. In some cases it will be essential to read out material which has to be placed before the court in order to make the submission fully intelligible. That, of course, is a matter of judgment, a judgment that should be made before the advocate rises to his feet. An advocate's ears are as important as his tongue. If, between his ears, he has a well-calibrated mind he will be able to detect which of his points are being favourably received and which are hopeless; he will also be able to pick up, adopt and develop a favourable line of argument that has been suggested from the bench. The court as currently constituted does not sit silently recording counsel's speeches. It responds, asks questions and debates the issues with counsel. The test of a good advocate is how well his preparation and properties of mind enable him to engage in that forensic debate. Normally, the advocate is given only one opportunity to speak. So he must anticipate his opponent's argument and try to meet it in advance. In particular he must refer to and attempt to distinguish (or to challenge) any authorities which are against his submission and which his opponent is likely to found upon. In some cases the advocate may be called upon to reply to some part of the submission made in response to his opening submission, so it is necessary to concentrate on that submission and to be ready to reply, if asked. It is perfectly proper to request an opportunity to reply to a point that has emerged since the end of the first submission, but only if the advocate has something new to say.

## 1.11 Assisting the court

In presenting his submission the advocate is endeavouring to inform the court as to the facts and the law. When statutes are referred to they should be described by reference to their short title (including the date) and their chapter number; although this will be unnecessary in the case of the most common statutes, such as the 1975 Act. If the version of the statute to be referred to is in the *Parliament House Book* or in *Statutes in Force* the volume and page reference should be given. The same information should be given if the reference is to the official bound volumes of statutes. As a part of his preparation the advocate must ensure that what is placed before the court is the statute as amended etc at the material time. The same detail is required for statutory instruments. Reported cases should be placed before the court by reference to the official reports, such as the Justiciary Cases. If the case is not reported (or not fully reported) in the official reports, counsel should refer to the best available report and should be in a position to assure the court that the case is not reported in official reports. All references to statutes, statutory instruments or reported cases should be enunciated clearly and the advocate should observe to see that the judges have recorded the reference, and, if necessary, have found the report, before reading excerpts from it. Textbooks and articles in learned journals may properly be referred to but it is important to ensure beforehand that the judges have access to such material or copies of the relevant pages. It is a matter of courtesy to spell out any very unusual names, of cases etc, to assist the judges to make an accurate note. It is important for the advocate to make it crystal clear to the court, preferably at the first opportunity, what propositions in law he is to advance (if any) and precisely what it is that he is inviting the court to do.

## 1.12 Terminology

A person who appeals against a decision at a preliminary diet or, in summary proceedings, under section 334(2A), is referred to as **the appellant** and his opponent is **the respondent**. A person who appeals after conviction on indictment is properly described as **the appellant**, although in the forms used to give intimation of intention to appeal [Form 37] and in the note of appeal [Form 38] and in other forms he is variously described as 'the convicted person', 'the applicant', 'the petitioner' or 'the appellant'. In court he is usually referred to as 'the appellant'. Section 279 provides that, unless the context otherwise requires, appellant includes a person who has been convicted and desires to appeal under this part of this Act. A person who appeals by way of stated case after summary conviction is referred to as the **the appellant** even at the stage of the application for a stated case.[1] If he appeals by bill of suspension he should be referred to as **the complainer**. In either case the procurator fiscal (or other prosecutor) is **the respondent**. The person (whether he is the accused or the prosecutor) who brings a bill of advocation is called **the complainer**. Those on the other side (including perhaps the co-accused) are **respondents**.[2] A person who petitions the High Court to use the *nobile officium* **is a petitioner** and those answering the petition are **respondents**. In recent years it has become common in criminal proceedings to refer to the victim of a crime (eg of assault) as 'the complainer'. Purists would say that, as it is the procurator fiscal in whose name any complaint runs, he is the one who should be described as 'the complainer'. But if the accused appeals by bill of suspension or advocation it is he who is then the complainer, which is very confusing. It would seem sensible to use relatively unambiguous terms like 'the appellant', 'the accused', 'the Crown', 'the victim', where the context allows, especially in the oral presentation of appeals. The judges from whose courts appeals are taken are described simply as **the justice (or the justices), the sheriff, the trial judge**. It is not necessary to preface every, or indeed any, reference to a judge with the epithet **learned**. The term 'High Court of Justiciary' is sometimes used in the plural[3] and sometimes in the singular.[4] The singular is more common and appears to be the better usage. **The Crown** is also singular.

1 s 444(1).
2 Cf *HM Advocate v McDonald* 1984 SCCR 229.
3 Eg s 256.
4 s 260 or Act of Adjournal (Consolidation) 1988, r 38.

## 1.13 Legal aid: availability for appeals

State-funded legal assistance is available for all types of criminal appeal, whether arising prior to trial (such as in the case of a bail appeal or a preliminary matter) or arising after the disposal of the case at first instance. It is also available for appeals on incidental matters which might arise by way of suspension or advocation, and for petitions to the *nobile officium*. The whole subject is discussed in detail later,[1] but a few general points may be made at this stage.

First, the system of legal aid, advice and assistance in Scotland is administered by the Scottish Legal Aid Board constituted under the provisions of the Legal Aid (Scotland) Act 1986. Under Part II of the Act, solicitors and counsel may provide preliminary advice and assistance on criminal appeals without application to the Board at all. Assistance by way of representation (ABWOR) is also given under Part II, and this is of relevance to certain types of appeal to the High Court in summary matters. Under Part IV of the Act, criminal legal aid is available for most other types of appeal proceedings on application to the Board.[2] Its Edinburgh office handles all applications for legal aid for criminal appeals, which applications are determined by its staff. They assess whether the applicant is financially eligible for legal aid and whether a grant of legal aid is justified on its merits. Neither the appeal court nor the court which heard the case at first instance has any functions under the 1986 Act in this regard, although the High Court can, in the case of an unrepresented appellant who appears before it in an appeal of complexity, adjourn the hearing and ask the Board to review any decision it has made to refuse legal aid.[3]

Secondly, an appellant does not automatically qualify for legal aid for an appeal arising from the disposal of his case in the court of first instance merely because he was legally aided there. Criminal legal aid is granted for various categories of 'distinct' proceedings; the conditions of eligibility for each category and the regulations which apply to each are different. Certain types of appeal proceedings, including appeals to the High Court of Justiciary against conviction, sentence or acquittal, are 'distinct' for these purposes and therefore require separate application to the Board and consideration by it.[4] But appeals arising as an incident of proceedings in the court of first instance, for example an appeal on a preliminary point such a competency or relevancy, are regarded as part of the original proceedings and are covered by any legal aid (or ABWOR) which applies there.[5]

Thirdly, while legal aid is commonly granted for representation at trial proceedings, it is more sparingly available for appeals. This is partly because the tests of eligibility are different and also because, in appeals against conviction, the presumption of innocence has been displaced. In respect of appeals against conviction, sentence or acquittal, the Board must be satisfied not only that the expenses of the appeal are beyond the applicant's means, but also (1) that he has substantial grounds for making the appeal (if he is the appellant) and (2) that it is reasonable, in the particular circumstances of the case, that legal aid should be made available to him.[6] Both these tests have to be applied against the sole statutory ground upon which a conviction, sentence or (in a summary case) acquittal may be set aside, namely that there has been a miscarriage of justice[7] the Board therefore requires to scrutinise each application with this in mind to ensure that totally unmeritorious appeals (of which there are many) are not funded at public expense.

1 See chapter 8 below. On the subject of legal aid generally, see Stoddart: *Legal Aid in Scotland* (3rd edn, 1989; W. Green & Son).
2 Legal Aid (Scotland) Act 1986, s 25; Criminal Legal Aid (Scotland) Regulations 1987, reg 13.
3 See 8.13 below.
4 Criminal Legal Aid (Scotland) Regulations 1987, reg. 4(1).
5 See chapter 8.
6 Legal Aid (Scotland) Act 1986, s 25.
7 Criminal Procedure (Scotland) Act 1975, ss 228(2), 442(2).

# 2. Appeals by the accused: solemn jurisdiction

2.01 Right of appeal
2.02 Sentence fixed by law

## PRELIMINARY DIETS

2.03 Appeals from preliminary diets
2.04 Preliminary diet appeal procedure
2.05 Postponement of trial diet pending appeal
2.06 Time for appealing
2.07 Note of appeal
2.08 Procedure on lodging note of appeal; report
2.09 Disposal of the appeal from preliminary diet decisions

## APPEALS AFTER CONVICTION

2.10 Appeals against conviction only
2.11 Intimation of intention to appeal; timing; form
2.12 Note of appeal; form; timing; content
2.13 Written presentation of appeal
2.14 Bail pending appeal
2.15 Shorthand notes
2.16 Documentary productions
2.17 Appeals against sentence only
2.18 Note of appeal; form; timing; content
2.19 Stating the grounds
2.20 Written presentation of appeal
2.21 Shorthand notes
2.22 Appeals against both conviction and sentence
2.23 Other appealable orders
2.24 Appeals in respect of contempt of court
2.25 Leave to appeal
2.26 Grounds of appeal
2.27 Specifying the grounds

## EXTENSION OF TIME LIMITS



## ABANDONMENT



## JUDGE'S REPORT



## THE HEARING

## 2.01 Right of appeal

Before trial, a person upon whom an indictment has been served may have a right to appeal against a decision at a preliminary diet (see 2.03 below), or, by note of appeal, against the grant of an application to extend the periods mentioned in section 101 (viz. the 12 months and the 80 and 110 day periods there prescribed).[1] After trial, any person who has been convicted on indictment, whether in the High Court of Justiciary or in the sheriff court, has the right to appeal to the High Court against the conviction, against the sentence passed on such conviction or against both the conviction and the sentence.[2] His right to appeal includes the right to appeal against any of the various orders that may be made at the time of conviction or sentence (see Other appealable orders, at 2.23 below). Leave to appeal is not required after conviction. A person who has pled guilty may competently appeal against conviction, though such an appeal is unlikely to succeed unless the circumstances are wholly exceptional.[3] A person who has pled guilty to an indictment (or complaint) which is vitiated by some fundamental nullity may challenge his conviction on appeal, whether or not the point was taken when it should first have been taken.[4] Fundamental nullity is discussed in chapter 5.[5]

1 s 101(5).
2 s 228(1).
3 *Boyle v HM Advocate* 1976 JC 32; *Harvey v Lockhart* 1991 SCCR 83.
4 *Sangster v HM Advocate* (1896) 2 Adam 182.
5 See 5.26 *et seq.*

## 2.02 Sentence fixed by law

A convicted person has, however, no right of appeal against any sentence fixed by law.[1] A person aged 21 or over who is convicted of murder therefore cannot appeal against the sentence of imprisonment for life which is a sentence fixed by law.[2] Similarly, a person who is under the age of 18 years when he is convicted of murder cannot appeal against the sentence that he be detained without limit of time as this sentence is also fixed by law.[3] Where a person is convicted of murder and at the date of conviction is 18 or over but under 21 years of age his sentence is also fixed by law[4] and is not appealable. Although a sentence of life imprisonment for murder cannot be appealed the murderer has a right of appeal[5] against a recommendation made by the sentencing judge under section 205A(1) as to the minimum period which should elapse before release.

1 s 228(1), Proviso.
2 Cf s 205(1).
3 s 205(2).
4 s 205(3).
5 s 205A(3).

## PRELIMINARY DIETS

### 2.03 Appeals from preliminary diets

Section 76 of the 1975 Act (introduced by the Criminal Justice (Scotland) Act 1980) provides for a preliminary diet to be held to allow the court before which the trial is to take place to deal with certain issues that may or must be resolved before the trial. These issues include matters relating to competency or relevancy, the validity of the citation, pleas in bar of trial or for separation or conjunction of charges or trials and questions as to refusing or allowing the record of proceedings at the judicial examination to be read to the jury.[1] A party can also invite that court to exercise its discretion to order a preliminary diet to consider and deal with any matter which could in the opinion of that party be resolved with advantage before the trial.[2] An objection to the validity of the citation, on the ground of any discrepancy between the record copy of the indictment and the copy served on the accused, or on account of any error or deficiency in the service copy or in the notice of citation must be stated in a notice under section 76(1)(a) of the 1975 Act and argued at a preliminary diet.[3] If it is not taken and argued in this way the accused is held to have passed from and waived the objection. This was made clear in *HM Advocate v McDonald* in which the court held that section 108, as then worded, was badly drafted. The Full Bench construed it so that it applied to solemn proceedings both in the sheriff court and the High

Court and to objections at preliminary diets in both courts. It has since been amended.[4] Except by leave of the court on cause shown (a) no matter relative to the competency or relevancy of the indictment shall be raised; (b) no plea in bar of trial shall be submitted; and (c) no application for separation or conjunction of charges or trials shall be submitted, unless the intention to do so has been stated in a notice under section 76(1).[5] The court, if it orders a preliminary diet, may postpone the trial diet: cf section 76(4) and (5).

1 s 151(2).
2 s 76(1)(c).
3 s 108(1); *HM Advocate v McDonald* 1984 SCCR 229.
4 Law Reform (Miscellaneous Provisions) (Scotland) Act 1985, Sch 2, para 18.
5 s 108(2).

## 2.04 Preliminary diet appeal procedure

Appeals against any decision taken at a preliminary diet are governed by section 76A, and Rules 34–40 of the Act of Adjournal (Consolidation) 1988,[1] although (a) the prosecutor may bring such a decision under review of the High Court by bill of advocation[2] and (b) the full rights of appeal conferred by section 228 are preserved even if the accused does not at the end of the preliminary diet seek leave to appeal against the adverse decision. Leave to appeal to the High Court against a decision at a preliminary diet is required and must be sought by way of motion to the judge who has made the decision at the preliminary diet. The motion for leave to appeal must be made to the judge at the preliminary diet immediately following the making of the decision. The judge must grant or refuse leave as soon as he has intimated his decision and has been moved to grant leave.[3] The judge may grant leave *ex proprio motu*, that is to say even if there is no motion for leave.[4] Any party who appears at the preliminary diet hearing may seek leave to appeal. So, for example, the first of several accused might invite the court at a preliminary diet to separate the trials. It would be competent for any of the other accused persons to seek leave to appeal against the decision that followed that application. Again, the motion for leave must be made immediately and on the spot.

1 In this book a reference to a rule is to a rule of the Act of Adjournal (Consolidation) 1988, as amended; see chapter 1 at 1.06.
2 s 280A, and see 'Appeals by the Crown' in chapter 4, at 4.06.
3 Rule 34(1).
4 s 76A(1).

## 2.05 Postponement of trial diet pending appeal

If he grants leave the judge must decide if the trial diet should be postponed.[1] It will commonly be necessary to postpone the trial diet if leave is granted because most preliminary diets are heard in the week before the trial is due to begin and there is little time to complete the appeal process before the date fixed for the trial (see the interaction of the time limits in sections 76(7) and 75). If the court decides at the preliminary diet that the original trial diet should be postponed the court is allowed to discharge it and fix a new diet or give leave to the prosecutor to serve a notice fixing a new trial diet, under section 77A. The High Court itself may postpone the trial diet for such period as appears to that court to be appropriate and direct that the whole or part of the period is not to count in the computation of any time limit in respect of the case.[2] If the decision to postpone is taken by the High Court the Clerk of Justiciary has to inform the sheriff clerk (in a sheriff court case), all the parties and the governor of any institution in which any of the persons accused on the indictment in the case is detained.[3] Obviously the final determination of the issue may take months (as in *Khaliq v HM Advocate*[4]), and in appeals against preliminary diet decisions the possible need to invoke section 76A(2) should not be overlooked.

1 Rule 34(2)
2 s 76A(2).
3 Rule 38.
4 1983 SCCR 483.

## 2.06 Time for appealing

Any appeal to the High Court against a decision taken at a preliminary diet must be taken not later than two days after such decision.[1] It should be remembered, however, that the two days period is automatically extended by section 111A if the second of the two days falls on a Saturday, Sunday or court holiday; the period is then extended to and includes the next day which is not a Saturday, Sunday or court holiday.

1 s 76A(1).

## 2.07 Note of appeal

The appeal against a decision taken at a preliminary diet must be made by way of note of appeal in the form contained in Form 17.[1]

The completed form must be lodged not later than two days after the making of the decision (or such longer period as allowed by s 111A). If the case was one set down for trial in the High Court the note of appeal has to be lodged with the Clerk of Justiciary; in a case set down for trial in the sheriff court, with the sheriff clerk.

1 Rule 35.

## 2.08 Procedure on lodging note of appeal; report

Rule 36 regulates the procedure in an appeal from the sheriff court and imposes certain duties on the sheriff clerk once a note of appeal has been lodged with him. He is required to certify that leave to appeal has been granted and the date and time of lodging Form 17. He must as soon as possible send a copy of the note of appeal to all other parties or their solicitors. He must request a report from the sheriff on the circumstances relating to his decision appealed against and send the Clerk of Justiciary a certified copy of the indictment, the record of proceedings and any relevant document. The sheriff in turn must as soon as possible send his report to the Clerk of Justiciary. The Clerk of Justiciary thereafter has to send a copy of the sheriff's report to the parties or their solicitor, arrange for the appeal to be heard as soon as possible, and make copies of any documents that the appeal court may need.[1] Although there is no comparable provision in the 1988 Act of Adjournal or elsewhere relating to appeals from preliminary diets in the High Court they are in practice treated in the same way *mutatis mutandis*, although if the High Court judge has written an opinion explaining his decision he will not be asked for a separate report. A High Court judge who grants leave would usually write an opinion without being asked to do so and would certainly do so at the request of any party; but it is good practice to ask for a written opinion when obtaining leave to appeal. In any event the appeal court must have an opinion or report from the court below explaining the decision. It will be observed that in a sheriff court case it is not the indictment itself which is transmitted by the sheriff clerk but a certified copy only.[2] That has the consequence that if the Crown seeks to amend the indictment during the course of the hearing in the appeal court (eg to meet a criticism directed at specification or latitude) it cannot be done there and the Crown would have to undertake to seek leave to amend in the court below. In that circumstance the appeal court or the Clerk of Justiciary has to record in some unambiguous form what has transpired and what has been undertaken. The actual amendment must be effected to the record copy of the indictment which has been lodged (on or before the date of service) with the clerk of court before which the trial is to take place.[3]

1 Rule 37.
2 Rule 36(2).
3 See s 78(1) and s 123.

## 2.09 Disposal of the appeal from preliminary diet decisions

The appellant may abandon an appeal against a preliminary diet decision at any time before the hearing of the appeal.[1] He does so by lodging with the Clerk of Justiciary a completed version of Form 18 signed by himself or by his solicitor. In an appeal from the sheriff court, the Clerk of Justiciary informs the sheriff clerk. In all cases he informs other interested parties and the case resumes its progress towards trial. If the appeal proceeds, the powers of the High Court in this regard are governed by section 76A(3). The accused need not be present at the appeal court hearing.[2] The High Court may affirm the decision of the court of first instance. It may remit the case to that court with such directions in the matter as the High Court thinks fit. This power would allow the High Court, in a sheriff court case[2] where the Crown indicated at the appeal hearing that it was intended to amend the indictment, to direct the court of first instance to allow such amendment, if moved; and, failing such a motion, to dismiss the indictment (or otherwise as the circumstances may require). If the court of first instance has dismissed the indictment or any part of it the High Court may reverse that decision and direct the court of first instance to fix a trial diet; though such a direction will not be necessary if a trial diet has already been fixed as regards part of the indictment not dismissed at the preliminary diet. In cases from the sheriff court, the Clerk of Justiciary tells the sheriff clerk what the High Court has decided. If what the High Court has decided is to reverse a decision of the court of first instance which resulted in the dismissal of the case and, consequently, to direct the court of first instance to fix a trial diet that High Court direction is authority for the Clerk of Justiciary or the sheriff clerk, as the case may be, to issue a fresh warrant for citation under section 69 (warrants for citation). If the trial court has dismissed the indictment and the High Court reverses the decision it is not necessary for the trial court to fix another, or a continued, preliminary diet just for the purpose of requiring the accused to state how he pleads to the indictment[2] section 76(6) does not apply to the appeal court hearing.[3] If in reversing the decision of the court of first instance the High Court holds that the proceedings were and are incompetent, it will sustain the plea to the competency, as in *K v HM Advocate*,[4] a 110 day rule case.[5] If, as a consequence of delay occasioned by the taking and hearing of an appeal against a decision at a preliminary diet, the trial cannot commence within the 12 month period allowed by section 101(1) (the period from first appearance on petition to commencement of trial) the court may extend that period, retrospectively if necessary.[6]

1 Rule 40.
2 *HM Advocate v O'Neill* 1992 SCCR 130.
3 Rule 39(2).
4 1991 SCCR 343.
5 s 101(2)(b).
6 *HM Advocate v M* 1986 SCCR 624.

## APPEALS AFTER CONVICTION

### 2.10 Appeals against conviction only

Subject to the right of the Secretary of State to refer the whole case to the High Court under section 263,[1] the only procedure by which a convicted person may appeal after conviction on indictment is that prescribed by Part I of the 1975 Act, sections 228 to 282 and the relative Acts of Adjournal.

1 See 5.25 below.

### 2.11 Intimation of intention to appeal; timing; form

The first step is to lodge with the Clerk of Justiciary written intimation of intention to appeal and send a copy to the Crown Agent.[1] All appeals under section 228 following conviction on indictment are initiated in the Justiciary Office of the High Court, not in the sheriff court. The form to be used for giving written intimation of intention to appeal is Form 37 in the 1988 Act of Adjournal.[2] The written notice must be given within two weeks of the final determination of the proceedings. For this purpose the final determination of the proceedings normally occurs on the day on which sentence is passed in open court. However, if sentence is not passed at the time of conviction but is deferred under section 219 (which permits the court to defer sentence for a period on conditions) the two weeks period begins to run from the date on which sentence is first deferred in open court[3] (a court may defer sentence several times). In 'drug trafficking' cases (as defined in section 1(6) of the Criminal Justice (Scotland) Act 1987) in which a confiscation order[4] can be made, the court may, after conviction, require information before coming to a decision as regards making a confiscation order (under section 1 of the same Act) and may therefore postpone its decision for a period to enable the required information to be obtained. If it does so, an intention to appeal against conviction must be intimated within two weeks of the day on which the period of postponement commences,[5] which means the day on which the decision to postpone is made.[6] The two weeks period may be extended at any time by the High Court.[7] As Form 37 itself makes clear, an Intimation of Intention to Appeal must be signed by the convicted person or by his counsel or solicitor.[8] This Form, like all prescribed forms and related instructions, is available from the Clerk of Justiciary at the Public Office, Parliament House, Edinburgh EH1 1RQ. Section 271 requires him to furnish such forms and related instructions to any person who demands them, and to officers of court, to governors of prisons and others as he thinks fit. Each prison governor must make the forms and any related instructions available to prisoners desiring to appeal or to make an application (eg for bail or for extension of time) incidental to the appeal. There is no prescribed form of appeal for the note of appeal to be presented by an accused who is remanded under section 179. The governor has the responsibility for forwarding to the Clerk of Justiciary any written intimation of intention to appeal prepared by a prisoner.

1 s 231.
2 Rule 84.
3 s 231(4).
4 For appeal purposes this is a sentence: s 1(4) of the 1987 Act.
5 s 2(2) of the 1987 Act.
6 1975 Act, s 231(5).
7 s 236B(2); see below, 'Time Limits' at 2.31 *et seq*.
8 s 236C.

## 2.12 Note of appeal; form; timing; content

Within six weeks of lodging Form 37 (Intimation of Intention to Appeal) the convicted person may lodge a written note of appeal with the Clerk of Justiciary.[1] The six weeks period may, before it expires, be extended by the Clerk of Justiciary, if, for example, there has been a delay in making the transcript of the judge's charge available. The six weeks period may also be extended by the High Court itself.[2] The written note of appeal must be in the form prescribed by Rule 84 of the 1988 Act of Adjournal, namely Form 38, and signed by the convicted person, his counsel or solicitor: the latter must add his address and telephone number. All the grounds of appeal must be fully stated in the form. It is not competent for an appellant to found any aspect of his appeal on a ground not contained in the written note of appeal, unless the High Court, on cause shown, grants leave.[3] Accordingly, although the section says that the convicted person 'may' lodge a written note of appeal, it is clear that he must do so if he intends to proceed with the appeal. The grounds of appeal must be stated with sufficient specification to identify the particular criticism of the conviction which the appellant hopes to present to the High Court; if they are not so stated the appeal court will usually refuse to entertain submissions related to an unspecific ground.[4] The note of appeal must identify the proceedings which have resulted in the conviction of the appellant. Form 38 makes it clear what details are required. The date of final determination is the date derived from applying section 231(4) to the circumstances (see 2.11 above). The Note of Appeal (Form 38) effectively supersedes the written intimation (Form 37).

1 s 233.
2 See below at 2.32.
3 See below: 'Grounds of Appeal' at 2.26 *et seq*.
4 High Court of Justiciary Practice Note of 29 March 1985 reproduced at 2.27 below.

## 2.13 Written presentation of appeal

The appellant has the right to present his argument orally to the High Court (subject to the power of the High Court to determine questions of law alone summarily if it considers that the appeal is frivolous or vexatious).[1] If, however, he prefers instead to present it in writing he must so inform the Clerk of Justiciary at least four days before the diet (ie the date) fixed for the hearing of the appeal. He must at the same time lodge with the Clerk of Justiciary three copies of 'his case and argument' and send a copy to the Crown Agent. The High Court must consider the material submitted.[2] This method of proceeding by written presentation, dating from 1926, is unknown in modern practice and is not regulated in any way by the 1988 Act of Adjournal. It is not clear what is meant by 'his case'. It is, however, clear that if an appellant opted to present his argument in writing instead of orally the appeal court would study the written material presented. (That often happens when a party appellant comes to court on the day of his appeal and asks if, instead of listening to an oral presentation by him, the court will instead read some notes or other written material which he has prepared or collected. Such requests are invariably granted). Section 234(2) enables the High Court to direct the respondent to make a written reply to a written presentation but, in the absence of such a direction, the reply is oral. An appellant who opts for a written presentation is not entitled, without leave of the High Court, to present an oral argument.[3]

1 See Chapter 6 at 6.04.
2 s 234(1).
3 s 234(3).

## 2.14 Bail pending appeal

The High Court has a discretion to admit the appellant to bail pending the determination of the appeal on his application at any time after he has lodged a written intimation of intention to appeal. The application is made on Form 40. This is more fully treated in Chapter 9 at 9.08 *et seq.*[1]

1 s 238.

## 2.15 Shorthand notes

Shorthand notes have to be taken of the whole proceedings at a trial[1] and any party interested (which is defined to include the convicted person)[2] is entitled to be furnished with a transcript of the notes or part thereof if he pays the appropriate charge fixed by the Treasury.[3] Normally no transcript is made unless the Clerk of Justiciary so directs after the court has decided that it wishes to see a transcript. The appeal court may leave it to the parties to agree precisely which parts should be transcribed. The whole proceedings at a preliminary diet under section 76 are proceedings at the trial for the purposes of the application of section 274.[4]

1 s 274.
2 s 275(5).
3 ss 274, 275.
4 Rule 33.

## 2.16 Documentary productions

A party interested in an appeal whether against conviction or sentence (being one of those parties listed in section 275(5)) has the right to obtain from the Clerk of Justiciary a copy of any documentary production lodged by or for any party to the appeal upon payment of the appropriate charge fixed by the Treasury.[1]

1 s 275(4).

## 2.17 Appeals against sentence only

The only procedure by which a person may appeal against a sentence passed on conviction on indictment is that prescribed in Part I of the 1975 Act, sections 228 to 282 and the relative Act of Adjournal.[1] There is no right of appeal against any sentence fixed by law – see 2.01 above.

1 Subject to the Secretary of State's right under s 263 to refer the whole case to the High Court.

## 2.18 Note of appeal: form; timing; content

The first step in taking an appeal against sentence only is to lodge with the Clerk of Justiciary within two weeks of the passing of the sentence in open court a written note of appeal. The two weeks period may be extended at any time by the High Court.[1] The written note of appeal must be, as nearly as may be, in the form prescribed by the 1988 Act of Adjournal, namely Form 38. It must identify the proceedings; and it must contain a full statement of all the grounds of appeal.[2] It must be signed by the convicted person or by his counsel or his solicitor (who is required to add his address and telephone number). Form 38 may be obtained from the Clerk of Justiciary together with a copy of the related instructions. The prison governors have the forms and the related instructions and must make them available to such of their prisoners who desire to appeal or to make any application (eg for bail or for extension of time) incidental to the appeal; but, as pointed out at 2.11 above, there is no prescribed form for a section 179 note of appeal (remand of a convicted person before sentence) even although such a note of appeal has to be presented within 24 hours of the remand.

1 s 236B(2); see below: 'Time Limits' at 2.31 *et seq.*
2 s 233; and see 'Grounds of Appeal' at 2.26 *et seq* below.

## 2.19 Stating the grounds

As the note of appeal is the only document which the appellant places before the appeal court when the appeal is against sentence alone it is important that it should contain properly and fully formulated grounds of appeal. But as the convicted persons often obtain the forms (Form 38) direct from the prison authorities, complete them without legal advice and cause the completed forms to be sent direct to the Justiciary Office, the grounds of appeal are often badly stated. If a solicitor is instructed to act for a person who has completed and sent Form 38 himself he should, at the earliest possible moment take steps to ensure that, if necessary, amended grounds are presented in place of those contained in the Form 38 which the prisoner has caused to be lodged. This matter is dealt with below ('Grounds of Appeal' at 2.26 *et seq*) but it is an acute problem in relation to sentence-only appeals. In practice, when an appeal form is sent direct from a convicted person who is in prison the Justiciary Office sends a copy of that completed form to the agents who acted for him in the proceedings giving rise to the appeal and asks the agents if they are still acting for the appellant. This procedure allows the grounds to be amended and properly stated at an early stage. If amended grounds are submitted promptly by agents the amended grounds are simply substituted for those submitted by the convicted person.

## 2.20 Written presentation of appeal

As in the case of an appeal against conviction the appellant has the right to present his argument orally or in writing. There are no special considerations affecting appeals which are taken against sentence alone. Accordingly the considerations discussed at 2.13 above apply to such appeals also.

## 2.21 Shorthand notes

In some cases on appeal against sentence alone shorthand notes are available and in some they are not. In those cases in which the trial judge's charge to the jury is before the appeal court the transcript of the whole proceedings in relation to sentencing, in so far as they were completed on that one occasion, will be before the appeal court. But if sentence is deferred for any reason there will usually be no shorthand notes of the proceedings at the deferred diet. Nor will there be a shorthand record at a section 102 diet at which an accused pleads guilty. In practice, the appeal court does not order a transcript of the shorthand notes (if any exist) in relation to sentence-only appeals. It would not be incompetent to seek to lay such a transcript before the appeal court or for the appeal court to require one (if available) if the High Court thought that an examination thereof would be of assistance to the appeal court; but this is virtually unknown in practice.

## 2.22 Appeals against both conviction and sentence

The methods and forms of appeal which apply to appeals against both conviction and sentence, in indictment cases, are the same for most practical purposes as those which apply to appeals against conviction. In particular the forms to be used are Form 37 (Intimation of Intention to Appeal) and Form 38 (Note of Appeal). Reference should be made to 2.03 to 2.09 above for descriptions of the relevant methods and forms. A person who has appealed against both conviction and sentence may abandon the appeal in so far as it is against conviction and may proceed with it against sentence alone.[1] Form 41 specifically allows for this (see para (b) of Form 41). Although there is no equivalent express provision in the statute, an appellant can use Form 41 to abandon his appeal against sentence while proceeding with his appeal against conviction: see 2.34 below.

1 s 244(2).

## 2.23 Other appealable orders

In addition to the more familiar sentences, namely the imposition of a fine, of imprisonment or detention, the giving of an admonition[1] or an absolute discharge[2] the making of a probation order[3] or a community service order[4] the imposition of a requirement to find caution for good behaviour[5] and orders for the forfeiture of property[6] there are other less common orders which are appealable by note of appeal in the same manner as ordinary sentences. They are:

(1) Recommendations as to the minimum period which should elapse before the Secretary of State releases on licence a person convicted of murder.[7]
(2) Hospital orders, interim hospital orders, guardianship orders or orders restricting discharge.[8]
(3) Disqualification from holding a driving licence.[9]
(4) Compensation orders.[10]
(5) Recommendations for deportation[11]
(6) A confiscation order under Part I of the Criminal Justice

(Scotland) Act 1987,[12] made in relation to a drug-related offence mentioned in section 1 of that 1987 Act.

(7) Statutory disqualifications: several statutes empower courts to declare persons convicted of statutory offences to be disbarred or temporarily disqualified from holding or continuing to hold certain permits or licences or from entering certain licensed premises without the express consent of the licensee.[13]

1 s 181.
2 s 182.
3 ss 183–192.
4 Community Service by Offenders (Scotland) Act 1978.
5 *Renton & Brown*, para 17.37.
6 s 223 and also s 27 of the Misuse of Drugs Act 1971 and other examples in Nicolson: *The Law and Practice of Sentencing*, para 7.05; cf *Findlay v McNaughtan* 1991 SCCR 321.
7 s 205A.
8 s 280.
9 Road Traffic Offenders Act 1988, s 38(2).
10 Criminal Justice (Scotland) Act 1980, ss 58 and 63(1).
11 Immigration Act 1971, s 6; and Criminal Procedure (Scotland) Act 1975, s 279; cf *Caldowei v Jessop* 1991 SCCR 323.
12 s 1(4).
13 *Nicolson on Sentencing*, paras 7.17, 7.26, 7.22 and *Renton and Brown* paras 17.45, 17.46.

## 2.24 Appeals in respect of contempt of court

There is no appeal to the High Court of Justiciary against a sentence imposed for contempt of court in civil proceedings.[1] The remedy in such a case must be sought in the Court of Session. The Court of Session has full powers to deal with any matter of contempt arising in the course of proceedings in that court.[2] In matters of contempt of court an appeal against or review of a sentence for alleged contempt of court should follow the civil route to the Court of Session in civil cases and the criminal route to the High Court in criminal cases.[3] Section 230 of the 1975 Act provides that it shall not be competent to appeal to the High Court by bill of suspension against any conviction, sentence, judgment or order pronounced in any proceedings on indictment in the sheriff court; it was formerly held competent to proceed by way of bill of suspension to the High Court against a sentence of imprisonment imposed by a sheriff, during the course of a jury trial, on a witness whom he held guilty of contempt of court for prevarication.[4] But that decision was overruled by a bench of five judges in *George Outram & Co Ltd v Lees*.[5] Application to the High Court of Justiciary by petition to the *nobile officium* is the appropriate method of appealing in such circumstances; this method was held to be competent in the case of two Crown witnesses who having been cited to give evidence at a trial in the High Court of Justiciary entered the witness box but refused either to take the oath or to give evidence.[6] They had been detained in custody till the conclusion of the trial when they were brought before the presiding judge and sentenced to three years' imprisonment each.[7] An accused person may also be found guilty of contempt of court, eg by swearing at witnesses or refusing to leave his cell or to plead when brought to court.[8] In a solemn case, if the accused were not convicted of any charge contained in the indictment, he would need to petition the *nobile officium* in respect of any penalty imposed for contempt of court as there would be no other method of appeal open to him. If, however, he were convicted of a crime or offence contained in the indictment and if he appealed under section 228 there seems no reason to doubt that the court would hear submissions about the penalty imposed for contempt if adequate notice were given in the note of appeal.

1 *Cordiner, Petitioner* 1973 JC 16.
2 *Cordiner*, above at 18.
3 *Cordiner*, above at 19.
4 *Butterworth v Herron* 1975 SLT (Notes) 56.
5 1992 SCCR 120.
6 *Wylie v HM Advocate* 1966 SLT 149.
7 The maximum period is now two years: Contempt of Court Act 1981, s 15(2).
8 *Dawes v Cardle* 1987 SCCR 135; and see *Renton and Brown*, para 18-105 for examples of other conduct amounting to contempt of court.

## 2.25 Leave to appeal

After a decision at a preliminary diet, leave to appeal is required, though the judge may grant it without being asked to do so. Otherwise it must be applied for immediately following the decision: cf 2.04 *et seq* above where the strict timetable is described. Leave to appeal is never required after conviction, whether the appeal is against conviction or sentence, or both, or against any order properly forming part of the sentence.

## 2.26 Grounds of appeal

In Chapter 7 consideration is given to the meaning of the term 'miscarriage of justice' which appears in section 228(2): 'By an appeal . . . a person may bring under review of the High Court any alleged miscarriage of justice in the proceedings in which he was convicted . . .'.

The term 'grounds of appeal' is used to describe the detailed criticisms which are specifically related to the particular appeal. The expressions 'ground of appeal' and 'ground' were used in the Criminal Appeal (Scotland) Act 1926.[1] Thus the High Court was directed (subject to a proviso) to allow the appeal 'if they think that the verdict of the jury should be set aside on the ground that it is unreasonable or cannot be supported having regard to the evidence, or that the judgment of the court before whom the appellant was convicted should be set aside on the ground of a wrong decision of any question of law or that on any ground there was a mis-carriage of justice'. The word 'ground' was virtually synonymous with 'basis'. The words 'grounds of appeal' have changed their context in the new statutory provisions, but not their meaning. The grounds of appeal, therefore, consist of specific and distinct statements which identify the particular criticism or criticisms of the conviction or sentence which the appellant intends to present at the oral hearing of the appeal. Each distinct criticism should, where possible, be separately stated. All the grounds of appeal should be stated at the same time in Form 38. Each ground should be fully stated.[2] Additional evidence as a ground of appeal is considered in chapter 6 at 6.26 *et seq*.

1 ss 1 and 2.
2 s 233 and Form 38.

## 2.27 Specifying the grounds

The best guide as to how not to frame grounds of appeal is that contained (expressly and by inference) in the High Court of Justiciary Practice Note of 29 March 1985. It is in the following terms:

29 March 1985

**Appeals in solemn procedure and appeals against sentence in summary procedure**

All too often the time of the appeal court is wasted, and proper disposal of appeals is hampered, where the grounds stated in notes of appeal are wholly unspecific. In appeals against conviction, for example, it is common to find grounds stated thus:

(i) "Misdirection" without any specification whatever;

(ii) "Insufficient evidence" without any specification of the particular point, if any, which is to be taken, eg the absence of corroboration of evidence identifying the appellant as the perpetrator of the crime, or an alleged insufficiency of evidence to establish that the crime libelled, or a crime within the scope of the libel, was committed;

In appeals against sentence, for example, the ground of appeal is more often than not equally uninformative, eg "sentence excessive in the circumstances" or merely "severity of sentence". No hint is given of the circumstances to be relied on and it often happens that at the hearing the court is told of allegedly relevant circumstances which, it is said, were not before the judge or sheriff or which, it is said, the judge or sheriff ignored.

It will be appreciated that the consequence of the statement of unspecific grounds of appeal is that the trial judge or sheriff is unable to report upon them, and the appeal court is at a grave disadvantage in preparing for and hearing appeals without the benefit of the observations of the trial judge or sheriff upon the proposition which the appellant submits to the court without notice.

This practice note is intended to remind practitioners that grounds of appeal must be stated with sufficient specification to identify the particular criticism of the conviction or sentence which the appellant hopes to present at the hearing. In the case of notes of appeal lodged after the issue of this practice note the appeal court may be expected, save in exceptional circumstances and on cause shown, to refuse to entertain any appeal upon any unspecific ground'.

## 2.28 Criticism of unspecific grounds

The practice note reflects the concern of the court, repeatedly expressed,[1] that adequate notice of the points to be argued must be given in the note of appeal. In *Moffat*, simply because of the seriousness of the consequences of the conviction under review (18 years' imprisonment for each of two accused) the court entertained submissions that went beyond the stated grounds of appeal but added, '. . . the tabling of stated grounds of appeal does not open the door to a free for all . . .'. The court has also[2] criticised the practice of including in the note of appeal grounds of appeal which are departed from at the start of the hearing. It was stated[3] that, 'Since the judge's charge should now be available timeously, practitioners have a professional responsibility to see that criticisms of a judge's charge can be read out of the charge and do not stem from recollections which can be imperfect and unjustified'. To make unchecked and unwarranted criticisms of a judge's charge was said to constitute 'an unwarranted public criticism of the judge's professional competency and result in a waste of time and money'. It might be added that the advancing and last-minute abandoning of grounds of appeal is likely to try the patience of the appeal court judges who are required to read all the papers beforehand. It is not good advocacy needlessly to irritate the bench.

1 Eg *Moffat v HM Advocate* 1983 SCCR 121.
2 *McAvoy v HM Advocate* 1982 SCCR 263.
3 *McAvoy* at p 271.

## 2.29 Framing grounds of appeal - general

From some examples quoted in some detail in chapter 7[1] it is clear that the characteristics of a well-drawn ground of appeal are as follows:

*Accuracy:* any description of events or quotation from the proceedings should be accurate.

*Stateability:* if the ground of appeal is stateable, that is enough. Of course frivolous points should not be argued but it is bad advocacy to advance only those submissions which are bound to succeed. Between the frivolous and the unanswerable lies an unmapped territory in which knowledge of the law, experience, instinct and good judgment are the only guides.

*Clarity:* the ground should be clearly stated in language as simple and non-technical as can be achieved.

*Brevity:* the purpose of a ground of appeal is to give written notice of the point to be argued, not to argue the point in writing. The ground should be stated as shortly as is consistent with giving full notice of the circumstances said to have caused a miscarriage of justice. Repetition should be avoided although it may be necessary where, for example, one error gives rise to several distinct grounds of appeal, eg (a) that the judge allowed the jury to hear inadmissible evidence; (b) that he later misdirected the jury by telling them they could take it into account, and (c) that without the inadmissible evidence there was insufficient evidence in law to support his conviction.

*Informative:* if the appellant's advisers intend to draw attention to a particular case or statutory provision it can be helpful to the court to be given a reference to it in the grounds (though it is not necessary). Similarly, helpful references to parts of the charge or other written material can assist the court to focus more swiftly on the true issues.

*Responsibility:* those who frame grounds of appeal and present them and submissions in support of them have a responsibility not just to the appellant, but also to the appeal court, the court of first instance and, in some cases, to persons such as other accused or witnesses or court staff: grounds of appeal should not cast imputations upon the character or conduct or professional competence of others without a solid justification. Those who frame grounds of appeal are professionally responsible for their contents.

1 SCCR contains numerous other examples.

## 2.30 Late amending of the grounds of appeal

The written note of appeal whether against conviction or sentence or both must, as already noted, contain a full statement of all grounds of appeal.[1] It is not competent for an appellant to found any aspect of his appeal on a ground which is not contained in the note of appeal unless on cause shown he obtains the leave of the High Court. In the case of an appeal against conviction the appellant and his advisers will have had six weeks or more to consider and frame the grounds of appeal and will have had adequate opportunity to study a transcript of the charge to the jury. In practice, the six week period allowed for lodging grounds of appeal against conviction[2] is split up by the Justiciary Office into the 'first' and 'second' three week periods, in terms of the power contained in the proviso to section 233(1). The second three week period does not start to run until the transcript of the judge's charge has been obtained. The Justiciary Office then sends the appellant, or his solicitor, a letter (Form E) with copies of the indictment proceedings and charge giving a date some three weeks ahead on or before which the note of appeal (Form 38) must be lodged. That period may be further extended by the High Court if good grounds are presented to it for so doing.[3] Accordingly the High Court will not readily allow the late amending of grounds of appeal and may exercise its discretion to refuse to entertain additional or substituted grounds.[4] In the case of an appeal against sentence only, the appellant will have had only two weeks to prepare and lodge his written note of appeal and he may have obtained the necessary form in prison and lodged it without legal advice. A prompt altering of the grounds thereafter by his legal advisers is permitted. However, a most important consideration is the time when any such amendment or substitution is proposed. An amendment proposed before the judge who presided at the trial prepares his report is clearly more likely to be considered favourably then one proposed at any later stage. But the timescale is short. That is because upon receiving the note of appeal the Clerk of Justiciary immediately takes steps to intimate the grounds to all the interested parties and to obtain the judge's report. He sends a copy of the note of appeal to Crown Office, to the Legal Aid Board and to the Criminal Records Office. If the note of appeal has come direct from prison a copy is sent to the solicitor who acted for the appellant with a standard letter asking if he still acts for the appellant; this gives the solicitor an opportunity to substitute amended grounds for those prepared by the convicted person. If the note of appeal comes from a solicitor copies are sent to the prison where the appellant is detained. The judge who presided at the trial must furnish a report to the Clerk of Justiciary 'as soon as is reasonably practicable'.[5] In practice, if the report is not received within three or four weeks the Justiciary Office will take steps to see that the report is prepared. The High Court can order the report to be furnished, or, if it thinks fit, can hear and determine the appeal without obtaining the report.[6] On receiving the report the Justiciary Office sends a copy to the appellant or his solicitor, as well as to the Crown Office, and the appeal is ready to be put out on the rolls. Clearly once the judge's report has been prepared the High Court will be slow to allow amendment of the grounds. Although in a few serious cases the court has allowed later amendment of the grounds, sometimes necessitating a supplementary judge's report, the only responsible course is to state the grounds fully and accurately in the note of appeal and to approach the Clerk of Justiciary to seek any extension of time that can be justified and shown to be necessary before the note of appeal is lodged.

1 s 233(2).
2 s 233(1).
3 s 236B(2).
4 *Moffat v HM Advocate* 1983 SCCR 121.
5 s 236A.
6 s 236A(2).

## EXTENSION OF TIME LIMITS

### 2.31 The time limits

It has already been noted that

(1) written intimation of intention to appeal must be lodged within two weeks of the final determination of the proceedings[1] and a copy sent to the Crown Agent;
(2) a written note of appeal must be lodged within six weeks thereafter (subject to extension by the Clerk of Justiciary)[2] or by the High Court;[3] and
(3) a note of appeal against sentence only must be lodged within two weeks of the passing of the sentence in open court.[4] Each period is automatically extended by section 236B(1) if Justiciary Office is closed on the last day of the prescribed period.

1 s 231(1).
2 s 233(1).
3 s 236B(2).
4 s 233(1).

## 2.32 Application for extension

Any period prescribed by sections 231(1) and 233(1) may be extended by the High Court.[1] The application form (solemn appeals) is Form 39 which may be signed by the appellant, or by his solicitor or counsel. The form itself specifies an obvious and necessary requirement of the application, namely that it must state fully the reasons for the failure to lodge the written notice or note within the prescribed time. The application form is checked by Justiciary Office staff to ensure that it has been completed correctly and contains all the relevant information and, usually on the day following receipt (provided it is in order), is put before a single judge of the High Court (the bail judge or the vacation judge)[2] in chambers together with the indictment, the list of previous convictions and, in High Court cases, the copy book of adjournal. Unless there is some unusual feature about the application the single judge will usually grant it without the need for any appearance by the appellant or his lawyer. The reasoning of the court in *Clayton, Petitioner*,[3] (a summary case), would apply equally to a solemn case; thus even a very long delay in appealing (in that case, nearly two years) may be excused in exercise of the power conferred by section 247. If the appellant has to be represented, for example because the judge seeks further information or explanation, the appellant may appear personally or by counsel or be represented and appear by a solicitor alone. After the judge has considered the application and decided to grant or to refuse it the applicant is notified of the result on Form 42.[4] If the application is refused, the Clerk of Justiciary sends with Form 42 an application form (Form 43) to enable the applicant to exercise his right[5] to have his application determined by the High Court as fully constituted for the hearing of solemn appeals (quorum of three).[6] If the applicant does not apply properly on Form 43 within five days the refusal by the single judge is final.[7] If he duly applies for his application to be determined by the full court he has to state on the form if he desires to be present at the hearing of his application before the full court. If he is not to be legally represented (ie by counsel) he is entitled to be present at the hearing and does not need leave to be present[8] but he must nonetheless express on Form 43 his desire to be present. If he is to be legally represented at the hearing he is not entitled to be present, unless the court gives leave. If he expressly seeks leave to be present, the Clerk of Justiciary places his request before the High Court in chambers and notifies the applicant of that court's ruling on the matter. As for a full hearing (2.46 below), leave is automatically granted as a matter of course. If (whether with or without leave) the applicant is to be present at the hearing the Clerk of Justiciary must notify (a) the applicant, (b) the governor of the prison in which the applicant is in custody, and (c) the Secretary of State.[9] The single judge who refused the application may sit on the full court; but the applicant's solicitor has no right of audience before that court.[10]

1 s 236B(2).
2 s 247.
3 1991 SCCR 261.
4 s 251(1).
5 s 247.
6 s 251.
7 s 251(2).
8 s 251(3).
9 s 251(6).
10 See however, the Law Reform (Miscellaneous Provisions) (Scotland) Act 1990, s 24 which inserts section 25A into the Solicitors (Scotland) Act 1980, thus prospectively enabling solicitors to exercise extended rights of audience.

## ABANDONMENT

### 2.33 Express and deliberate abandonment by notice

An appellant may abandon his appeal by lodging with the Clerk of Justiciary a notice of abandonment (Form 41)[1] which must be signed by the appellant himself. He does not need leave of the court to abandon his appeal. But he must be sure to abandon in the manner prescribed by section 244(1) and lodge Form 41, if that is his intention, before the case calls in court. If he lodges a properly completed form the appeal is deemed to have been dismissed by the court.[2] But the time for lodging the notice ends when the case is called.[3] The court then becomes master of the procedure, and then has a discretion to refuse to permit the appeal to be abandoned. It may choose to hear the appeal and even to exercise its powers[4] to increase the sentence appealed against as in *Grant v HM Advocate*[5] where the sentences appealed against were substantially increased. (There is no such power if the appeal is against conviction alone).

1 s 244(1).
2 s 244(1).
3 *Ferguson v HM Advocate* 1980 JC 27.
4 s 254(3)(b).
5 1985 SCCR 431.

## 2.34 Partial abandonment by notice

An appellant who has appealed by note of appeal against both conviction and sentence may abandon the appeal in so far as it is against conviction but proceed with the appeal against sentence alone.[1] Form 41 allows for this in option (b). There is no similar express statutory provision for the case of a person who has appealed by note of appeal against both conviction and sentence and who wishes to abandon his appeal against sentence but to proceed with his appeal against conviction. Form 41 does not expressly provide for such a possibility. However, in practice, such an appellant uses Form 41 to indicate that he is abandoning his appeal against sentence but proceeding with his appeal against conviction. The court (and the Clerk of Justiciary) accept such a notice and the appeal proceeds against conviction alone.

1 s 244(2).

## 2.35 Finality of abandonment

A statutory abandonment is final[1] subject to two possibilities: (1) the Secretary of State's power under section 263, to refer a case to the High Court is not affected by a statutory (or a deemed) abandonment; (2) it is impossible to rule out an exercise of the *nobile officium* to permit an appeal to proceed after statutory abandonment. Where the appellant's legal representatives know that the appeal is to be abandoned (in whole or in part) they should so intimate to the Clerk of Justiciary and without delay lodge the notice of abandonment as soon as possible.

1 *Biondi v HM Advocate* 1967 SLT (Notes) 22.

## 2.36 Deemed abandonment

If an appellant has lodged a written intimation of intention to appeal (Form 37) but fails to lodge either a note of appeal (Form 38) or an application (Form 39) for extension under section 236(B)(2), the Justiciary Office prepares a letter stating that as no note of appeal has been lodged and no application for extension of time received the proceedings are deemed to have come to an end. Such a letter goes to the Crown Office, Criminal Records Office, the Legal Aid Board, the prison governor, the judge, the sheriff clerk (in the case of a sheriff court appeal) and to the convicted person and his solicitor. If that evokes no response from the convicted person the appeal comes to an end. The convicted person may respond by choosing to apply for an extension of time and, if an extension is granted, to present a late note of appeal; cf 2.32 above.

## 2.37 Abandonment by non-appearance

'Where no appearance is made by or on behalf of an appellant at the diet appointed for the hearing of an appeal and where no case or argument in writing has been timeously lodged,[1] the High Court shall dispose of the appeal as if it had been abandoned'.[2] That means that 'the appeal shall be deemed to have been dismissed by the court' (section 244(1)). Thus an appellant against sentence who wishes to abandon his appeal but has neglected to lodge Form 41 (notice of abandonment) might be able to avoid the consequences seen in *Ferguson v HM Advocate*[3] by not appearing at the diet either personally or by counsel. The wording of section 257 thus suggests that the time when the court becomes master of the procedure might not be when the case calls, as stated *obiter* in *Ferguson* (above), but the time when the appellant or his counsel appears at the diet after the case has been called. However, section 238(2) which ordains an appellant who has been admitted to bail to 'appear personally in court on the day or days fixed for the hearing of his appeal [or application for leave to appeal (sic)]' gives to the court, in the event of the appellant's not appearing, powers which appear to be at odds with the peremptory terms of section 257. Section 238(2) empowers the court inter alia to consider and determine the appeal even if the appellant fails to appear. Section 257 requires the court to dispose of the appeal as if it had been abandoned. The only safe course for one who decides to abandon an appeal against sentence is to do so as soon as possible by notice (Form 41) under section 244, and certainly before the case is called.

1 Cf 2.10 above.
2 s 257.
3 1980 JC 27; cf 2.47 above.

## 2.38 Agents withdrawing from acting

Agents and counsel may decide that they are to withdraw from acting for the appellant. Such a decision may follow a refusal of legal aid, or the legal representatives may conclude that the appeal is unstateable or that the risks of having the sentence increased are such that it would be folly to proceed. The normal and proper procedure to follow is to advise the appellant of the situation as early as possible and, unless he instructs abandonment, then, whether or not he has been told orally, for the solicitor to send him at his bail and/or his last-known address a recorded delivery letter telling him clearly and simply of the situation (and possibly the reasons for it), advising him of the date and place of the diet fixed for his appeal hearing and of his rights and duties in relation to abandonment or to continuing with the appeal in person or instructing new agents and reminding him of his duty to surrender his bail. The appeal court requires to be satisfied that timeous intimation has been given to the appellant so any such letter should be sent as long before the hearing as circumstances allow. A copy of the letter should be sent to the Clerk of Justiciary as soon as possible.

## 2.39 Consequences of abandonment

Once it is clear that the appeal has been wholly abandoned and is not to proceed (however that result has to be achieved) the effect is the same as if the appeal has been determined and simply dismissed by the court. The Clerk of Justiciary ascertains if the appellant was on bail pending the determination of the appeal. Intimation of the (deemed) dismissal goes to the Crown Office, the appellant's agent, the prison governor (where necessary), Criminal Records Office, the Legal Aid Board, the judge or sheriff and the sheriff clerk (to enable him to release Crown productions). If the appellant was on bail, Justiciary Office prepares, and a single High Court judge signs, an interlocutor recalling his bail order and authorising the Clerk of Justiciary to grant warrant to officers of law to apprehend the convicted person and to convey him to prison to serve the remainder of his sentence: see section 268(3). Unlike summary appeal procedure, which requires the matter to go back to the procurator-fiscal for an application to the court for enforcement of the warrant, the solemn warrant can be executed immediately. Thus an appellant on bail who also attends Parliament House on the day fixed for the hearing but chooses to abandon the appeal without going into court can surrender himself to the court (the clerk will provide Form 41 for him to sign) and the warrant will be executed at once. Otherwise the Crown Office receives the principal warrant from the Clerk of Justiciary and a copy of the interlocutor recalling bail. If the ex-appellant is then in custody in connection with some other matter, the principal warrant and a copy of the interlocutor are sent direct to the governor of the prison where the ex-appellant is held.

## JUDGE'S REPORT

### 2.40 Report to be furnished timeously

The judge who presided at the trial leading to the appellant's conviction or who passed sentence following the appellant's plea of guilty to any charge on indictment receives from the Clerk of Justiciary a copy of the written note of appeal.[1] It is then his duty to furnish the Clerk of Justiciary with a report in writing giving the judge's opinion on the case generally and on the grounds of appeal contained on the note of appeal.[2] He must furnish his report as soon as is reasonably practicable. If the Clerk of Justiciary does not receive it within four weeks action is taken by him to ensure that the report is provided. If necessary, the High Court can order it to be furnished and may specify a period within which that must be done.[3] The judge cannot decline to furnish a report because the grounds are inadequate in some way, such as failing to meet the requirements of the Practice Note of 29 March 1985[4] as to specification of the grounds.[5] The Clerk of Justiciary sends a copy of the report to the convicted person or to his solicitor (ie the solicitor known to be his agent in relation to the appeal proceedings).

A report will be called for in the same way in a case which is referred to the High Court by the Secretary of State under section 263(1).[6] The judge's report is available only to the High Court and the parties;[7] but copies are in practice made available to those who report proceedings of the High Court in legal periodicals.

1 s 233(1).
2 s 236A(1).
3 s 236A(2).
4 Cf 2.38 above.
5 *Henry v Docherty* 1989 SCCR 426.
6 s 236A(1).
7 s 236A(3).

### 2.41 The judge must report

As section 236A says, the report must give the judge's opinion on the case generally and on the grounds contained in the note of appeal. In summary cases, where the trial judge has to draft a stated case and different statutory provisions apply, sheriffs have declined to state a case in circumstances in which the statement of matters which the appellant desired to bring under review disclosed no relevant ground of appeal[1] or failed to specify or focus the issue sufficiently clearly and unambiguously to enable the sheriff to understand what the point of the appeal was.[2] In solemn cases, it is clear that the judgment as to the adequacy of the grounds is one for the High Court to make[3] and the reporting judge must furnish a report, regardless of the judge's opinion of the shortcomings of the grounds of appeal.[4] If he does not report, or prepares and sends what purports to be a report but which the High Court regards as inadequate, he will be required by the High Court to provide a (supplementary) report containing the information which the High Court needs and any other information which the judge considers is relevant to the appeal.

1 *McQuarrie v Carmichael* 1989 SCCR 370.
2 *Durant v Lockhart* 1986 SCCR 23; *Galloway v Hillary* 1983 SCCR 119.
3 *Smith v HM Advocate* 1983 SCCR 30.
4 *Henry v Docherty* 1989 SCCR 426.

## 2.42 Contents of judge's report

There are obviously no rigid rules as to the contents of the report; and the curious statutory desideratum 'the judge's opinion on the case generally' might appear to open a surprisingly wide door, particularly given the circumstance that in solemn cases the jury alone determines all questions of fact, including credibility and reliability.[1] But there is no barrier to the judge's expressing an opinion on any aspect of the case and indeed - given that he must give his opinion on the grounds contained in the note of appeal, regardless of his view as to their relevancy - he may be obliged to do so. Thus in *Rubin v HM Advocate*, above, the additional ground of appeal contained the assertion, 'That the evidence of the Crown witness number 15 ... was *and is* [emphasis added] so deficient with regard to its character, quality and strength as to render it insufficient to substantiate or materially corroborate the Crown case'. Another appellant had a similarly worded ground of appeal. Clearly, despite the rule that 'questions of the reliability and credibility of witnesses are essentially questions for the jury',[2] the reporting judge must report his opinion on any ground so stated, and that would appear to necessitate some comment on matters of fact and evidence. In *Mitchell v HM Advocate*[3] and in the later associated case of *Chapman v HM Advocate* (unreported) both trial judges in their respective reports made comment about the evidence. It is clear that, in any particular case, such opinions might assist the High Court to decide if a miscarriage of justice has occurred. If the final judgment about whether or not a miscarriage of justice has occurred is one that has to be made against the whole known background of the case - and it is - then the trial judge's opinion about the quality and coherence of the evidence is a factor which can be taken into account in making any necessary assessment of the quality or sufficiency of the evidence. But comments upon the witnesses are not appropriate where the issue is purely one of sufficiency.[4]

1 *Rubin v HM Advocate* 1984 SCCR 96.
2 *Rubin* at 103 per the Lord Justice General.
3 1989 SCCR 502.
4 *Horne v HM Advocate* 1991 SCCR 248 at 253.

## 2.43 The report and the evidence

The purpose of the report is to assist the High Court to appreciate the background against which the appeal is taken and the context in which the grounds of appeal arise. When the case is put out for hearing the judges of the High Court will not have the evidence before them but, where the appeal is taken against conviction, they will have a transcript of the judge's charge to the jury. The judge in preparing his report should be able to make reference to parts of the charge if there can be found there any account of the evidence or of any other circumstance which is relevant to any ground of appeal. Whatever needs to be added should be added with such economy as the author can command.[1] If one issue in the appeal is the sufficiency of the evidence the High Court will expect to find all the evidence upon which the Crown is able to found referred to in the judge's charge. Thus in *McGougan v HM Advocate*[2] the court expressed surprise that, while the trial judge's report referred to certain evidence in which corroboration might be found, the charge to the jury did not refer to some of that evidence. That, taken along with a misdirection, was enough to persuade the court that a miscarriage of justice had occurred.

1 *Horne v HM Advocate* 1991 SCCR 248 at 252 per Lord Justice Clerk Ross.
2 1991 SCCR 49 at 53, 54.

## 2.44 The report and alleged misdirections

As in the case of judges' reports on sentence (cf 2.45 below) the report should be more concerned to explain the circumstances in which the direction complained of came to be given than to justify or defend them. The court of appeal can read what was said to the jury and needs only to be advised fully and accurately as to its context. If the reporting judge considers that the transcript is inaccurate in any material particular he should point out the inaccuracy. If he considers that the alleged misdirection ought for completeness to be considered along with other passages in the charge he should direct attention to them. If he thinks on reflection that the direction given was faulty he may choose to say so in his report; but unless it is clearly wrong he is perfectly entitled to leave it to the court of appeal to assess the charge as a whole; after all the appeal may not go ahead, and, in any event, the real issue is whether or not a miscarriage of justice has occurred; and that is not a matter for the reporting judge to decide.

### 2.45 The report and sentence

The purpose of the report when dealing with a sentence or order appealed against is to explain why the sentencing judge acted as he did. It is also very important for him to disclose fully, but concisely, what information was placed before him and what representations were made to him, which of these matters he considered of real or of little or no importance and whether or not he took into account any notorious circumstance known to him and considered relevant, such as the prevalence of the type of offence in the locality. If he has pronounced sentence after trial and the appellant has also appealed against conviction then the Appeal Court will have the charge to the jury and also the transcript of the sentencing proceedings. So, if when imposing sentence the trial judge has publicly and fully explained why he was imposing the sentence imposed, the report may be short and may explain the sentence by reference to the contemporary transcript. It is proper for a judge who on mature reflection has come to the conclusion that the sentence he imposed was too severe to say so and to indicate the lesser sentence he now feels he should have imposed.

## THE HEARING

### 2.46 Obligation or entitlement to be present

Some appellants are in custody; some have been admitted to bail and are at liberty; some are at liberty but not on bail (eg those given a non-custodial sentence). An appellant who has been admitted to bail and who is at liberty must, unless the High Court otherwise directs, appear personally in court on the day or days fixed for the hearing of the appeal: section 238(2). An appellant who is in custody is entitled to be present (subject to the exceptions contained in section 240); but he is not obliged to be present[1] – unless he has been admitted to bail and is back in custody on another matter; and the High Court can always excuse attendance.[2] In practice all appellants who are in custody (whatever the reason) are brought to court on the day or days appointed for the hearing of the appeal. Leave to attend is necessary if an appellant in custody wishes to attend any High Court proceedings preliminary or incidental to the appeal itself but in practice leave is always given and appellants in custody are brought to court for matters not dealt with by a single judge under section 247. According to section 240, leave is also needed 'where the appeal is on some ground involving a question of law alone', but, in practice, this provision is a dead letter and leave is neither sought nor required for an appellant who is in custody (whether in respect of the offence appealed against or in respect of a separate matter). Thus, despite the terms of sections 240 and 241, if an appellant is in custody, the Clerk of Justiciary, who will have prepared a list of appeals and appellants three to four weeks before the week in which the appeal is to be heard, notifies all the persons specified in sections 241 and 242 of the probable date of the hearing. This notification enables the Secretary of State to take the necessary administrative measures to ensure that the appellants will be able to appear and also be able to consult their legal advisers (if any). Appellants appearing from custody must appear in 'ordinary civilian clothes'.[3] Appellants who are neither on bail nor in custody include those who were admonished or given an absolute discharge but are appealing against conviction, persons who received a non-custodial sentence (eg a fine), those who have completed their sentences, those on deferred sentence, those who have escaped from custody and those who have died. If no appearance is made by or on behalf of an appellant the appeal is disposed of as if it had been abandoned and is dismissed for want of insistence.[4] Appellants who have received a non-custodial sentence are entitled but not obliged to be present and their counsel may present their appeals in their absence. If an appellant dies, his appeal dies with him.[5]

1 *Manuel v HM Advocate* 1958 JC 41.
2 s 238(2).
3 s 242.
4 ss 257 and 244(1).
5 *Keane v Adair* 1941 JC 77.

## 2.47 Conduct of appeal

Certain aspects of the appeal hearing are discussed in chapter 6 (Powers of the Appeal Court) and in chapter 1 at 1.08 *et seq*. The appeal court consists of three or more Lords Commissioners of Justiciary, who may include temporary or retired judges. Five or more will sit if it is necessary to reconsider previous decisions of the High Court.[1] Five judges will sit to hear an appeal on an issue if the trial judge has decided the issue after consulting two other judges.[2] The High Court (or a single judge exercising powers under section 247) may continue the hearing of any appeal or application to a date fixed or to be fixed.[3] The High Court has a wide discretionary power to excuse non-compliance with many provisions of the Act or with any rule of practice in force under the Act of Adjournal, so far as relating to appeals.[4]

Appellants who have received a non-custodial sentence are entitled but not obliged to be present and their counsel may present their appeals in their absence. If an accused person dies after the verdict in a trial, any appeal relating to the verdict or sentence dies with him: *Keane v Adair*.[5] One court's powers in relation to handcuffing the accused or otherwise exercising security controls are discussed in *Ralston v HM Advocate*.[6]

1 *Leggate v HM Advocate* 1988 SCCR 391; *Morrison v HM Advocate* 1990 SCCR 235; both cases where a bench of seven judges overruled a decision by a bench of five judges.
2 *HM Advocate v McDonald* 1984 SCCR 229; *Hay v HM Advocate* 1968 JC 40.
3 s 259.
4 s 277.
5 1941 JC 77.
6 1988 SCCR 590.

## 2.48 Bill of suspension

Section 230 excludes appeals to the High Court by bill of suspension from any conviction, sentence, judgment or order pronounced in any proceedings on indictment in the sheriff court. This provision did not prevent the taking of a bill of suspension by a witness who had been dealt with for contempt of court in solemn proceedings in the sheriff court in *Butterworth v Herron*[1] but this case has now been overruled: see 2.24 above. There is no provision for appeal by bill of suspension in relation to proceedings in the High Court.

1 1975 SLT (Notes) 56.

# 3. Appeals by the accused: summary jurisdiction



## APPEALS BY STATED CASE

## 3.01 Right of appeal

Before trial, an accused person upon whom a complaint has been served has a right of appeal (but only with leave of the court of first instance) against a decision of that court relating either to any objection which he has taken to the competency or relevancy of the complaint or the proceedings, or in relation to a denial issued by or on behalf of the accused that he is the person charged by the police with the offence.[1] He may also appeal by note of appeal against the grant of an application under section 331A(2) to extend the 40 days maximum detention period prescribed by section 331A(1)[2]. After trial, any person who has been convicted on a summary complaint, whether in the sheriff court or the district court, has the right to appeal to the High Court against the conviction, against the sentence or against both conviction and sentence.[3] His right of appeal includes the right to appeal against any of the various orders that may be made at the time of conviction or sentence (see 2.23 above). Leave to appeal is not required after conviction. As in solemn cases (see 2.01 above) a person who has pled guilty may competently appeal against conviction. The accused's right to appeal to the High Court by bill of suspension against a conviction is preserved to the extent specified in section 453A.

1 s 334(2A).
2 s 331A(3).
3 s 442(1).

## 3.02 Appeal before trial

The right to appeal before trial in respect of matters of competency, relevancy or the identity of the accused is contained in section 334(2A). The procedure is regulated by Rule 128 (as amended in 1992), and Form 78.[1] A plea in relation to such matters may, prior to pleading, be stated by or on behalf of the accused at the first calling of the case whether he is present or absent but legally represented (by counsel or by a solicitor).[2] Such a plea, if not taken then, may not be taken later, except with the leave of the court, which may be granted only on cause shown.[3] Leave of the court which has decided the issue raised by such a plea (prior to pleading to the complaint) is required for an appeal[4] under section 334 against the decision.[5] Such leave may be granted on the motion of the accused or by the court *ex proprio motu*. If leave is refused, that refusal is not appealable.[6] If leave is granted by the court it cannot proceed to trial at once, as otherwise permitted by section 337 paragraph (a);[7] the presiding judge must adjourn[8] the case to a diet for trial or some other fixed diet. The High Court, once the appeal has been taken, may postpone the trial diet (if one has been fixed) for such period as to that court seems appropriate and has a discretion to direct that the whole or any part of that period is not to count towards any time limit applying in respect of the case.[9] If the High Court makes an order postponing the trial diet under section 334(2B), with or without a direction, the Clerk of Justiciary intimates to all the persons specified in Rule 128(9) of the Act of Adjournal (Consolidation) 1988, ie the appropriate clerk of court, to any accused who are not parties to the appeal, or to their solicitors, and to the governor of any institution in which any of the accused is detained.

1 See 3.03.
2 s 334(1) and (2).
3 s 334(1).
4 (Ie an immediate appeal).
5 Without prejudice to any rights of appeal under s 442 (after conviction or acquittal) or s 453A (suspension or advocation).
6 s 334(2A).
7 s 334(2C).
8 s 334(2C) and s 337, paragraph (b).
9 s 334(2B).

## 3.03 Appeal procedure (pre-trial)

The procedure governing such an appeal is that prescribed by the Act of Adjournal (Consolidation) 1988, Rule 128, as amended. An accused whose plea to competency or relevancy has been repelled must state to the court which has repelled the plea how he pleads to the charge or charges set out in the complaint before he applies for leave to appeal. If he pleads guilty, he can still competently appeal to the High Court after conviction (by stated case or by bill of suspension) *Harvey v Lockhart*.[1] The provisions of Rule 128(1) applied expressly only to objections stated to the competency or relevancy; but section 334(2A) allows an appeal also against the ruling of the court of first instance in relation to a denial by the accused that he was the person charged by the police with the offence. It is not clear in what circumstances an accused could appeal against an adverse ruling on such an issue, which is one of fact and to which the limited[2] presumption contained in section 26(5) of the Criminal Justice (Scotland) Act 1980 applies at any time. However, it is conceivable that the form in which the issue was raised could result in the courts making an appealable decision, as apparently envisaged by section 334(2A).[3] There appeared to be a lacuna in the Act of Adjournal,[4] as suggested by *Renton and Brown* at paragraph 14–25, footnote 3. If leave to appeal is granted, the clerk of court enters the necessary details in the minutes of proceedings.[5] The appeal must be by way of note of appeal in the form of Form 78 of Schedule 1 to the Act of Adjournal (Consolidation) 1988. Form 78 needs no explanation, except to note that it does not deal explicitly with an appeal in respect of a ruling against a person whose objection is that he is not the person charged by the police with the offence. However, the necessary details in connection with such an appeal can go under heads (2) and (3) in Form 78. Only two days are allowed for lodging the note of appeal with the clerk of the court that granted leave,[6] subject, however, to the automatic extension allowed by section 451(1) if the second of the two days falls on a Saturday, Sunday or court holiday prescribed for the relevant court. Once the note of appeal is lodged, that clerk sends a copy to the respondent or his solicitor, requests a report from the presiding judge and transmits the note of appeal, and certified copies of the complaint, the minutes of proceedings and relevant documents to the Clerk of Justiciary. The presiding judge must send his report as soon as possible to the Clerk of Justiciary who furnishes copies to the parties or their solicitors. The Clerk of Justiciary arranges for the Appeal Court (ie three judges of the High Court) to hear the appeal as soon as possible and it is his responsibility to copy any documents that that court may need.

1 1991 SCCR 83, a stated case.
2 *Smith v Paterson* 1982 SCCR 295; *Hamilton v Ross* 1991 SCCR 165.
3 See, for example, *Tudhope v Lawson* 1983 SCCR 435 and *Benton v Cardle* 1987 SCCR 738.
4 Now amended
5 Act of Adjournal (Consolidation) 1988, r 128(3).
6 s 334(2A).

## 3.04 Disposal of the appeal (pre-trial)

Any appeal against a preliminary diet decision may be abandoned at any time prior to the hearing of the appeal.[1] Form 79 should be used to effect the abandonment. When the minute of abandonment is lodged, the Clerk of Justiciary informs the appropriate clerk of court and the respondent or his solicitor of the abandonment and the court of first instance may then proceed as accords,[2] that is to say, the procedural process at first instance resumes, as near as may be, just as if no appeal had been taken. In disposing of an appeal the High Court may affirm the decision of the court of first instance or may remit the case to it with such directions in the matter as the High Court thinks fit.[3] In a case where the court of first instance has dismissed the complaint, or any part of it, and a successful appeal is taken by the prosecutor against that decision the High Court will, if necessary, direct the court of first instance to fix a trial diet. In that situation, the accused (ie the unsuccessful respondent) will not have pled in common form; but there is no statutory provision requiring that a special diet be fixed to allow him to plead.

1 Rule 128(10).
2 Rule 128(12).
3 s 334(2D).

## 3.05 Methods of appeal after conviction

The principal method of appeal against sentence alone is by note of appeal (see 3.39 below); but the proviso to section 442B preserves the right of a convicted person to proceed by way of a bill of suspension in respect of any alleged fundamental irregularity relating to the imposition of the sentence. In cases where the sentence is not the only issue, the principal method of appeal after conviction is by stated case. But in some circumstances, discussed below,[1] an accused may proceed by bill of suspension choose to.[2] There are also certain special methods of seeking review, or the like. They are discussed elsewhere. They are (1) petitions to the *nobile officium*;[3] and (2) references to the Court of Justice of the European Communities.[4]

1 See 3.06 *et seq.*
2 s 453A.
3 See 5.01 *et seq.*
4 See 5.10 *et seq.*

## 3.06 Choice of method of appeal (against conviction or conviction and sentence)

Although, in some circumstances, more than one method of appeal may be open to a party,[1] usually one method is competent and appropriate and others are not. Sections 442, 442A and 444 allow any person convicted in summary proceedings to appeal to the High Court, so as to bring under review any alleged miscarriage of justice in the proceedings, by applying for a stated case, against conviction alone, or against both conviction and sentence. This right to appeal by stated case is, however, conferred without prejudice to any right of appeal under section 453A. Furthermore, section 449(2), which provides that once the stated case has been lodged with the Clerk of Justiciary[2] the appellant shall be held to have abandoned any other mode of appeal which might otherwise have been open to him, is specifically made subject to section 453A, so that, if section 453A applies, this deemed abandonment does not occur. Accordingly, section 453A allows an accused to appeal to the High Court by bill of suspension against a conviction (which, for this purpose, includes conviction and sentence) on the ground of an alleged miscarriage of justice in the proceedings if an appeal under section 442 would be incompetent or would in the circumstances be inappropriate. If an application for a stated case has already been made and in that application (or in any duly made amendment or addition to it)[3] the same alleged miscarriage of justice is referred to, the appeal by bill of suspension cannot proceed without the leave of the High Court until the appeal by way of application for a stated case has been finally disposed of or abandoned.[4] The effect of these provisions is that, if an appellant raises the same point of alleged miscarriage of justice both in a stated case and in a bill of suspension, the bill cannot proceed (without leave of the High Court) until the stated case has been disposed of whether by the court[5] or by abandonment by minute.[6] Section 453A(3) provides that the provisions of section 453A(1) and (2) are to be without prejudice to any rule of law relating to bills of suspension or advocation in so far as such rule of law is not inconsistent with those provisions. And section 455(1) provides that the provisions regulating appeals shall, subject to the provision of Part II of the Act (summary procedure), be without prejudice to any other mode of appeal competent. A similar saving is contained in section 443. The result of these provisions is that in deciding which method of appeal to adopt the appellant and his legal advisers have to be familiar with the old (pre-1980) law as well as the recent statutory procedures. On the other hand, the preservation of some pre-1980 appeal procedures means that there is a rich variety of instruments for raising matters which an appellant desires to bring under review.

1 Eg advocation or note of appeal, in *Lafferty v Jessop* 1989 SCCR 451 – though there was no conviction in this case.

2 s 448(4).
3 Under s 444(1B).
4 Proviso to s 453A.
5 ss 452A, 453D, 453E.
6 s 449(1).

## 3.07 General rule governing choice of procedure

Appeal by stated case is the normal method of appeal by a person who has been convicted in summary proceedings and who seeks to appeal against his conviction on its merits. In *Handley v Pirie*[1] the High Court, though allowing an appeal brought by way of a bill of suspension, said, 'We ... wish to cast no doubt upon the general rule, which will be enforced, that a challenge of a conviction on its merits will, save in exceptional circumstances, only be entertained when the matter is brought before the court by a stated case in which the considered views of the trial judge will be expressed.' In that case, however, the circumstances were said to be 'instantly verifiable' and the only point to be divided was 'a crisp issue of competency' which could be resolved by applying the terms of the statute to the known and agreed facts and circumstances which were set out in the minutes of procedure. The only point falling to be decided in that case resolved itself into a simple question of law, viz 'Did the trial begin on 3 November 1975 when the accused appeared at the diet ordained for trial and pleaded not guilty or on 28 November 1975, the date to which the trial was adjourned, no evidence having been led after the recording of the plea.' If, as a matter of law, the trial had begun on 3 November it was not in dispute that the conviction could not stand; if the trial had begun on 28 November it was not in dispute that the conviction must stand. Thus neither the facts nor the merits of the case itself were in issue, the trial judge's view of them was irrelevant, and the only 'fact' that needed to be known was instantly discoverable from the minutes of procedure. The general rule clearly enunciated in *Handley v Pirie* is still applicable and any exceptions to it must derive from the statutory provisions referred to. Accordingly, if, for any reason, a convicted person considers that a method of appeal other than by stated case might be adopted, he must decide (1) if appeal by stated case is competent or incompetent, (2) if the alternative contemplated is competent, and (3) (if both methods under consideration are competent) which of them is the more appropriate. In practical terms, appropriateness and competency tend to raise the same or similar considerations.

1 1977 SLT 30.

## 3.08 Competency of proceedings by stated case

As stated in the preceding paragraphs, appeal by stated case is competent against conviction or against both conviction and sentence and is effectively the only competent process for reviewing the merits of a conviction. Until he has been convicted, an accused person cannot appeal by stated case. Others, for example witnesses dealt with for contempt, or an accused person acquitted of the charge(s) in the complaint but punished for contempt, or a solicitor found guilty of contempt,[1] have no right to appeal by stated case; the appropriate procedure for them is to raise a bill of suspension. Similarly, if a purported conviction has been recorded but the whole proceedings have been vitiated by some essentially procedural or jurisdictional flaw and are inept, that matter ought to be brought before the court by a method other than by stated case. But if a stated case is taken and such a flaw emerges the court is likely to entertain and decide the point.[2] If the whole proceedings are incompetent and, as a result, fall to be treated as entirely null and void, then any acquittal or conviction therein or any sentence pronounced is incompetent. That kind of incompetency has been held to be not properly reviewable by stated case because the essence of the ground of appeal is that what purports to be a conviction (or acquittal or sentence) is in law and in reality nothing of the kind. It is just a sham. The person 'convicted' accordingly does not qualify for the statutory description of 'any person convicted in summary proceedings', because those proceedings were inept, null and void. This was the situation in *MacNeill v MacGregor*.[3] When that case first called in court the accused's solicitor tendered a plea of guilty in the absence of the accused; the plea was accepted and duly recorded and sentence was imposed. On the next day the same solicitor appeared and explained that the plea had been tendered in error. The sheriff allowed the plea to be withdrawn and recalled the sentence. The case thereafter proceeded to trial. It was held that the result of the trial (which was an acquittal) could not be challenged (by the prosecutor) in an appeal by stated case because the trial itself, and indeed everything else that had happened since sentence had been passed on the guilty plea, had been *ultra vires* and inept. The foundation for a stated case did not exist. Although, as noted in 3.09 below, procedural irregularities, and other irregular proceedings, including oppression, may be able to be brought under review by bill of suspension, it is usually competent in relation to such matters to proceed by way of stated case following conviction.

1 Eg as in *McKinnon v Douglas* 1982 SCCR 80.

2 See Fundamental Nullity, 5.26 *et seq*.
3 1975 JC 55.

## 3.09 Bill of suspension

'Suspension is a competent method of review, available in summary proceedings only[1] when some step in the procedure has gone wrong, or some factor has emerged which satisfies the court that a miscarriage of justice has taken place resulting in a failure to do justice to the accused': *MacGregor v MacNeill*.[2] This case was the sequel to *MacNeill v MacGregor*;[3] in an appeal brought by bill of suspension after the failure of the stated case, the conviction recorded following the plea of guilty tendered in error was quashed. *Renton and Brown* defines suspension more generally:[4] 'Suspension is a process, restricted to criminal cases, whereby an illegal or improper warrant, conviction or judgment issued by an inferior judge may be reviewed and set aside by the High Court'. If the appellant is detained in custody the process becomes one of suspension and liberation. Suspension is not open to the prosecutor: he proceeds by bill of advocation, or by stated case, or by petition to the nobile officium. 'A bill of suspension is particularly appropriate when the appeal is based either on defects which appear on the face of the proceedings themselves or on irregular or oppressive conduct on the part of the judge or the prosecutor'.[5] Thus, more generally, where there has been some material procedural irregularity, some jurisdictional defect or some clear departure from the rules of natural justice or other such circumstance which it appears may have affected the proceedings and resulted in justice not having been done to the appellant, he may competently appeal by bill of suspension against the conviction or purported conviction or against a sentence or purported sentence.[6] Suspension is competent, and appears to be the more appropriate form of appeal, where what is suggested is that the summary trial judge should have declined jurisdiction because of some personal connection with the accused or the case and the related principle that justice must be seen to be done.[7] Alleged oppressive conduct by the trial judge can competently be brought under review by bill of suspension.[8] The procedure was properly and successfully used in *Stewart v Lowe*[9] where the sheriff, after trial, convicted the accused without having given the accused's solicitor any opportunity to make submissions. Where there has been a plea of guilty it would be competent, and probably more appropriate, to proceed by bill of suspension.[10] Procedure by bill of suspension is available only where there is a conviction or sentence to suspend[11] (apart from the exception that exists in respect of incidental warrants, such as search warrants, which do not form part of the case.[12] It is competent for a convicted person to present a bill of suspension to the High Court if the judge who convicted him cannot sign the stated case because of illness or death and by means of such a bill to bring under review any matter which might otherwise have been brought under review by stated case.[13] If the accused seeks to bring under review *pendente processu* alleged irregularities in the preliminary stages of a case, being irregularities that seriously put at risk the prospects of there being a fair trial, he may proceed by bill of advocation.[14] There is no time limit for bringing a bill of suspension but it should be done as soon as possible: acquiescence in the judgment complained of may be inferred from undue delay: *Low v Rankine*[15] and *McPherson v Henderson*,[16] in which the imposition of a period of disqualification was challenged by means of a bill of suspension twenty years after the event. The challenge failed on other grounds, but the court appeared to suggest that the appellant might have been barred by acquiescence. What might amount to undue delay is judged in the light of the whole circumstances and any judgment on such a matter is, to some extent, discretionary.[17]

1 *Butterworth v Herron* 1975 SLT (Notes) 56, to the contrary effect, was overruled in *George Outram & Co Ltd v Lees* 1992 SCCR 120.
2 1975 JC 57 per Wheatley LJC.
3 1975 JC 55.
4 *Renton and Brown*, para 16–133.
5 Thomson Report (Third Report) Cmnd 7005, para 9.01
6 See proviso to s 442B (fundamental irregularity).
7 See *Harper of Oban (Engineering) Ltd v Henderson* 1988 SCCR 351; *Robertson v MacPhail* 1989 SCCR 693 and *McPherson v Hamilton*; *Penman v Hamilton* 1990 SCCR 270.
8 See *Kane v Tudhope* 1986 SCCR 161; *Bradford v McLeod* 1985 SCCR 379 (sheriff stating on a social occasion before trial of miners that he would not grant legal aid to miners).
9 1991 SCCR 317.
10 See editor's comments, at page 87 in *Harvey v Lockhart* 1991 SCCR 83, an unusual case in which the accused took a plea to the competency of the proceedings, pled guilty when it was repelled, did not then apply for leave to appeal, was sentenced and then successfully appealed by stated case.
11 *Durant v Lockhart* 1985 SCCR 72.
12 Cf *Morton v McLeod* 1981 SCCR 159 at 164, per Lord Cameron and editor's commentary in *Durant v Lockhart* above.
13 s 444(2).
14 *Durant v Lockhart* 1985 SCCR 72; see 3.12 *et seq* below.
15 1917 JC 39.
16 1984 SCCR 294.
17 Trotter: *Summary Criminal Jurisdiction*, p 66; *Watson v Scott* (1898) 2 Adam 501; *Macfarlan v Pringle* (1904) 4 Adam 403; *Muirhead v McIntosh* (1890) 2 White 473; *Renton and Brown* 16–152.

## 3.10 Bill of suspension - style and procedure

The bill is prepared and signed either by a solicitor or by counsel.[1] If the solicitor does not practise in Edinburgh he may (but no longer needs to) appoint an Edinburgh agent to act for him.[2] The signed bill is lodged in the Justiciary Office. An order for service is craved and there may be a crave for interim liberation, if the accused is in custody, or for any other interim order, such as interim suspension of disqualification. The bill is dealt with in the first instance by a single judge. He may, if he thinks the bill discloses no substantial ground, remit the case to a quorum of the High Court who may refuse the bill. In the normal case an order for service will be granted and the bill may be served by any officer of law.[3] The prosecutor is the respondent. Where a bill contains a prayer for interim suspension of any order or for interim liberation, the judge before whom the bill is laid for a first deliverance must assign a diet at which counsel, or a solicitor who has a right of audience in the High Court of Justiciary, may be heard on the interim prayer.[4] The Clerk of Justiciary must forthwith give notice of that diet to the parties.[5] Any application for interim regulation must be dealt with within seven days. Such matters are dealt with by a single judge whose decision is final. If interim liberation is granted it is not effective until the bill has been served on the respondent, and the complainer or his solicitor has returned to the Clerk of Justiciary the principal bill and first deliverance endorsed by the clerk of the sentencing court with a certificate that an execution or acceptance of service has been exhibited to him. On certifying the bill, the clerk of the sentencing court must send a certified copy of the complaint and the relative minute of proceedings to the Clerk of Justiciary[6] at the same time as he returns the bill. It is preferable practice to serve the bill and a copy thereof on the clerk of the sentencing court rather than simply attend and hand it in. It is now the practice for the Clerk of Justiciary, when ordering service, to send a copy of the bill to the sentencing judge together with a letter suggesting that he may wish to comment on the terms of the bill. Such comments take the form of a report which is prepared and sent to the Clerk of Justiciary and is used to assist the court in consideration of the bill. It is the duty of the solicitor for the complainer (ie the appellant), or the complainer himself if not represented, to uplift from the Clerk of Justiciary the complaint, the bill and relative minute of proceedings and to arrange for printing and to return the process to the Clerk of Justiciary not later than seven days before the hearing.[7] In other respects the duties of solicitors, or of party appellants (complainers), are those specified in Rules 135 to 138 discussed below at 3.34. As with stated cases, the prosecutor, if not prepared to maintain the judgment appealed against, may consent to the setting aside of the conviction. This matter is more fully discussed in chapter 4 at 4.15. The respondent is not obliged to lodge written answers to a bill of suspension though he may choose to do so.

1 Styles may be found in Trotter *Summary Criminal Jurisdiction* in Appendix III at pages 537 to 539. More recent examples are printed as an appendix, below.
2 Rule 135, as amended by Act of Adjournal (Consolidation Amendment No 3) 1991.
3 s 455(2).
4 Rule 139, as amended in 1991 (Consolidation Amendment No 3).
5 Rule 139.
6 Rule 133.
7 Rule 136.

## 3.11 Suspension of warrants and incidental orders

The High Court has power to suspend an illegal search warrant which is *ex facie* valid,[1] but the trial judge cannot do so.[2] An application by bill of suspension (or advocation) to suspend such a warrant is competent both before trial[3] and after trial.[4] The procedure may be used *pendente processu* to challenge as oppressive a warrant granted by a sheriff for the taking of a blood sample (for blood grouping purposes) from an accused person.[5] As in the case of a search warrant the granting of the warrant can be challenged after conviction.[6] The process of suspension is available to challenge other warrants such as a warrant to take fingerprints[7] - a bill of advocation by the procurator fiscal, but the same principles apply - a warrant to place an accused person on an identification parade,[8] or a warrant to take a sample of pubic hair.[9] A bill of suspension may still be competent (eg more than twenty-four hours after the order has been made) to suspend an order made by a court whereby a first offender is ordered to be detained in custody pending the pursuit of inquiries whose purpose is to discover if there is some method of dealing with him other than by imposing a custodial sentence;[10] but the competency of such a bill must now be in doubt, and the correct method of proceeding is by note of appeal presented to the High Court under section 380(2).[11] This can be heard promptly by the bail judge in chambers. Proceeding by bill of suspension would be appropriate for a challenge to an order made in relation to bankers books.[12]

1 *Bell v Black and Morrison* (1865) 5 Irv 57.

2 *Allan v Tant 1986 SCCR 175.*
3 *Paterson v Macpherson* 1924 JC 38; and *HM Advocate v Gerald Rae* 1992 SCCR 1, *obiter* opinion of trial judge; cf also *Oldfield, Complainer* 1988 SCCR 371 (bill of advocation).
4 *Bell v Black and Morison* (1865) 5 Irv 57.
5 See *Wilson v Milne* 1975 SLT (Notes) 26.
6 *Hay v HM Advocate*1968 JC 40.
7 See *Lees v Weston* 1989 SCCR 177.
8 *Currie v McGlennan* 1989 SCCR 466.
9 *McGlennan v Kelly* 1989 SCCR 352 also a Crown bill of advocation.
10 *Morrison v Clark* 1962 SLT 113.
11 See s 179, for solemn cases.
12 Cf *Jessop v Rae* 1990 SCCR 228 – this was also a Crown bill of advocation.

## 3.12 Advocation - generally

'Advocation, which is literally the calling up or removal of a cause from an inferior to a superior Court, seems to have been originally not strictly speaking a process of review, but a removal of the cause at its commencement or during its course, on account of some objection to the jurisdiction of the inferior Judge, or on account of partiality or incapacity on his part, in order to its being proceeded with before the superior Court or before some other tribunal or Judge . . . By degrees advocation came to be used also as a mode of review; as such it is strictly speaking the appropriate remedy for errors committed in the course of and during the dependence of the trial or criminal process, and before final judgment or sentence'.[1]

Until recently it had come to be accepted in practice that advocation was the means whereby the prosecutor might seek review, and that an accused would use suspension and not resort to advocation.[2] In 1969, the Lord Justice General (Clyde) said, 'In modern times this procedure has become very rare, and for practical purposes is really out of date'.[3] In the same case Lord Cameron said: 'The limited sphere of competence of the process of advocation lies in the correction of irregularities in the preliminary stages of a case, though recourse to the process is incompetent until the cause is finally determined, unless in very special circumstances'.[3] Recently, however, despite the provision of various other statutory means of review, the process of advocation has taken on a new lease of life, both for prosecutors and for accused persons, albeit in a limited sphere, and has been competently used before the final determination of the cause.

1 *Moncrieff on Review in Criminal Cases* (1877) p 163.
2 See the Thomson Committee (Third Report) chapter 15; see also Trotter: *Summary Criminal Jurisdiction* pp 68–69; *Hume* ii 509; *Alison*, ii 26, para 15.
3 *MacLeod v Levitt* 1969 JC 16 at 19.

## 3.13 Advocation by accused

It is now clear that advocation is still available in summary criminal proceedings *pendente processu* to enable an accused person to challenge some procedural irregularity (including any 'order or procedure' in the course of a trial or criminal process in an inferior court)[1] which threatens to deprive him of a fair trial. In *Durant v Lockhart*,[2] a case had been set down for trial but repeatedly adjourned without the trial being started; the accused took a bill of suspension against the fourth such adjournment and maintained that advocation as a form of review for accused persons was obsolete. In holding the bill of suspension incompetent because there was no conviction or sentence to be suspended, the court, after a brief reference to the history of advocation, concluded that there might be circumstances where procedure by way of advocation would still be open to an accused, and stated:[3]

> 'Accordingly we conclude that in very special circumstances where grave injustice to an accused would result from an irregularity in preliminary procedure, which injustice could not be reasonably rectified by a bill of suspension brought after the determination of the case, a bill of advocation would be appropriate'.

In *Grugen v Jessop*[4] an accused brought a bill of advocation to bring under review an alleged abuse of process which, it was complained, resulted from a sheriff's decision to continue a partly heard trial for eight days even although the forty-day period[5] had previously expired and had already had to be extended. The High Court dealt with the issue on its merits without suggesting that there was any question mark over the competency of proceeding by bill of advocation in the course of a trial. The High Court took the same approach in *Platt v Lockhart*,[6] raising no issue as to the competency of proceeding by bill of advocation in circumstances in which the accused's complaint was that it was incompetent for a sheriff to allow a new trial to commence against him, the first (partly-heard) trial not having been completed owing to the illness of the judge who had been hearing that trial. In *Hoyers (UK) Ltd v Houston*[7] the accused company competently proceeded by bill of advocation, before trial, against an interlocutor and decision of the sheriff allowing an amendment to the complaint by substituting therein the true version of the accused company's name in place of an inaccurate version. The **procedure for advocation** by an accused person in a summary case is the same as that for a bill of suspension, as described at 3.10 above. A style may be found in *Trotter*, Appendix

III, page 539, and a more recent example in the appendix to this book.

1 *Alison* ii 26.
2 1985 SCCR 72
3 At 74.
4 1988 SCCR 182.
5 Cf s 331A.
6 1988 SCCR 308.
7 1991 SCCR 919.

## 3.14 Appropriateness of different methods of appeal

It is clear that circumstances may arise in which it is competent to proceed by stated case but it would also be competent to proceed by suspension or by advocation. The first consideration must be one of timing. In relation to an ordinary trial resulting in conviction and sentence, procedure by stated case or by suspension is not available until the proceedings in the trial court have been concluded. Advocation is available at an earlier stage. If the point to be taken is one that may competently be taken either before or after trial (or even in the middle of an adjourned trial, as in *Grugen v Jessop*),[1] it is a matter of judgment in all the circumstances of the case which method is the most likely to produce the most expeditious result. Thus, for example, the complaint might be that the judge who is to try the case is disqualified by reason of some personal connection with the case or some conduct reflecting on his impartiality – as was alleged in *Bradford v McLeod*:[2] in that case the sheriff attended a social function and it was reported that in the course of a conversation about miners on picket lines he had remarked that he personally would not grant legal aid to miners. On the basis of such a report, agents appearing some months later for miners in a series of trials arising out of picket-line disturbances moved the sheriff to disqualify himself from considering the case. He declined to do so. The convictions of those who were convicted were then quashed on appeal, the appeal having been brought by bill of suspension. Obviously, however, the point, which was known about for some time before the trial, might have been taken before the trial by bill of advocation, if it had been known that the sheriff in question was to preside at the trial. The most important rule in such matters must be that it is necessary to consider whether or not the point, if not taken at the earliest opportunity, may be lost altogether, in the sense of being regarded as waived by not being taken timeously. This consideration is of vital importance in those cases in which some statutory provision prescribes a point of time (or procedural stage) beyond which the objection cannot be entertained: cf section 454(1).[3]

1 1988 SCCR 182.
2 1985 SCCR 379.
3 And see s 108(1): *HM Advocate v McDonald* 1984 SCCR 229, a solemn case.

## APPEAL BY STATED CASE

### 3.15 Stated case procedure

Any person convicted in summary proceedings may appeal to the High Court against his conviction or against both conviction and sentence by applying for a stated case. The sections of the 1975 Act governing the procedure are sections 442, 442A, 444, 446–453, 453D, and 453E. The Act of Adjournal (Consolidation) 1988, Chapter 2, Part IV also has effect, notably rules 127, 129, 131, 132, 134, 135–137, and forms 70–73, 75 and 80. The practitioner would be well advised to refer directly to these statutory provisions in relation to any step which has to be taken and not to rely solely on any summary or paraphrase thereof which appears in this or any other text. In relation to the detailed steps of procedure this text is intended not to take the place of the statutory provisions but to assist the practitioner to obtain access to them and to see how they are applied in practice.

### 3.16 Time for applying [section 444]

A stated case must be applied for 'within one week of the final determination of the proceedings'. The convicted person who applies for a stated case is referred to as 'the appellant'. The final determination of proceedings occurs on the day on which sentence is passed in open court,[1] unless sentence is deferred,[2] in which event the proceedings are deemed to be finally determined on the day on which sentence is first deferred in open court.[3] But in either event (sentence passed or first deferred) the final determination is not deemed to occur until the finding and sentence (or order deferred) are entered in the record of proceedings.[4] The one-week period is automatically extended by section 451(1) if the last day of that week falls on a Saturday, Sunday or court holiday (in the convicting court); the period then expires at the end of the next day which is not a Saturday, Sunday, or court holiday in the convicting court. The period of one week starts to run on the day after sentence is passed (or deferred) and entered in the record of the proceedings.[5] The application must be in the hands of the clerk of court within the week; mere posting within the week is not enough.[6] Only the High Court has a discretion to decide that a further period of time may be afforded to the applicant[7] who must apply in writing for the exercise of such a discretion to the Clerk of Justiciary, stating the grounds for the application, all in accordance with the requirements of section 444(4). Notification of the application must be made by the appellant or his solicitor to the clerk of the court from which the appeal is taken. That clerk must thereupon transmit the complaint, documentary productions and any other proceedings in the cause to the Clerk of Justiciary.[8] The High Court disposes of an application for further time to comply (section 444(3)) in the same manner as it deals with bail appeals (ie by a single High Court judge in chambers) but may dispense with a hearing: it almost invariably does.

**1** s 451(3).
**2** s 432.
**3** s 451(3).
**4** *Tudhope v Campbell* 1979 JC 24; *Williams v Linton* (1878) 6 R(J)12: see also s 430(1) and 434(2).
**5** *Hutton v Garland* (1884) 5 Couper 274; *Smith v Gray* 1925 JC 8 at 12, per Lord Anderson.
**6** *Elliot, Applicant* 1984 SLT 294.
**7** s 444(3).
**8** s 444(4).

## 3.17 The manner of applying [section 444]

The application, signed by the appellant or his solicitor, should be in the form prescribed by Form 71. It must be lodged with the clerk of the convicting court;[1] and the appellant must, within the same one week (or extended) period, send a copy to the respondent or the respondent's solicitor. The clerk of court enters in the record of proceedings the date when the application was lodged with the clerk of court. The appellant has the right to amend any matter stated in the application or to add new matters.[2] He effects such amendment or addition to the terms of the application by intimating in writing to the clerk with whom the application was lodged and must intimate any such alteration to the respondent or the respondent's solicitor. The period allowed for such alteration or addition, after lodging the initial application, (unless it is extended by the High Court under section 448(6)) is approximately five weeks. The actual period allowed for alteration/addition, after lodging the initial application, comprises (1) the two weeks or thereby between the lodging of the application and the issue of the draft stated case, plus (2) the three week adjustment period allowed by section 448(1), plus (3) an extra day or so, if appropriate, automatically allowed by section 451(1), plus (4) any extension allowed by the sheriff principal.[3]

1 s 444(1).
2 s 444(1B).
3 s 451(2).

## 3.18 The content of the application

The written application[1] must contain a full statement of all the matters which the appellant desires to bring under review and, where the appeal is also against sentence, a statement of that fact.[2] Clearly, if the appellant desires to bring under review particular points bearing upon sentence (being points upon which the sentencing court should have the opportunity to comment) they must be included and specified in the full statement; it is not enough merely to state (in the words of the form), 'The appeal is also against sentence'. Nor is it enough to aver something such as 'sentence too severe for the crime that I committed'.[3] As Form 71 indicates, the matters to be brought under review should, if possible, be distinctly specified in separate paragraphs. As Form 71 also indicates, the appellant should use that form to crave the court for bail, for interim suspension of an order for disqualification imposed under the Road Traffic Acts, or for any other order in terms of section 446(1) of the 1975 Act, which refers to bail, sist of execution and 'and other interim order'.[4]

1 Form 71.
2 s 444(1).
3 *Henry v Docherty* 1989 SCCR 426 where it was emphasised that the High Court might refuse to entertain such an appeal: see also 3.19 below.
4 See eg s 443A.

## 3.19 The statement of matters for review

The requirements in section 444(1)(b) are that the statement should be full and be a statement of all matters which the appellant desires to bring under review. It is not competent for an appellant, without leave of the High Court on cause shown, to found any aspect of his appeal on a matter not contained in his application under section 444(1), or in a duly made amendment or addition to that application.[1] In *MacLean v Mackenzie*[2] the court allowed the (party) appellant to raise an issue not raised in the stated case: exactly why is not clear, but it appears that the magistrate had acted *ultra vires*; it can be surmised that if the point is recognised as being a sound one as in *Aitken v Lockhart*[3] the court is more readily persuaded to entertain it. The practice note of 29 March 1985[4] applies in terms only to appeals in solemn procedure and appeals against sentence in summary procedure. However, the same principles apply to the statement of matters which an application for a stated case has to contain; section 233 of the 1975 Act, dealing with solemn appeals, also contains a requirement for 'a full statement of all the grounds of appeal'. If the matters to be brought under review are not sufficiently specified, the trial court may be unable to report upon them and the appeal court will be put at a grave disadvantage. The Crown may well found upon the same circumstances as causing an inexcusable disadvantage to the Crown. In an extreme case, the sheriff, or justice, is entitled to refuse to state a case; cf *Dickson v Valentine*[5] though he may not refuse to do so on the ground that the matter which it is desired to raise is not relevant; because that is for the High Court to decide.[6] In *McQuarrie v Carmichael*[7] the sheriff declined to state a case but simply wrote a short note asserting (correctly, as the appeal court acknowledged) that the matter desired to be brought under review was not a matter that could be brought under review in a stated case (ie the truthfulness of witnesses). The court, agreeing with the sheriff, said that he could not be compelled to state a case upon a clearly unstateable, ie obviously irrelevant, ground. In *Dickson v Valentine* above the sheriff — although not obliged to state a case because of the unspecific character of the matter ('the sheriff erred in law') — in fact stated a case: in the circumstances, the appeal court entertained the appeal, and refused it. An extreme example, in a solemn case, is *Mitchell v HM Advocate*[8] where, despite the fact that the appellant had been convicted of murder at a trial in which he pled diminished responsibility, the High Court, referring to the Practice Note of 29 March 1985, refused to entertain an appeal upon a ground stated as follows: 'The learned trial judge rehearsed incorrectly the crucial evidence of the psychiatric witness and in so doing misdirected the jury'. The Court regarded that as entirely lacking in specification and refused the appellant's motion to adjourn the case. In *Anderson v McClory*[9] the court, accepting the Crown's submission, declined to entertain an argument that a police request to a motorist to provide a specimen was not in accordance with section 7(1)(b) of the Road Traffic Act 1988, the only matter raised in his application being whether, as on the facts stated, the sheriff was entitled to convict the accused on charge (2). What is necessary is that the statement should explain in some detail what it is that the appellant is seeking to bring under review so that the court when stating the case can be in no doubt as to what the particular issue is: *Durant v Lockhart*.[10] Accordingly, if, for example, the point which it is desired to raise is a point as to sufficiency of evidence, it is not enough just to say, 'The evidence was insufficient to justify conviction'. The particular alleged weakness must be identified in such a way that the inferior court can state in the findings in full all matters relevant to the point which is to be taken. In *Durant v Lockhart*,[10] the point which it was desired to raise was whether or not it was necessary to adduce certain additional evidence to buttress, and thus to enable the Crown to depend upon, a statutory presumption contained in the Gas Act 1972, viz. that proof of one state of facts 'shall be *prima facie* evidence of' [the facts necessary to establish guilt]. What, therefore, should have been put into the application was some such form of words as: 'The provision as to '*prima facie* evidence' contained in the Gas Act 1972, Sch 4, para 20(3), did not, without additional evidence, provide sufficient evidence to infer guilt: there was no other sufficient evidence to establish guilt.' It is equally to be stressed that the point must be stated clearly and unambiguously.[11] It is not possible to spell out any more general rule or statement of what section 444(1)(b) requires: see eg *MacDougall, Petitioner*[12] where, although the ground was misconceived, the court held that the sheriff should have stated a case, and remitted to him to do so. As the considerations which apply in framing 'a full statement of all matters which the appellant desires to bring under review' (section 444(1)(b)) are effectively the same as those that apply to 'a full statement of all the grounds of appeal' (section 233(2)), reference should be made to the treatment of grounds of appeal in solemn cases in chapter 2.[13] The parties should propose the questions which are to be submitted for the opinion of the court. In certain instances, if this is well done, nothing more may be required in order to satisfy the requirement (on the appellant) of making a full statement of the matters he desires to bring under review: see 3.25 below (Form of questions or stated case). If an applicant for a stated case lodges an application which the court regards as not falling within the statute, the court's refusal to state a case disposes of the matter. If the seven day period has not expired it is competent to submit another application and, if it meets the statutory requirements, the court must state a case.[14] In *Galloway v Hillary*[15] the sheriff allowed a timeous, but insufficient, application to be amended after the expiry of the seven days: this seems a sensible way to proceed, though its competency might be open to question.

1 s 452(3).
2 1986 SCCR 482.
3 1989 SCCR 368.
4 cf 2.03 above.
5 1988 SCCR 325.
6 *McTaggart, Petitioner* 1987 SCCR 638; see also *MacDougall, Petitioner* 1986 SCCR 128.
7 1989 SCCR 371.
8 1991 SCCR 216.
9 1991 SCCR 571.
10 *Durant v Lockhart* 1986 SCCR 23.
11 *Durant v Lockhart* at 27.
12 1986 SCCR 128.
13 At 2.26 et seq.
14 *Singh, Petitioner* 1986 SCCR 215.
15 1983 SCCR 119.

## 3.20 *Interim* regulation if appellant in custody

If a convicted person who is in custody appeals under section 444, the convicting court may do all or any of the following: (1) grant bail;[1] (2) grant a sist of execution; (3) make any other interim order.[2]

1 See 9.10 et seq below.
2 See 9.10 et seq below; s 446(1).

## 3.21 Preparation of the draft stated case

The draft stated case must be prepared within three weeks of 'the final determination of the proceedings' (see 3.16 above; the same considerations apply as to when that period starts to run).[1] The three weeks period for preparation of the draft stated case may be extended by the sheriff principal for such period as he considers reasonable if a sheriff or justice against whose judgment an appeal is taken is temporarily absent from duty and the court at which the judgment was pronounced is situated within his sheriffdom.[2] The draft stated case must be issued 'forthwith' to the appellant or his solicitor and a duplicate issued to the respondent or his solicitor.

1 s 447(1).
2 s 451(2) and Form 75.

## 3.22 Form of stated case

The stated case (and the draft) must be, as nearly as may be, in the form of Form 72. It must 'set forth the particulars of any matters competent for review which the appellant desires to bring under the review of the High Court and of the facts, if any, proved in the case, and any point of law decided, and the grounds of the decision'.[1] Form 72 makes it clear that the case (the same applies to the draft) is to begin by stating 'concisely and without argument the nature of the cause and the facts if any admitted or proved in evidence, any objections to the admission or rejection of evidence taken in the proof, the grounds of the decision and any other matters necessary to be stated for the information of the superior court'. It is not normally necessary to narrate in the stated case all the charges contained in the complaint, as the appeal court judges are each provided with copies of all relevant papers, including the complaint. It is, therefore, preferable (unless there is some good reason to the contrary) for the narrative in the stated case to say something such as: 'The appellant faced five charges: (1) assault, (2) assault, (3) breach of the peace, (4) vandalism, (5) a Bail Act offence, all as set forth in the complaint; the Crown asked me to convict the appellant on charges (1), (3) and (4)'. 'Findings in fact . . . ought to be crisp, clear and certain', and not 'a mere recitation of the evidence'.[2] All the facts relevant to conviction must be stated. And, in a case where an appeal is taken against sentence as well, all facts that bear upon the sentence imposed must also be stated, so that the High Court may understand precisely the basis upon which the sentence rests.[3] The fullness with which the facts need to be stated depends to some extent upon the terms of the statement of matters lodged by the appellant under section 444(1), including any amendment or addition thereto; but all the relevant facts must be stated. If in the light of the appellant's statement of matters some matters of fact which are germane to the decision(s) are peripheral to the points to be brought under review they should be stated with brevity; but no fact which is material to the result (conviction, acquittal, sentence) can be omitted. All the facts which are important in the light of the matters to be brought under review must be fully stated. 'The findings in fact ought to include all findings of fact made by the sheriff (or justice) and if the sheriff has drawn an inference from the facts, then the inference which he has drawn ought to be recorded as part of his findings in fact'.[4] It is a mistake, therefore, when inferences of fact are made from the primary facts to put those inferences into the note, though they may be referred to there. They should go into the findings in fact. If the accepted evidence from witnesses A and B is that 'All admirals are sailors', and from C and D, that 'X is an admiral', the inference drawn by the sheriff that X is a sailor is as much a matter of fact as any other fact testified to directly by a witness speaking to his own observation. Of course, in a case where the inference is not a necessary or mechanical one (as in the example quoted) the justice or sheriff should (if it is germane to the review matters) explain why he made the inference; but the inference itself, if one is properly made, is always a fact which has its proper place in the findings in fact. A stated case may raise questions which were decided by two different sheriffs, one deciding a preliminary matter of competency and relevancy, the other deciding the case on the basis of the proof.[5]

1 s 447(2).
2 *Gordon v Allan* 1987 SLT 400 per LJG Emslie.
3 *Industrial Distributions (Central Scotland) Ltd v Quinn* 1984 SCCR 5.
4 *Mundie v Cardle* 1991 SCCR 118.
5 *Beattie v Tudhope* 1984 SCCR 198.

## 3.23 The evidence and the facts

The facts are not the evidence. The evidence given on oath may enable the judge to hold facts proved by the evidence; but the facts are effectively a creation or composition of the court, using the material provided by the evidence. Facts may be established in various ways, for example, by formal admission or agreement[1] or by inference from other facts or by the effect of a presumption[2] or from judicial knowledge, as well as by the normal method of the court's accepting as a fact that which a reliable witness swears he observed. But, when constructing or making findings in fact, the decision to hold a particular 'fact' established must be based upon a consideration of the whole evidence bearing upon that 'fact': *Jordan v Allan*[3] in which, although the findings in fact warranted the conviction of failing to stop at a traffic-light controlled junction, the court quashed the conviction because the court was not satisfied that the justice had considered all the evidence. In that case, the Lord Justice General said[4], 'The difficulty in the case is . . . that the justice appears to have made these findings in fact without considering the evidence of the appellant himself, giving an explanation for the manner of, or the timing involved in, the crossing at the junction. The stated case sets out the findings . . . and proceeds as follows: 'The appellant then gave evidence on his own behalf as follows:' [a summary of the appellant's evidence was then given]. The justice does not say whether he took it into account. He does not say whether he believed the appellant's explanation. He does not say that he disbelieved the appellant's explanation. In that state of play, the findings in fact cannot be treated as the findings in fact made upon the whole evidence, and what we shall do is to answer the question in the case in the negative and quash the conviction'.

See also *White v Allan*[5] for an example of a wholly inadequately stated case, and where the court, as a result, allowed, the accused's appeal. There is, however, no universal rule of law that every relevant piece of evidence must be separately addressed in the judge's note and assessed, weighed and counted.[6] If evidence has been led and it contradicts the evidence on which the finding in fact is based that evidence should be discussed in the note and the judge should explain why he has chosen the one piece of evidence as dependable and rejected the contradicting evidence. A bald statement of preference is not enough. There must be some indication as to the mental process that resulted in the conclusion; there must be stateable and defensible reasons for the choice made.[7] It follows that the findings in fact should not set out the evidence.[8] 'If discussion of evidence is relevant for the purposes of an appeal the place for that discussion is in the note which follows the findings which, upon the evidence, the justice has found himself able to make'.[9] This must be understood subject to section 448(2D) (proposed adjustments) — see 3.30 below. Facts bearing upon 'special reasons' for not disqualifying or 'exceptional hardship' which derive from the evidence should go into the findings in fact, if sentence is a subject of review; but all reasoning on such matters belongs in the note.

1 s 354.
2 eg as in *Durant v Lockhart* 1986 SCCR 23.
3 1989 SCCR 202.
4 At p. 203.
5 1985 SCCR 85.
6 *Mowbray v Guild* 1989 SCCR 535.
7 *Petrovich v Jessop* 1990 SCCR 1; see also *Bowman v Jessop* 1989 SCCR 597 at 598E/F.
8 Cf *Pert v Robinson* 1956 SLT 23, a case under the 1954 Act.
9 *Gordon v Allan* 1987 SLT 400.

## 3.24 Form of case — submission of no case to answer

If at the end of the Crown case the defence make a submission of no case to answer the submission may be upheld, in which event there will be no evidence led for the defence. Alternatively, it may be rejected and evidence may or may not be led for the defence.

If the submission is rejected, a conviction may or may not follow. In *Wingate v McGlennan*[1] the appeal court offered general guidance to inferior courts as to how cases should be stated where submissions have been made in terms of section 345A. Three different situations were identified and dealt with as follows:

'(1) Where a submission of no case to answer in terms of section 345A has been upheld, and the accused has been acquitted, the Crown may appeal against that decision of the sheriff. In that event the stated case should not contain any findings in fact, but should simply set out the evidence adduced by the prosecution and any inferences drawn[2] therefrom by the sheriff (*Keane v Bathgate* 1983 SCCR 251).

(2) Where a submission of no case to answer in terms of section 345A has been made and has been rejected, the accused may choose to lead no evidence. If the sheriff proceeds to convict the accused in such circumstances, and the accused then appeals against conviction, and the stated case includes a question asking whether the sheriff was justified in rejecting the submission of no case to answer, the stated case should contain findings in fact in the usual form. Normally there will be no need for the sheriff to set out separately the evidence adduced by the prosecution and the inferences drawn from it because, since no evidence was led by the defence, his findings in fact must necessarily be based solely upon the evidence adduced by the prosecution, and must accordingly represent what the evidence for the prosecution established. The sheriff should, however, in the note annexed to his findings in fact explain briefly upon what evidence his findings were based. There may, however, be exceptional cases where questions arise as to whether the evidence led justified the sheriff in drawing particular inferences and in such cases the sheriff may require to set out in detail the evidence adduced by the prosecution. In making the findings in fact, the sheriff may not have accepted all the Crown evidence, but the court will usually be able to ascertain the evidence adduced by the prosecution from the findings in fact and from what the sheriff says about the evidence in the note annexed to the findings in fact. If the sheriff has not accepted certain evidence in making the findings in fact, the accused who is contending that there was no case to answer cannot be prejudiced if no reference is made in the case to such evidence. In a case where the accused had led no evidence, the issue which is raised by the question whether the sheriff was justified in rejecting the submission of no case to answer is virtually the same as that raised by the question whether the sheriff on the facts stated was entitled to convict.

(3) Where a submission of no case to answer in terms of section 345A has been made and has been rejected, and the accused has proceeded to lead evidence and has thereafter been convicted, he may appeal against his conviction. If the stated case contains a question as to whether the sheriff was justified in rejecting the submission of no case to answer, the stated case will require, first, to set out the evidence adduced by the prosecution and any inferences drawn therefrom and secondly, to set out the findings in fact which, of course, must be made on the whole evidence

that has been led before the sheriff.[3] As was observed in *Keane v Bathgate* if the defence has led evidence, findings in fact can be made only by considering the evidence led by the prosecution against any evidence which the defence has thereafter adduced. In a case where the accused has led evidence, the question whether the sheriff was justified in rejecting the submission of no case to answer raises a different issue from that raised by the question whether the sheriff on the facts stated was entitled to convict.

Categories (2) and (3) represent exceptions to the general rule that where a stated case contains findings in fact, it should not set forth the evidence upon which the findings are based unless there is a question asking whether there was sufficient evidence to entitle the sheriff or justice to make a specific finding'.

The submissions of both parties on the section 345A submission should be narrated by the judge and he should indicate his view in relation to them. So in a case[4] where one of the sheriff's questions was, 'Was I correct in upholding the defence submission of no case to answer . . .?' the High Court was unable to answer that question because the sheriff had not stated what those submissions were. In *Wingate v McGlennan*, above the appeal court dealt with three situations. There is a fourth; the judge may repel the submission, hear evidence from the defence and acquit. In that event, the Crown might wish to appeal.[5] The most appropriate form of appeal is still by way of stated case. The Crown, of course, will have no appeal against the ruling on the section 345A submission but the defence may decide to raise this issue and would be entitled to do so. In that event, the judge should state the case as if it fell under head (3) in *Wingate v McGlennan, mutatis mutandis*.

1 1991 SCCR 133.
2 It respectfully appears to be premature to *draw* inferences at this stage: it would be better simply to indicate what inferences of fact pointing to guilt would appear to be open on the evidence adduced.
3 *Bowman v Jessop* 1989 SCCR 597.
4 *Cardle v Wilkinson* 1982 SCCR 33.
5 On a point of law: s 442(1)(b).

## 3.25 Form of questions in stated cases

Neither the 1975 Act nor Form 72 of the 1988 Rules prescribes the form of questions which are to be added at the end of the stated case. There are, however, many reported cases containing comments upon questions which have been submitted, approving or disapproving the form of questions asked. As a matter of general principle, each question should be as succinct and pointed as the circumstances allow. Simplicity is the paramount virtue in such matters. If the questions are couched in terms of impenetrable obscurity, it may be less difficult for the appellant to persuade the appeal court that the judge in the inferior court has not understood the point. Each question should raise a different point from each other question in the same case. If there is, as there usually is, a logical sequence to the questions, such that question 2 cannot be answered except in the light of the answer to question 1, that logical order should be observed in the presentation of the questions. The questions should be closely related to the statement of matters which the appellant desires to bring under review.[1] Whatever questions are asked, they may simply be superseded, if they are not considered to be appropriately worded, as in *Robertson v Aitchison*[2] (a fundamental nullity case), or ignored, as in *Marshall v Smith*[3] or reformulated by the appeal court. If the question in the stated case contains an obvious error the court will simply amend the error and answer the amended question.[4] In *Waddell v MacPhail*[5] the appellants had been convicted of the common law crime of attempting to pervert the course of justice, in respect that when asked by the police, who were then exercising a statutory power to require information from the appellants as to the identity of the driver a car, they gave false replies. The court rewrote the justices' question[6] so that it read, 'Was I entitled to allow the evidence of the replies to a statutory requirement to support a common law charge when there was a statutory charge available?', and disposed of the case by answering that question. In *Conner v Lockhart*[7] there was no question directed to the question of conviction at all but the court, having formed the view that the sheriff had erred in law by permitting cross examination of the appellant about his previous convictions when he should not have done so, held that a miscarriage of justice had occurred and that the conviction should be quashed even in the absence of an appropriate question.

1 s 444(1).
2 1981 SCCR 149.
3 1983 SCCR 156.
4 *McCuaig v Annan* 1986 SCCR 535.
5 1986 SCCR 593.
6 Cf 1986 SCCR at p. 595
7 1986 SCCR 360.

## 3.26 Standard questions

In all cases in which there has been a conviction there must be a standard question:

'On the facts stated, was I entitled to convict the appellant?'.

Similarly, where, on the basis of the facts established at trial, the judge has acquitted, the standard question will be:

'On the facts stated, was I entitled to acquit the respondent?'.

Whenever, by way of stated case, the appellant challenges both conviction and sentence the standard question on sentence will be:

'Was the sentence I imposed excessive?' or, if there were several convictions each resulting in its own distinct penalty, the question will be:

'Was the sentence I imposed on charge X excessive?'.

## 3.27 Questions related to evidence

In a number of cases the real issues have related to the evidence. The following examples are worth studying. In *Peebles v MacPhail*[1] the real issue was whether or not the sheriff was entitled to infer *mens rea* in a case where the appellant had become angry, slapped her two year old child on the face with moderate force, knocking him off balance and leaving a red mark on his face. Having set out the facts and his reasoning the sheriff asked, 'On the facts admitted or proved, was I entitled to find that the appellant possessed the necessary *mens rea* to commit the offence of assault? 2. On the facts stated was I entitled to convict the appellant?'. The court found these questions satisfactory and answered them.

In *Girdwood v Houston*,[2] a case well worth studying as a model, the charge was one of reset. The evidence enabled the sheriff to make findings in fact including, '13. The appellant reset the four fishing rods, the rod bag, the three fishing reels and the gun-clearing rod'. The questions were in the following terms, '1. Did I err in law in repelling the submission made on behalf of the appellant in terms of section 345A of the Criminal Procedure (Scotland) Act 1975? 2. Was there sufficient evidence in law to entitle me to make finding 13? 3. On the facts stated was I entitled to convict the appellant? 4. Was the sentence imposed excessive?'. The case serves as a model of how to draft clear findings in fact and reasons in support of the court's conclusion, as well as clear questions.

In *Watt v Annan*[3] the vital issue of fact was whether or not a Stihl saw found in the appellant's possession was the same saw as one proved to have been stolen about six months earlier. The sheriff's conclusion that it was (that conclusion being an inference from the other evidence) was stated in the findings in fact as, '7 The Stihl saw stolen as narrated in finding 3 and the Stihl saw found in the appellant's house are one and the same'. There followed two questions, 'On the evidence, was I entitled to make finding in fact 7?

2. On the facts stated, was I entitled to convict?'. The court was able to answer the first question in the affirmative but answered the second question in the negative on the basis that the conviction referred to therein was one of theft and should properly have been one of reset. However, the court went on to find that on the facts the sheriff was entitled to convict the appellant of reset and should have done so. The result was to substitute a conviction of reset for one of theft and the penalty was reduced. In any case in which the findings in fact contain a vital finding which is clearly an inference from the other findings the case should always include a question directed as to whether or not the vital finding was one which the court was entitled to make in the light of the evidence or, more properly, as an inference from the other findings in fact based upon the evidence.[4] In *Kincaid v Tudhope*[5] the only issue at the trial was whether the appellant had demonstrated that he had had a reasonable excuse for having an offensive weapon in his possession at the time and place alleged in the complaint. The justice was not satisfied that the appellant had discharged the onus upon him of demonstrating that he had a reasonable excuse for such possession. It was said by the appeal court that the question should properly have been: 'Was there material in the case upon which I was entitled not to be satisfied that there was reasonable excuse for the possession [by the appellant] of the offensive weapon at 4 o'clock in the morning in Walnut Street in Glasgow on 28 March 1982?'. If the issue is whether or not upon evidence (which is narrated in the case) the judge was entitled to make a particular finding there should be a question such as 'Was I, upon the evidence narrated, entitled to make finding N?'.

1 1989 SCCR 410.
2 1989 SCCR 578.
3 1990 SCCR 55.
4 *Argo v Carmichael* 1990 SCCR 64.
5 1983 SCCR 389.

## 3.28 Mixed questions

It may be necessary to ask a question which is effectively a mixed question of fact and law.

In *Coull v Guild*[1] the issue was whether or not the appellant by possessing a sheath knife in the grounds of a hospital was guilty of an offence under section 1(1) of the Prevention of Crime Act 1953. Two questions were asked, '(1) Was I entitled to hold it proved that the ground of Victoria Hospital, Kirkcaldy was a public place in terms of the Prevention of Crime Act 1953? (2) Was I entitled to hold that the knife, label production No. 1, was *per se* an offensive weapon?'. The Lord Justice Clerk stated, 'Somewhat surprisingly there was no question in the form, 'On the facts set forth was I entitled to find the appellant guilty as libelled?'. This reflects the rule that there should always be such a question when the appellant challenges a finding of guilt. The two questions put were satisfactorily framed. In the event, the court answered question No. 2 in the negative and quashed the conviction. In *Valentine v McPhail*[2] the issue was whether or not the sheriff (who had sustained a section 345A submission) was entitled to hold that it could not be established, on the basis of the material before him, that the Camic breathaliser was an approved device within the meaning of section 8(1) of the Road Traffic Act 1972. The questions in the case were in the following terms, '(1) Was I correct in holding that it was necessary for the Crown to prove the device in question was an 'approved device'? (2) Was I entitled to sustain the defence submission under section 345A of the Criminal Procedure (Scotland) Act 1975 that there was no case to answer?'. The court (and both parties) considered that these questions were not in the proper form and substituted therefor one question in the following terms, 'Was it essential, in order to prove that the device was of an approved type, to produce and prove the Breath Analysis Devices (Approval) Order 1983?'. This was selected as the correct question because it was plain from the stated case itself that had the Crown produced and proved the said 1983 order the sheriff would have been satisfied that the device was 'approved'. The court held that having regard to judicial knowledge the proper inference to be drawn from the facts was that the device was of a type approved by the Secretary of State. The court accordingly answered the amended question in the negative and remitted the case to the sheriff to proceed as accords.

In *Robertson v Gateway Food Markets Ltd*[3] the sheriff had sustained a section 345A submission on the basis that a quantity of steak taken from a packet sold by a shop to a customer and tested by analysis was a 'sample' within the meaning of a statutory provision. The Crown appealed on the ground that the material was not a 'sample'. In these circumstances the appropriate questions were, '(1) Was I entitled to hold that the environmental health officers dealt with a sample in relation to the packet of steak delivered to them by Mrs McDowell [the purchasing customer]? (2) Was I correct in holding that the respondents have no case to answer?'.

1 1985 SCCR 421.
2 1986 SCCR 321.
3 1989 SCCR 305.

## 3.29 Procedural questions

In *Brown v McLeod*[1] the question was whether or not the sheriff was entitled in the circumstances of the case to grant the prosecutor's motion to amend the complaint's description of the locus where a driving offence was said to have occurred. The question which the court was content to entertain said simply, 'Did I err in permitting the Crown to amend the complaint'. This is a good example of the virtue of simplicity.

In *Turnbull v Allan*[2] the only issue was whether the sheriff's refusal to grant an adjournment to the appellant was oppressive and resulted in a miscarriage of justice in respect that the appellant was unable properly to present his case. Nonetheless, quite properly, the sheriff stated the facts upon which the conviction was based and asked the following questions: '(1) On the facts stated, was I entitled to find the appellant guilty as libelled? (2) Did I act oppressively in refusing to grant an adjournment at the trial? (3) Did my refusal to grant an adjournment at the trial cause a miscarriage of justice?'. All these questions were regarded as satisfactory and were answered by the court. The more logical order might have been (2), (3), (1).

In general, it may be said that, if a particular legal issue has been raised by the appellant in the application, a question of law must be framed to put that issue clearly before the court and in a way that separates it from all other issues. Although from time to time the High Court may allow an argument to be presented that is not properly encapsulated in one of the questions it is impossible to approach the framing either of the application or of the stated case upon the assumption that the court might be indulgent. There are ample opportunities to put the issue properly into the case, and there are serious disadvantages for the administration of justice if that is not properly done. Accordingly such indulgence is sometimes not granted.

The case of *Thomson v Allan*[3] provides a model for a stated case in relation not only to the findings in fact but also to the whole structure, content, character and quality of the note. It also contains three model questions for a case in which the sheriff has rejected a section 345A submission and proceeded to convict: '(1) Did I err in rejecting the appellant's submission of no case to answer? (2) Was the police officer entitled to make a second requirement of the appellant to provide two specimens of breath for analysis after the appellant had failed to provide two specimens of breath following upon the first requirement? (3) On the facts stated, was I entitled to convict the appellant?'. The aim when framing the questions must always be to keep them short, simple, clear and exhaustive of the issues placed before the appeal court.

1 1986 SCCR 615.
2 1989 SCCR 215.
3 1989 SCCR 327.

## 3.30 Adjustment of case

Within three weeks of the issue of the draft stated case each party must cause to be transmitted to the court and to the other parties or their solicitors a note of any adjustments he proposes be made to the draft case; alternatively, he must intimate that he has no adjustments to propose. If the appellant does not lodge adjustments and does not intimate that he has no adjustments to propose he is deemed to have abandoned his appeal.[1] If he is thus deemed to have abandoned his appeal and has previously been granted bail the inferior court has power to grant warrant to apprehend and imprison him for such period of his sentence as at the date of his bail remained unexpired, such period to run from the date of his imprisonment under such warrant.[2] Section 448(6) empowers the High Court to direct that an applicant who has failed within the three weeks specified in section 448(1) may be afforded further time to comply with the requirement imposed by subsection 1. Obviously the granting of such further period of time avoids the consequence that an appellant who has not lodged adjustments or intimated that he has none to propose shall be deemed to have abandoned his appeal, at least until the further period of time has expired. An application for a direction from the High Court that the appellant/applicant be afforded further time has to be made in writing to the Clerk of Justiciary, which writing must state the grounds for the application.[3] The High Court has the usual power to dispose of such an application in like manner to the disposal of bail appeals, coupled with power to dispense with a hearing or to make further enquiry.[4] In practice such applications are dealt with in chambers without a hearing. The Clerk of Justiciary informs the clerk of the inferior court of the result of the High Court's decision. If adjustments are proposed within the three weeks (or any extended period) or if the judge desires to make any alterations to the draft case there must, within one week of the expiry of the period allowed for adjustment, be a hearing (unless the appeal has been abandoned or has been deemed to be abandoned). The hearing is for the purposes of considering such adjustments or alterations.[5] Even if a party is not represented at the hearing, the hearing proceeds. At the hearing, where any adjustment proposed by a party and not withdrawn is rejected by the judge, or any alteration proposed by the judge is not accepted by all the parties, that fact must be recorded in the minute of the proceedings of the hearing. Form 73 contains the minutes of procedure in an appeal by stated case and includes the matter of adjustment and alteration. Within two weeks of the date of the hearing or, if there is no hearing, then within two weeks of the expiry of the adjustment period, the judge (except in the case of abandonment) must state and sign the case. He must append to the case any adjustment proposed under section 448(1) and rejected by him, a note of any evidence rejected by him which is alleged to support that adjustment and the reasons for his rejection of that adjustment and evidence; and also a note of the evidence upon which he bases any finding of fact which is challenged on the basis that it is unsupported by the evidence, such challenge having been advanced by a party attending an adjustment hearing. *Wilson v Carmichael*[6] provides a good example of this process at work in a case where the appellant proposed radical adjustments to the vital findings in fact, and the appeal court took some account of material rejected by the sheriff. The court which receives adjustments or representations at a hearing must take care to deal fairly with the representations and must give adequate and defensible reasons for rejecting significant adjustments. Thus in *Ballantyne v MacKinnon*[7] the court found that the sheriff's treatment of the adjustments was so unsatisfactory that the conviction could not be allowed to stand; the sheriff had rejected a proposed adjustment of importance for a wholly improper reason. The court in fact effectively accepted the rejected adjustments in concluding that the conviction fell to be quashed. In *O'Hara v Tudhope*[8] the sheriff rejected a proposed adjustment whereby a question relating to corroboration would have been added to the stated case: the appeal court allowed the appellant to argue the corroboration point and did not find it necessary to remit the case to the sheriff with a direction to add the necessary question. *McLeod v Campbell*[9] is a good example of the importance of raising during the period of adjustment any important issue which is not in the draft stated case or which arises out of the draft stated case. There the court held that the respondent in a Crown appeal, not having taken the opportunity to raise a material issue during the period of adjustment, was not to be allowed to raise it at the hearing of the appeal. It is important to observe, however, that any proposed adjustments have to relate to evidence heard (or purported to have been heard) at the trial and not to additional evidence not heard at the trial, such as is referred to in section

442(2).[10] The period of one week during which the hearing must take place[11] or the two weeks allowed by section 448(2D) for final statement and signature of the case may be extended by the sheriff principal exercising powers under section 451(2). Any period of time prescribed under section 448 is automatically extended by section 451(1) if the prescribed period expires on the Saturday, Sunday or court holiday prescribed for the relevant court. The extension is into the next day which is not a Saturday, Sunday or such court holiday.

1 s 448(2).
2 s 446(4).
3 s 448(7).
4 s 448(8).
5 s 448(2A).
6 1982 SCCR 528.
7 1983 SCCR 97.
8 1986 SCCR 283.
9 1986 SCCR 132.
10 s 448(1) proviso.
11 s 448(2A).

## 3.31 Signature and transmission of stated case

Once the case has been signed the clerk of court must send the case to the appellant or his solicitor and a duplicate of the case to the respondent or his solicitor and transmit the complaint, productions and any other proceedings in the cause to the Clerk of Justiciary.[1] Within one week of receiving the case (unless that period is extended by the High Court under the procedure contained in section 448(6), (7) and (8)) the appellant or his solicitor as the case may be must cause it to be lodged with the Clerk of Justiciary. The clerk of court retains label productions unless the Clerk of Justiciary asks for them to be sent to him. If the appellant or his solicitor fails to lodge the case timeously with the Clerk of Justiciary he is deemed to have abandoned his appeal (see also 3.32 below). Where there are several appellants it is good practice (though it is not specifically prescribed by the Act or the Rules) for each to be supplied with a stated case to lodge.

1 s 448(3).

## 3.32 Abandoning the appeal

An appellant who proceeds by stated case may at any time prior to lodging the case with the Clerk of Justiciary abandon the appeal by minute signed by himself or his solicitor written on the complaint or lodged with the clerk of the inferior court, and intimated to the respondent or the respondent's solicitor.[1] The Clerk of Justiciary has then to notify the other interested parties as prescribed by Rule 131 (as amended). Such abandonment is without prejudice to any other competent mode of appeal, review, advocation or suspension.[2] Section 449(2) provides, 'Subject to section 453A of this Act, on the case being lodged with the Clerk of Justiciary, the appellant shall be held to have abandoned any other mode of appeal which might otherwise have been open to him'. Section 453A provides:

'(1) Notwithstanding section 449(2) of this Act, a party to a summary prosecution may, where an appeal under section 442 of this Act would be incompetent or would in the circumstances be inappropriate, appeal to the High Court, by bill of suspension against a conviction, or as the case may be by advocation against an acquittal, on the ground of an alleged miscarriage of justice in the proceedings: Provided that where the alleged miscarriage of justice is referred to in an application, under section 444(1) of this Act, for a stated case as regards the proceedings (or in a duly made amendment or addition to that application) an appeal under subsection (1) above shall not proceed without the leave of the High Court until the appeal to which the application relates has been finally disposed of or abandoned'.

Accordingly, unless the leave of the High Court is obtained, the appellant must abandon his stated case before proceeding by any other method of appeal. Failure to lodge the stated case timeously has the effect that the appellant is deemed to have abandoned the appeal, and such deemed abandonment brings section 446(4) into operation, allowing the inferior court to grant warrant to apprehend and imprison in the circumstances there specified.[3] But the High Court has power retrospectively to allow late lodging.[4] In practice, up until the actual calling of the case in court for oral hearing, an appellant is allowed to abandon by this minute procedure. If the case is actually called, the appellant, if he then wishes to abandon, should seek leave of the court to abandon at the bar of the court. A motion made at the bar, before any submissions are made, is in practice always granted. After submissions have started, the court may refuse leave to abandon and may go on to increase the sentence.

1 s 449(1).
2 s 449(1).

3 s 448(5).
4 s 448(6).

## 3.33 Record of procedure in appeal

When an appeal is taken by way of stated case the clerk of the inferior court must record on the complaint the different steps of procedure in the appeal, and that record is evidence of the dates on which the various steps of procedure took place. The form of procedure is that contained in Form 73.[1]

1 s 450.

## 3.34 Duties of solicitors: lodging, printing etc

The Act of Adjournal (Consolidation) 1988[1] sets forth the duties incumbent upon solicitors who are acting in relation to appeals once they have reached the Clerk of Justiciary. These duties may be carried out by a solicitor who practises in Edinburgh ('Edinburgh solicitor') but it is not now mandatory to appoint an Edinburgh solicitor. The appellant's solicitor is required to 'enter appearance' and lodge the stated case timeously.[2] In practice, what has happened hitherto is that the appellant's local (non-Edinburgh) solicitor, when marking the appeal, has informed the clerk of court who his Edinburgh correspondents were to be. The clerk of court told the Clerk of Justiciary in turn and the Clerk of Justiciary gave whatever information or notification was necessary to the Edinburgh agents. The appellant's solicitor (or the appellant himself, if unrepresented) must have the complaint, the minutes of proceedings and the stated case (or bill) printed.[3] The Clerk of Justiciary issues a list of appeals with the dates for hearing appeals in the Justiciary roll and gives the solicitors representing all parties at least 14 days notice that their appeal has been listed for hearing.[4] The appellant's solicitor (or the unrepresented appellant) must return the process to the Clerk of Justiciary not later than seven days before the hearing and provide a copy of the print to each of (a) the Clerk of Justiciary, and (b) the solicitor for the respondent.[5] The papers should be accompanied by an Inventory of Process listing the complaint, the stated case and all other documents lodged with the case. The Clerk of Justiciary has power to postpone the hearing of the appeal by dropping it from the roll if the appellant's solicitor (or the party appellant) intimates with reasons, at least seven days before the hearing, that he cannot comply with the requirements of Rule 136(1). If a solicitor or the appellant wants to have a case taken off the roll he should write to the Clerk of Justiciary as soon as possible after the printed roll has been issued setting out fully his reasons for wanting the case to be withdrawn. The Clerk of Justiciary then consults the chairman of the particular division of the court before which the appeal has been set down and the decision of the chairman is then communicated to the solicitor or appellant. The reason has to be convincing eg illness, or awaiting the outcome of a legal aid application. The unavailability of a particular counsel is not normally considered a good reason for withdrawing a case from the roll. If the chairman refuses to withdraw the case from the roll it is, of course, always open to counsel or the appellant to renew the motion at the hearing of the appeal. Often a continuation is granted on the express understanding that, even if the problem is still unresolved when the appeal is next put out on the roll, the hearing must then proceed. If the Clerk of Justiciary does not accede to any request to drop the case from the roll, the High Court at the hearing may either drop the case from the roll or dismiss the appeal. The print will usually contain the stated case itself, and, as an annex, copies of the complaint, of the minutes of proceeding, and any relevant documents which the High Court may require to see in order properly to dispose of the appeal. Party appellants are sometimes excused failure to comply with these detailed rules if the court (and the Crown) can deal with the appeal on the basis of what is made available.

1 Rules 135, 136 and 138, as amended by Act of Adjournal (Consolidation Amendment No. 3) 1991, SI 1991/2676.
2 Rule 135(3).
3 Rule 136(1).
4 Rule 137(2).
5 Rule 136(1).

## 3.35 Time limits — extension

The various periods allowed by the Act for the taking of any necessary procedural steps have been noted in the text describing those steps, and it has also been noted that the periods may in some cases be extended. In summary, the position is as follows:

THE LIMITS

(a) lodging of application for stated case and sending copy to the other party — within one week of final determination;[1]

(b) issuing of draft case — within three weeks of final determination;[2]
(c) intimation of or regarding adjustments — within three weeks of the issue of the draft stated case;[3]
(d) alteration of the application and intimation to the other party — within the same three week period mentioned in (c);[4]
(e) the adjustment hearing (if necessary) — within one week of the end of the period in (c);[5]
(f) signing of the case — within two weeks of the adjustment hearing (if any) or, if no such hearing, within two weeks of the end of the period in (c);[6]
(g) sending of case to appellant (duplicate to other party) — as soon as the case has been signed;[7]
(h) transmitting complaint etc to Clerk of Justiciary — as soon as the case has been signed;[8]
(i) lodging of signed case with Clerk of Justiciary — within one week of the appellant (or his solicitor) receiving the signed case;[9]
(j) abandonment by minute — at any time before lodging case; in practice, abandoning by minute is allowed up to the calling of the case[10] (see 3.32 above);[11]
(k) returning the process to the Clerk of Justiciary — not later than seven days before the High Court hearing;[12]
(l) providing copies of prints to the Clerk of Justiciary and the other side — at the same time as (k);[13]
(m) issuing list of appeals — 14 days notice of the date fixed (given by Clerk of Justiciary).[14]

## EXTENSION OF FOREGOING LIMITS

(1) All the foregoing periods of time [except those mentioned in (k), (l) and (m)] are automatically extended by a period (of up to four days) if section 451(1) applies:

'If any period of time specified in any provision of this Part of this Act relating to appeals expires on a Saturday, Sunday or court holiday prescribed for the relevant court,the period shall be extended to expire on the next day which is not a Saturday, Sunday or such court holiday'.

(2) The power of the sheriff principal to extend, for such period as he considers reasonable certain prescribed time limits on account of the temporary absence of a judge in his sheriffdom[15] extends to (b), (e) and (f) above, and, as a result, delays the dates in (g), (h) and (i).

(3) The powers of the High Court to direct that a further period of time be afforded to the applicant for the procedural steps in a stated case[16] extend to (a) above and to (c), (d) and (i) above respectively. These powers are exercised *after* a failure to comply with a prescribed timetable;they are not available to grant an extension before the period has expired. When the High Court grants an extension of the period in s 444(1)(a) the effect in practice,unless it is otherwise stated, is that the date of granting the extension is treated as if it were the date of final determination. Equally, any other extension has the effect of postponing any dependent deadlines to the extent appropriate.

## USE OF *NOBILE OFFICIUM* TO EXCUSE PROCEDURAL FAILURE

Extensions of time (or *post facto* indulgence for failure to act timeously) are obtainable under these statutory provisions and are not obtainable by petition to the *nobile officium* if the circumstances narrated in the petition are such that they disclose that the statutory procedure could have been used.[17] However, the *nobile officium* is there to fill all gaps and, if one appears, may be invoked — as in *Rae, Petitioner*[18] in which a judge neglected to consider a statutory application at all on its merits. The High Court when considering an application for extension of time under these provisions of the Act, has a duty to exercise its discretion under reference to all the known, relevant circumstances drawn to its attention.[19]

**1** s 444(1).
**2** s 447(1).
**3** s 448(1).
**4** s 444(1B).
**5** s 448(2A).
**6** s 448(2D).
**7** s 448(3)(a).
**8** s 448(3)(b).
**9** s 448(4); Rule 135(3).
**10** s 449(1); Rule 131.
**11** Rule 136(1)(b).
**12** Para 3.22.
**13** Rule 136(1)(c).
**14** Rule 137(2).
**15** s 451(2).
**16** s 444(3) and s 448(6).
**17** *Berry, Petitioner* 1985 SCCR 106.
**18** 1981 SCCR 356.
**19** *Berry*, above at 109 per the report of Lord Wheatley.

## 3.36 Additional evidence

An appellant whose appeal is against conviction or sentence or both may bring under review of the High Court any alleged miscarriage of justice in the proceedings on the basis of the existence and significance of additional evidence which was not heard at the trial and which was not available and could not reasonably have been made available at the trial.[1] (The Crown cannot appeal on the basis of additional evidence). The wording of the provision is the same in summary as in solemn appeals[2], so the legal considerations are the same. These considerations bearing upon the right of appeal are discussed in chapter 6 at 6.26 et seq. This ground of appeal is available to a convicted appellant whether his appeal is by way of stated case or otherwise. In *Marshall v Smith*[3] the appellant, proceeding by way of stated case, founded in the matters to be brought under review upon an alleged 'miscarriage of justice in respect of additional, significant evidence which was not heard at the trial and which was not available and could not reasonably have been made available at the trial, namely . . .'. In fact, no new evidence was led, as the Crown conceded at the appeal court hearing that an examination of the police record showed that material police evidence which the sheriff had believed was untrue. The court, without considering why the police record could not reasonably have been made available at the trial, quashed the conviction, despite the sheriff's curious observation in the stated case that such additional evidence 'would not have materially assisted the case for the defence'.

1 s 442(2).
2 s 228(2).
3 1983 SCCR 156.

## 3.37 Abandoning appeal against conviction; continuing with appeal against sentence

A person who has appealed against both conviction and sentence may abandon the appeal in so far as it is against conviction but proceed with the appeal against sentence alone.[1] The procedure is governed by Rule 129 of the Act of Adjournal (Consolidation) 1988. The appellant makes an application by minute (using Form 70) signed by him or his solicitor and intimated by him to the respondent. He has to lodge the minute with the clerk of the court which imposed sentence — or with the Clerk of Justiciary if the stated case has already been lodged; in that event, the Clerk of Justiciary must immediately send a copy of the minute to the clerk of the court which imposed sentence. If before the minute has been lodged prints of the stated case and relative proceedings have been lodged with the Clerk of Justiciary those prints are used for the High Court hearing on sentence. Once the minute has been lodged the procedure is regulated by section 453B(3) to 453E as if the minute were a note of appeal against sentence lodged in terms of section 453B(1) and (2): see 3.39 below.

1 s 442A(2).

## 3.38 Appeals against hospital orders etc

Where a hospital order,[1] interim hospital order[2] (but not a renewal thereof), guardianship order[3] or an order restricting discharge[4] has been made by a court in respect of a person charged or brought before it, he may, without prejudice to any other form of appeal under any rule of law, (or, when an interim hospital order has been made, to any right of appeal against any other order or sentence which may be imposed), appeal against that order in the same manner as against sentence[5] ie by note of appeal on Form 76.

1 s 376.
2 s 375A.
3 s 376.
4 s 379 (a 'restriction order').
5 s 443.

## 3.39 Appeal against sentence alone

The statutory right of a person convicted in summary proceedings to appeal against the sentence passed on conviction is contained in section 442(1)(a)(ii). Section 453A (appeal by bill of suspension or advocation on ground of miscarriage of justice) applies only to appeals against conviction or acquittal. A person who desires to appeal against sentence alone must pursue the appeal by note of appeal;[1] but the proviso to section 442B specifically saves the common law right to proceed by way of a bill of suspension in respect of any alleged fundamental irregularity relating to the imposition of the sentence. In addition to the more common and familiar sentences there are other less common orders which are also appealable by note of appeal in the same manner as ordinary sentences: see chapter 2 at 2.23.

1 ss 442B and 453B(1).

## 3.40 Note of appeal against sentence alone

The note of appeal against sentence alone has to be in the form prescribed in Form 76. It has to be lodged, within one week of the passing of the sentence, with the clerk of the court from which the appeal is to be taken.[1] If the appellant has failed to comply with the requirement to lodge his note of appeal within the week he may thereafter apply to the High Court for a direction that further time be afforded him to enable him to lodge his note of appeal out of time.[2] The procedure for dealing with such an application is exactly the same as that prescribed in respect of a failure by an appellant to apply for a stated case within the one week allowed in section 444(1).[3] (The statute is perhaps inaccurate in providing that the additional time will allow him 'to comply' with the requirement; *ex hypothesi* it is too late to comply). If the High Court extends the period for lodging the note of appeal the periods of one week[4] and two weeks[5] are deemed to run from the date which is two days after the date on which the court makes the order extending the period, not from the date when sentence was passed'.[6] Rule 130(2) delays that deemed date still further if it would run from a Saturday, Sunday or court holiday, so the period starts to run on the next day which is not a Saturday, Sunday or court holiday.

1 s 453B(2).
2 s 453B(6).
3 s 444(3)–(5).
4 s 453B(2).
5 s 453B(4).
6 Rule 130(1).

## 3.41 Grounds of appeal

The only statutory ground of appeal is 'any alleged miscarriage of justice'.[1] In appeals against sentence the test is no longer (as before 1980) whether the sentence was harsh and oppressive but whether it was excessive.[2] Thus the considerations which are discussed in relation to grounds of appeal generally in solemn cases are applicable in summary cases:[3] see 2.26 et seq in Chapter 2. See also *Renton and Brown* 16-46 to 16-59 where there is also some discussion of the pre-1980 'harsh and oppressive' cases. Clearly, most circumstances which would have led to a sentence being characterised as 'harsh and oppressive' in the past would be likely to be regarded now as indicative that the sentence was excessive and that accordingly a miscarriage of justice had occurred. And, although 'excessiveness' is the primary criterion, the appeal court has been known to look at other matters, including 'comparative justice', or the public interest, in arriving at the conclusion that a sentence which would not normally be regarded as excessive should be quashed in the special circumstances.

1 s 442(2).
2 *Addison v MacKinnon* 1983 SCCR 52; *Donaldson v HM Advocate* 1983 SCCR 216, a solemn case.
3 s 444(3)–(5)

## 3.42 Interim regulation if appellant in custody

Section 446 is applied to appeals against sentence alone by section 453B(8). Reference should therefore be made to 9.14 below for a description of the procedure; see, generally, chapter 9 at 9.10 *et seq*.

## 3.43 Procedure following lodging of note of appeal

On receiving the note, the clerk of court from which the appeal is taken must send a copy to the respondent or his solicitor and obtain a report from the judge who imposed the sentence against which the appeal is taken.[1] That report should be provided without delay, ie within one week. Within two weeks of the passing of the sentence the clerk of the sentencing court sends the Clerk of Justiciary the note of appeal, together with the report of the sentencing judge, a certified copy of the complaint, the minute of proceedings and any other relevant documents and also sends copies of the judge's report to the respective parties or their solicitors.[2] The two weeks period may be extended by the sheriff principal of the sheriffdom in which the judgment was pronounced, if the sheriff or justice concerned is temporarily absent from duty. In relation to the contents of the judge's report nothing need be added to what is said in relation to the judge's report in solemn appeals, notably in chapter 2 at 2.40 et seq, (although the statutory provisions are different). If the judge's report is not furnished timeously the High Court may extend the period for it to be made available or may hear and determine the appeal without the report. However, the sentencing judge may be directed to produce a report even when the ground contained in the note of appeal is inadequate: this is clear from *Henry v Docherty*[3] where the sheriff, faced with wholly inadequate grounds, wrote a brief report stating that he was of opinion that there was no other appropriate method of dealing with either appellant otherwise than by a sentence of six months' detention. The court, however, stated that the sentencing judge should be able to produce a report describing the circumstances of the offence,[4] the circumstances of the appellant, the reasons he had for imposing the sentence under appeal and any other information which he considers relevant. This certainly includes the terms of any plea in mitigation and the effect given to it by the sentencing judge. The appeals in *Henry v Docherty* were remitted to the sheriff in order that he could provide to the court 'a supplementary report containing the minimum information outlined in the opinion of the court of even date and any other information he considers is relevant to the appeal'.

1 s 453B(3).
2 s 453B(4).
3 1989 SCCR 426.
4 Cf *Steele v MacKinnon* 1982 SCCR 19 as to the importance of narrating the circumstances.

## 3.44 Abandonment of appeal against sentence

An appellant may abandon his appeal by minute (Form 77) signed by himself or his solicitor lodged (a) if the note of appeal has not yet been sent to the Clerk of Justiciary, with the clerk of the sentencing court; or (b) in any other case, with the Clerk of Justiciary. In either event, intimation must be made to the respondent.[1] The Clerk of Justiciary or the clerk of the sentencing court, as the case may be, on the lodging with him of the minute abandoning the appeal must notify the Crown Agent or prosecutor, as the case may be, of the lodging of the minute; and the Clerk of Justiciary, where the minute is lodged with him, notifies the clerk of the sentencing court immediately.[2]

1 s 453B(7).
2 Rule 131, as amended.

## 3.45 Record of procedure in appeal

As with stated case procedure, the clerk of court must record on the complaint the different steps of procedure in the appeal, and such record is evidence of the dates on which the various steps of procedure took place: Form 74 is the prescribed form. It conveniently sets out the procedural steps in the order in which they should be taken.

## 3.46 The hearing: duties of solicitor etc

he High Court fixes the date for the hearing. The Clerk of Justiciary, after consultation with the Lord Justice General and the Lord Justice Clerk, issues a list of appeals with the respective dates of hearing on the justiciary roll. A copy is sent to the solicitors for the parties (and the appellant himself if he is unrepresented) at least 14 days prior to the hearing.[1] Intimation to the appellant is made by recorded delivery and first class post at the address given in any bail order, if he is on bail, or to the address he has given in his note of appeal. It follows that if an appellant has changed his address without informing the Clerk of Justiciary he will not receive intimation of his appeal and may be held not to be insisting in his appeal. The appeal is therefore likely to be refused for want of insistence and, if appropriate, a warrant will be issued for his arrest. (The powers of the court are discussed in Chapter 6.) The provisions of Rules 135-139 (as amended in 1991) of the Act of Adjournal (Consolidation) 1988 apply to appeals against sentence — see 3.34 above. Where an appellant has been granted bail, he must appear personally in court at the diet appointed for the hearing of the appeal. If he does not appear, the appeal court, in the absence of any explanation, usually drops the case down the roll to allow further opportunity for the appellant to appear, or for an explanation of his absence to be furnished. If he later appears, his appeal may be allowed to proceed. If he does not appear at all and no satisfactory explanation is forthcoming the court may, on cause shown, permit the appeal to be heard in his absence[2] or drop the case from the roll but will usually treat the case as abandoned, in which event the inferior court has power to grant a warrant for the apprehension and imprisonment; though in practice the High Court itself grants the warrant. As section 446 is applied (by s 453B(8)) to appeals against sentence alone the provisions of section 446(5) apply as well as those of section 446(4).[3] As a result, *Proudfoot v Wither*[4] applies; accordingly when the abandoning appellant is in custody serving a sentence imposed subsequently to the sentence appealed against and the sheriff is contemplating ordering that the unexpired portion of the sentence appealed against should run other than concurrently with any sentence imposed subsequently to the sentence appealed against, intimation should be given to the appellant of what the sheriff has in contemplation so that the appellant may make representations to the court on the matter: the court may in its discretion decide to have a hearing on the point. It would appear that, at least in those cases in which it can be seen that such a situation is likely to arise, it would be better to allow the inferior court to grant the warrant.

1 Rule 137 as amended.
2 s 453E.
3 Cf. s 453E, para (a).
4 1990 SCCR 96.

## 3.47 Conviction not to be quashed on certain grounds

Section 454 provides as follows:

'454. No conviction, sentence, judgment, order of court or other proceeding whatsoever under this Part of this Act shall be quashed for want of form or, where the accused had legal assistance in his defence, shall be suspended or set aside in respect of any objections to the relevancy of the complaint, or to the want of specification therein, or the competency or admission or rejection of evidence at the trial in the inferior court, unless such objections shall have been timeously stated at the trial by the solicitor of the accused'.

The problem is to distinguish between what is mere want of form and what is error of substance.[1] The same underlying principles and reasoning as to the timeous taking of points of admissibility, relevancy, competency and procedural irregularities apply also where there has been an acquittal rather than a conviction.[2] However, defective proceedings which may materially prejudice the accused cannot be regarded as affected by want of form only.[3]

1 See, for example *Ogilvy v Mitchell* (1903) 4 Adam 237; *Smith v Sempill* (1910) 6 Adam 348; *Dunsire v Bell* (1908) 5 Adam 625, and other cases quoted in *Renton and Brown* 16-21.
2 *Skeen v Murphy* 1978 SLT (Notes) 2.
3 *Cameron v Waugh* 1937 JC 5; *Ogilvy v Mitchell* (1903) 4 Adam 237: *Johannesson v Robertson* 1945 JC 146; *Beattie v McKinnon* 1977 JC 64; *Scott v Annan* 1981 SCCR 172.

# 4. Appeals by the Crown

## 4.01 Right of appeal: general

The Crown[1] may, with the leave of the court of first instance, appeal to the High Court against a decision at a preliminary diet under section 76A but has no right of appeal against acquittal or in respect of sentence in solemn proceedings. But during the proceedings, or after they have been effectively dismissed without evidence being led, the Crown has a limited right to seek review by the process of advocation. Advocation may be used to appeal, without leave, against a decision at a preliminary diet, see 4.06 below. And after an acquittal, though without challenge to the acquittal itself, the Lord Advocate may take a reference to the appeal court on a question of law: see 4.04 below. In summary proceedings, the prosecutor may appeal,[2] but only on a point of law, against an acquittal[3] in or a sentence passed in such proceedings. By such an appeal the Crown may bring under review any alleged miscarriage of justice in the proceedings. The Crown cannot, however, submit that an acquittal or a sentence should be reviewed on the basis of additional evidence. Advocation is also available to the Crown in summary proceedings. The Crown may competently apply by petition to the *nobile officium* in appropriate circumstances.[4] The prosecutor has a right in summary proceedings to consent to set aside a conviction.[5] The Crown has the right to appear at the hearing of any criminal appeal, although Crown counsel who appear there instructed by the Crown Agent are not called upon to address the court on matters of sentence, except where the point at issue is one of competency or the appeal has raised some question of fact upon which the Crown might be able to shed some light. In both solemn[6] and summary[7] proceedings the Crown may appeal against the refusal of any application to extend the maximum periods prescribed to prevent delay in criminal proceedings.[8]

1 A private prosecutor enjoys the same right of appeal as the Crown (but no right under s 263A).
2 s 442(1)(b).
3 See 4.07 below.

4 Cf chapter 5.
5 s 453(1); see 4.15 below.
6 S 101(5).
7 s 331A(3).
8 ss 101 and 331A.

## 4.02 Appeals from preliminary diets

Section 76 of the 1975 Act provides for a preliminary diet to be held to allow the court before which the trial is to take place to deal with certain issues before the trial: see chapter 2, at 2.03 et seq. The Crown is a party within the meaning of the section and may give written notice thereunder of an intention to raise a preliminary matter. It is difficult to envisage a situation in which the Crown would seek to raise matters in relation to the competency or relevancy of the indictment[1] but the Crown has the right to raise at a preliminary diet some point which in the opinion of the prosecutor could be resolved with advantage before the trial. Thus in *McDonald v HM Advocate*; *Valentine v McDonald*[2] the defence had lodged what purported to be a section 82(1) notice of special defence (effectively asserting a conspiracy against him by various criminal authorities). The Crown lodged a notice under section 76(1)(c) challenging the competency and relevancy of the special defence and asking the court to hold that certain witnesses cited by the defence should be excused from complying with their citations; the sheriff's decisions were appealed to the High Court and the Crown's submissions were upheld. It is clear that the Crown may lodge a notice under section 76(1) and appeal against the decision of the court thereon and also appear as a party at a preliminary diet hearing which follows a notice under section 76 given by any other party to the proceedings and at the hearing of any appeal by another party. The Crown's right to appeal is governed by section 76A. See, generally, chapter 2.

1 s 76(1), para (a).
2 1989 SCCR 165.

## 4.03 Preliminary diet appeal procedure

As with appeals by accused persons the Crown's right of appeal is governed by section 76A and Rules 34-40 of the Act of Adjournal (Consolidation) 1988 and leave is required. The procedure is no different in Crown appeals from that governing appeals by accused persons: reference should be made to chapter 2, at 2.04 to 2.09, *mutatis mutandis*.

## 4.04 Lord Advocate's Reference

Where a person tried on indictment is acquitted of a charge, the Lord Advocate may refer a point of law which has arisen in relation to that charge to the High Court for the opinion of that Court[1]; the Clerk of Justiciary must send to that person and to any solicitor who acted for him at the trial a copy of the reference and intimation of the date fixed by the appeal court for a hearing. The person acquitted (though he may have been convicted on another charge) has a right to participate in the reference proceedings. In pursuance of that right, he may, not later than seven days before the date fixed for the hearing, intimate in writing to the Clerk of Justiciary and to the Lord Advocate (per the Crown Agent) either (a) that he elects to appear personally at the hearing, or (b) that he elects to be represented there by counsel.[2] Except by leave of the court on cause shown he cannot participate personally or through counsel in the hearing proceedings if he has not intimated his election in writing as permitted by section 263A(2); this rule is without prejudice to 'his right to attend'. His right to attend presents no problem if he is at liberty; but if he is in custody on another matter he has no statutory 'right' to be brought from custody to attend a reference hearing in respect of which he has made no written election under section 263A(2). Where there is no intimation by the acquitted person that he elects to be represented at the hearing by counsel, the High Court appoints counsel to act at the hearing as *amicus curiae*[3] to act as a contradictor. The Lord Advocate meets the taxed costs of the elected representation by counsel or, alternatively, of the *amicus curiae*.[4] The opinion of the High Court on the point of law referred by the Lord Advocate has no effect upon the acquittal. It is perhaps unfortunate that an acquittal is the necessary precondition for a Lord Advocate's reference because there are often important points of law decided against the Crown's submissions in the course of a trial, for example, in relation to the admissibility of evidence, which deserve to be tested on appeal but which cannot be made the subject of a reference because there has been no acquittal. The proviso to section 113(4) which allows two or more judges in the High Court to preside for the whole or any part of the trial is rarely invoked, so it does not often provide a forum for an authoritative ruling). A High Court judge may report a case to the whole court (three judges) as in *HM Advocate v Cunningham*.[5]

1 s 263A(1).
2 s 263A(2).
3 s 263A(3).
4 s 263A(4).
5 1963 JC 80.

## 4.05 Lord Advocate's Reference — points of law

The Lord Advocate's Reference procedure has been little used. The first example of its use was *Lord Advocate's reference (No 1 of 1983)*.[1] The reference was presented in the form of a petition, the terms of which are set forth on pages 64-65 of the 1984 SCCR report. It narrated the material circumstances with commendable brevity and the court was supplied with transcripts of the material parts of the proceedings. Two questions of law were specified and 'referred' in the petition. The acquitted person did not elect to be represented by counsel and senior counsel was appointed *amicus curiae* by the court in terms of section 263A(3); he received his instructions from the Clerk of Justiciary. The same procedure was followed in *Lord Advocate's Reference (No 1 of 1985)*,[2] except that the acquitted person was represented at the hearing by senior counsel. As Sheriff Gordon's editorial commentary in the latter case makes clear[3] the same trial had led to certain convictions and closely related points of law were considered by a differently constituted High Court on appeal. There seems to be no good reason why a Lord Advocate's Reference should not be put out for hearing at the same time and before the same court as an appeal arising from the same proceedings.

1 1984 JC 52; 1984 SCCR 62.
2 1986 SCCR 329.
3 1986 SCCR 329 at 338/9.

## 4.06 Advocation in solemn proceedings

Section 280A(1) of the 1975 Act provides:

> 'Without prejudice to section 76A of this Act, the prosecutor's right to bring a decision under review of the High Court by way of bill of advocation in accordance with existing law and practice shall extend to the review of a decision of any court of solemn jurisdiction'.

This provision was added to the 1975 Act by the 1980 Act. The 'existing law and practice' there referred to was built up in relation to bills of advocation for sheriff and jury proceedings; but there were few examples of the use of this procedure and 'the existing law and practice' is somewhat ill-defined. The procedure was used in *HM Advocate v McCann*[1] to bring under review a sheriff's decision on a matter of competency and to seek the recall of his order declaring the accused (respondent) forever free from all questions or process for the crime for which he was charged. The sheriff had erroneously sustained a plea to the competency based on a misreading of the 110 day rule[2] (as it was then worded). The court passed the bill and recalled the order. There was no issue raised as to the competency of the procedure. Nowadays, however, such a matter would probably be able to be dealt with by preliminary diet procedure;[3] but proceeding by bill of advocation was not abolished when preliminary diet procedure was introduced[4] and may be used even in circumstances in which preliminary diet procedure would be available or where the judge at the preliminary diet has refused the Crown leave to appeal.[5] The use of advocation procedure has increased in recent years and it is not clear what limits may yet be placed upon its use to seek a remedy against some acting of a trial judge which the Crown considers restricts its rights. Thus a bill of advocation was used in *HM Advocate v McDonald*[6] to bring under review a decision by the trial judge (with two consulted judges) — upholding a plea to the competency of an indictment: the plea was taken when the diet of trial was called in the High Court and it was successfully argued then that the proceedings were vitiated by a fundamental nullity. The accused lodged answers to the Lord Advocate's bill of advocation. A court of five judges upheld the Crown's submissions, passed the bill and recalled the decision of the trial judge. In *HM Advocate v McKenzie*[7] the trial judge, after the accused had pled guilty to serious assaults upon a woman, continued the case on the matter of sentence and required the Crown to contact the woman to ask her (but only if she was willing to assist the court) if she was prepared to say what she felt in relation to the disposal of the case. The Crown, by bill of advocation, asked the appeal court to hold that the judge's requirement was incompetent, erroneous and contrary to law and should be set aside. The appeal court agreed, passed the bill, relieved the Crown of the 'requirement' and directed the judge to proceed as accords (ie to deal with sentence in the ordinary way). The court considered the question of competency and concluded that 'there are present here such special and peculiar circumstances ... that it is right for us to entertain this bill'. In *Carmichael v Sexton*[8] the Crown successfully appealed against a refusal by a sheriff for an order under the Bankers' Books Evidence Act 1879 at the stage in proceedings at which persons had been fully committed on petition but no indictment had been served. In *Carmichael v JB*[9] the procurator fiscal successfully appealed to the High Court by bill of advocation against that part of the sheriff's interlocutor which allowed a witness's solicitor to be present when the witness was to be precognosed on oath in relation to a possible offence of rape, at a time when no person had appeared in court in respect of the alleged rape. Accordingly, in solemn proceedings, and in addition to the right of appeal created by section 76A (preliminary diet), it is competent for the Crown to appeal by way of bill of advocation before the indictment is served, after the case has been effectively dismissed as flawed by fundamental nullity, and even, in special circumstances, after conviction. All that seems to be required is that in the course of criminal proceedings a court has made an improper order (or improperly neglected or declined to make an order) resulting in depriving the Crown of some right or privilege which the public prosecutor was entitled to exercise or imposing upon the Crown some duty or responsibility which should not have been imposed, with the result that the due administration of criminal justice is put at material risk.

1 1977 JC 1.
2 s 101.
3 ss 76 and 76A; see 4.02 above.
4 See opening words of s 76A.
5 See *Walkingshaw v Robison and Davidson Ltd* 1989 SCCR 359, a summary case, and *HM Advocate v Mechan* 1991 SCCR 812 at 820, note 3 by the editor.
6 1984 SCCR 229.
7 1989 SCCR 587.
8 1985 SCCR 333.
9 1991 SCCR 715.

## 4.07 Advocation against acquittal in summary proceedings

Although the usual method of appealing against an acquittal on a point of law is by stated case[1] the prosecutor's right to appeal by advocation against an acquittal in a summary prosecution on the ground of an alleged miscarriage of justice in the proceedings is expressly recognised in section 453A. The proviso to that section, however, (which also applies *mutatis mutandis* to proceedings by bill of suspension)[2] enacts that if the prosecutor has already applied for a stated case against the acquittal,[3] and in that application (or in any duly made amendment to it)[4] the same alleged miscarriage of justice is referred to, the appeal by bill of advocation cannot proceed without the leave of the High Court until the appeal by way of application for a stated case has been finally disposed of or abandoned. Reference should also be made to section 449(2) which provides that on a stated case being lodged with the Clerk of Justiciary the appellant shall be held to have abandoned any other mode of appeal which might otherwise have been open to him; but this deemed abandonment is subject to section 453A. Thus, even although the prosecutor has a 'live' application for a stated case or has lodged a stated case he may, in an exceptional case and with the leave of the High Court, proceed by bill of advocation in respect of an acquittal.

1 See 4.10 below.
2 See chapter 3 at 3.06 et seq.
3 Under s 444(1).
4 Cf s 444(1B).

## 4.08 Choice of procedure: advocation or stated case

The considerations that are relevant to the choice to be made by a convicted person between appealing by stated case or by bill of suspension are effectively the same *mutatis mutandis* as those governing the choice the prosecutor has to make between appealing by stated case or by bill of advocation against an acquittal. Those considerations are discussed in chapter 3, at 3.05 to 3.14. In summary, the position is as follows:

(1) In all but the most exceptional cases any appeal by a prosecutor against an acquittal, in summary proceedings, on the ground of a miscarriage of justice related to the merits should be taken by stated case, not by bill of advocation, so that the considered views of the trial judge will be properly and fully placed before the appeal court.

(2) Appeal by stated case against such an acquittal is always competent, provided the trial judge is able to sign the stated case and there are proper grounds of appeal; though the right to appeal may be lost by a failure to take an essential procedural step timeously; but appeal by bill of advocation against an acquittal is not always competent and will usually be inappropriate if appeal by stated case is available and appropriate.

(3) If the right to appeal by stated case has been lost so that the prosecutor can no longer competently appeal his right to appeal by bill of advocation may survive.

(4) Unless he obtains the leave of the High Court, the prosecutor cannot, at the one time, found upon the same alleged miscarriage of justice in a stated case (including an application for one) and also in a bill of advocation.

(5) If both methods of appeal are open to the prosecutor, he must consider if unusual circumstances exist so that proceeding by bill of advocation might be more appropriate, having regard to the nature of the alleged miscarriage of justice, the necessity for and the value of placing the trial judge's considered views before the appeal court, and the savings that may be achieved in speed, in time and in effort by proceeding by way of advocation when the

point at issue is crisp and clear and does not depend upon some considered assessment by and judgment of the trial judge.

(6) The powers of the court in sections 452(4)(a) to (e), 452A(1)(d) (authorising new prosecution), 452A(3) (substituting different sentences) and 452B (new prosecution procedure) are available whether the appeal is by stated case or by bill of advocation.[1]

1 s 453A(2).

## 4.09 Advocation: other uses

As in the case of solemn proceedings[1] advocation is the normal procedure used by the prosecutor to bring under review any improper order made by an inferior court, any neglect or refusal by such a court to make an order that it would be appropriate to make, or any other step, or proceeding or neglect, the effect of which is to deprive the prosecutor of some right or privilege or procedural step or device to which he is properly entitled in the exercise of his public responsibility in the conduct of criminal proceedings. In *Walkingshaw v Robison and Davidson Ltd*[2] a bill of advocation was successfully used to invite the High Court to direct a sheriff to hear the pleas of parties on questions of competency and relevancy, the sheriff having dismissed the complaint upon wholly erroneous grounds. In *MacKinnon v Craig*,[3] where the sheriff refused to deal with a number of cases because the procurator fiscal depute was not in court when the sheriff was on the bench ready to deal with them, the Crown obtained an order upon the sheriff to proceed as accords, ie to deal with the complaints in the ordinary way: the bill was held competent despite there being no relevant entry in the minute of proceedings. An improper refusal of a search warrant, which the procurator fiscal had sought by petition, was successfully advocated in *MacNeill*[4] prior to the taking of proceedings against any person.[5] In *Tudhope v Mitchell*[6] a sheriff's unjustified refusal to grant the Crown an adjournment and his decision to desert the diet simpliciter were successfully appealed by bill of advocation. In that case, the accused lodged answers to the bill and appeared at the appeal court hearing to oppose the bill; it is not necessary, however, to lodge answers. See also *Carmichael v Monaghan*[7] where the sheriff unwarrantably deserted a diet in the course of the Crown evidence because a witness volunteered information revealing that the accused had a previous conviction. The procedure was successfully used in *Wilson v Caldwell*[8] to challenge an order by the sheriff upon the procurator fiscal to produce at a future adjourned diet copies of photographs of a road accident locus, the appeal court agreeing with the procurator fiscal that it was not necessary for the sheriff to have such copies for the proper conduct of the case. In *Carmichael v JB*,[9] discussed in 4.06, the procedure was used to challenge part of a sheriff's interlocutor directing that a witness's precognition be taken on oath, in the presence of her solicitor.

1 See 4.06 above.
2 1989 SCCR 359.
3 1983 SCCR 285.
4 1983 SCCR 450.
5 See also *Carmichael v Sexton* 1985 SCCR 333 and *Lees v Weston* 1989 SCCR 177, a petition case (warrant to take fingerprints).
6 1986 SCCR 45.
7 1986 SCCR 598.
8 1989 SCCR 273.
9 1991 SCCR 715.

## 4.10 Appeal by stated case

The prosecutor in summary proceedings may appeal to the High Court on a point of law under section 442. The prosecutor's right of appeal is more limited than that of an accused person. In the first place, his right is limited to an appeal on a point of law. On that basis he may appeal against an acquittal or against a sentence passed in summary proceedings. However he cannot raise any question as to the leniency of the sentence: ie he has no appeal which is the counterpart of a convicted person's right to argue that his sentence was excessive. If, however, the judge has neglected to impose a sentence which he was obliged to impose on the basis of the facts the Crown may appeal; as in *Copeland v Pollock*[1] where the sheriff, though obliged by statute to disqualify a driver who had pled guilty to a statutory charge of driving with excess alcohol in his blood, decided against doing so upon the basis that the circumstances were exceptional and that to disqualify the driver, who was disabled, would be to punish him unduly: the question at issue was a point of law as to the meaning of 'special reasons' in the statute. The ground of appeal must be alleged miscarriage of justice. The Crown cannot, however, found upon the existence of additional evidence not heard at the trial to support its assertion that a miscarriage of justice has occurred. Thus even although the criminal authorities may have discovered vital new evidence pointing overwhelmingly to the guilt of a person who has been acquitted they cannot found upon such evidence. As the appeal must be on a point of law, it follows that if the prosecutor argues for a conviction upon the basis of the facts stated he must usually go so far as to say that, on the facts stated, no reasonable judge could have acquitted. The appropriate question in the stated case would therefore be 'On the facts stated, was I entitled to acquit the respondent?'. If the judge's note reveals that he did not in fact approach or make his decision in a reasonable manner, it may be easier for the appeal to succeed.

1 (1976) SCCR Supp 111.

## 4.11 Stated case procedure

The sections of the 1975 Act governing the procedure are sections 442(1)(b) and (2), 442A(1), 444 [other than 444(2)], 447-453, 453D and 453E. The prosecutor's right to consent to set aside a conviction (including conviction and sentence) is discussed below: see 4.15. Stated case procedure is also governed by rules in Chapter 2, Part IV of the Act of Adjournal (Consolidation) 1988, notably rules 127, 130, 131, 136 and forms 70-73, 75. The procedure described in chapter 3 (3.15 onwards) applies to appeals by the Crown, which is subject to the same timetable constraints (see 3.33 above) and uses the same forms *mutatis mutandis*.

## 4.12 Bail and other incidental applications

The Crown receives notice of all applications by a convicted person incidental to the appeal and is represented at any hearing into such matters assisting the court if required. In all bail appeals (other than interim liberation applications) the Crown intimates to the bail judge whether or not an accused's appeal is opposed.

## 4.13 Appeals against hospital orders

Reference is made to 3.37 in chapter 3. The Crown will, as in the case of an ordinary appeal against sentence, take no part in the appeal court hearing regarding hospital orders, guardianship orders or orders restricting discharge, except at the invitation of the court, or, with leave of the court, if it has information that ought properly to be laid before the court.

## 4.14 Lodging answers to bills

It is usual but not strictly necessary for the Crown to lodge answers to bills of suspension or of advocation brought by convicted persons and intimated to the Crown. The answers will respond, as far as possible, to all the matters contained in the averments in the bill, at least so far as within the knowledge and sphere of responsibility of the Crown. Pleas in law are usually added to the Crown's answers to make clear what attitude the Crown is to take when the case calls before the appeal court for hearing. An example may be studied in *Durant v Lockhart*[1] where, before conviction, an accused sought to appeal by bill of suspension against a decision by a sheriff to adjourn a diet of trial. The Crown lodged answers containing two pleas in law:

'(1) The bill being premature and thereby incompetent should be dismissed.

(2) In any event, there having been no miscarriage of justice or oppression the bill should be refused'.

Bills of suspension are not appropriate when there is an issue on the facts: *O'Hara v Mill*.[2] However, if in the answers lodged by the Crown matters of fact averred by the complainer (ie the appellant who brings the bill) are disputed by the Crown, the appeal court usually proceeds upon the Crown's assertions of fact[3] though the court has power to remit to any fit person, such as the sheriff principal, to inquire and report in regard to any matter or circumstance affecting the appeal.[4] In a case in which the Crown has no real interest or knowledge, answers may not be lodged and the Clerk of Justiciary, on the instructions of the Appeal Court, may seek a report from the judge in the inferior court: as in *Craig v Smith* 1990 SCCR 328 where the matter raised in the bill was the competency of imposing imprisonment in the event of future default (as allowed under section 407(1)(a)) after a section 398 inquiry. However, as the issue was a pure legal question of competency, the Crown made submissions to the court supporting the sheriff's reasoning.

1 1985 SCCR 72.
2 1938 JC 4.
3 Cf *O'Hara v Mill* above.
4 Cf ss 453A(2) and 452(4)(e).

## 4.15 Consent by prosecutor to set aside conviction

Once a person has been convicted in criminal proceedings, the conviction cannot be altered, or quashed or set aside in whole or in part except by the High Court.[1] The prosecutor can, however, make it clear to the court that he does not support a conviction or some part of it or that there is some flaw which undermines the sentence in whole or in part; or the prosecutor may concede that the court below erred in some specified way. If the prosecutor intimates to the court that there is some such flaw, the court will usually accept that a conviction or sentence which depends on the matter that the prosecutor no longer supports should be quashed or set aside accordingly, or, at least, that the concession was well-founded and properly given.[2] Nonetheless, the appeal court retains the right to decide the matter for itself and frequently delivers an opinion of the court to explain precisely what is wrong with the conviction which is being quashed or why the sentence is being altered. Thus, for example, in *Jones v HM Advocate*[3] the court held that an important concession by the Crown was well-founded, but went on to hold, contrary to the Crown's next and related submission, that a miscarriage of justice had resulted.

1 *O'Brien v Adair* 1947 JC 180 and *Boyle v HM Advocate* 1976 JC 32.
2 See, for example, *Brannon v Carmichael* 1991 SCCR 383.
3 1991 SCCR 290.

## 4.16 Minute of consent to set aside

Section 453 of the 1975 Act, an amended version of section 73 of the Summary Jurisdiction (Scotland) Act 1908 empowers the prosecutor in summary proceedings, if he is not prepared to maintain the judgment appealed against, to prepare a minute stating that he consents to the conviction and sentence being set aside, either in whole or in part.[1] This right arises once an appeal has been taken, whether by stated case or otherwise, and intimated to the prosecutor. On some occasions the prosecutor writes the minute on the complaint or lodges a minute with the clerk of court; on other occasions the Crown does not make its position clear until the hearing of the case has begun in the appeal court. The Crown cannot lodge such a minute in relation to sentence only but if the Crown becomes aware that a sentence is fatally flawed, Crown counsel will intimate that to the appeal court and explain why. Section 453 contemplates that the accelerated special procedure which it authorises should be initiated immediately upon an appeal being taken, ie as soon as practicable after the appeal is intimated to the prosecutor.[2] The primary object of the section is to save expense and delay wherever the conviction is untenable or where some fatal flaw in the proceedings has been uncovered or when new facts have come to the prosecutor's knowledge. It is not designed to enable the prosecutor to reverse the sheriff or justice on a question of law; so, for example, when the prosecutor submitted at the end of the trial that the evidence was sufficient, and the judge agreed, and convicted, the question then arising, viz. 'Was the judge *entitled* to convict?', was held to be a question of law to be answered by the appeal court not by the prosecutor; cf *O'Brien v Adair*.[3] The minute under section 453 must set forth the grounds on which the prosecutor is of opinion that the judgment of the inferior court cannot be maintained. The minute is signed by the prosecutor and written on the complaint or lodged with the clerk of court. The prosecutor must send a copy of the minute to the appellant or his solicitor and it is the duty of the clerk of court to ascertain as soon as possible from the appellant or his solicitor whether the appellant desires to be heard by the High Court before the appeal is disposed of. He notes on the record whether or not the appellant so desires and transmits the complaint and relative proceedings to the Clerk of Justiciary.[4] He in turn lays those papers before a single judge of the High Court. That judge hears parties if they desire to be heard. Then, whether or not he has heard parties, the single judge may set aside the conviction in whole or in part and award expenses to the appellant (not exceeding £60[5] though this amount may be altered by the Secretary of State).[6] Alternatively, he may refuse to set aside the conviction, in which case the proceedings are returned to the clerk of the inferior court; the appellant is then entitled to proceed with his appeal in the same way as if it had been marked on the date when the complaint and proceedings were returned to the clerk of the inferior court.[7] As pointed out in *Renton and Brown* at paras 16-71 to 16-74 the provisions of subsections (4) and (5) of section 453 do not cohere very well with each other, or with the words 'on the appeal being intimated to them' in subsection (3).[8] However, the strict time limits in the section would probably not be enforced.[9] Accordingly their effect appears to be: (a) the prosecutor should make up his mind as soon as possible after the appeal is intimated to him and process his minute before any stated case is drafted; (b) if he does so, the preparation of the draft stated case is delayed until the High Court has decided what to do in respect of the minute and all the matters to which it relates; (c) despite the requirement on the prosecutor to proceed as swiftly as possible, he is allowed to sign and process such a minute at any time within the two weeks after he has received the draft stated case, or two weeks after the intimation to him of the bill of suspension; (d) it is not clear what attitude the court would take to a minute tendered later than the period in (c), but it is not a matter of practical importance, as the court will always attach due weight to the attitude of the Crown even if it is not made clear until the hearing itself.

1 s 453(1).
2 *O'Brien v Adair* 1947 JC 180 at 181.
3 1947 JC 180.

4 s 453(2)
5 The Appellants (Increase in Expenses) (Scotland) Order 1991, 1991/810.
6 s 289D(1A)(e).
7 S 453(3).
8 *O'Brien v Adair*, above.
9 *O'Brien v Adair* at 181, per LJG Cooper.

# 5. Special procedures

## NOBILE OFFICIUM



## REFERENCE TO COURT OF JUSTICE OF THE EUROPEAN COMMUNITIES

# NOBILE OFFICIUM

## 5.01 Petitions to *nobile officium*

The High Court of Justiciary has an inherent and necessary jurisdiction to take effective action to vindicate the authority of the court and to preserve the due and impartial administration of justice.[1] It is an exclusive power enabling the court to provide a remedy for all extraordinary or unforeseen occurrences in the course of criminal business before any criminal court.[2] It may be exercised to provide a remedy to a person adversely affected by criminal proceedings, eg as a witness or a potential witness. It is an extraordinary power which is exercised *inter alia* to fill gaps in the procedural law, an example of which has been mentioned at 2.24, contempt of court. It may be invoked by the Crown, by an accused or convicted person, by witnesses or persons cited as witnesses,[3] by solicitors involved in proceedings[4] and by others, eg persons who are the owners of goods forfeited from the possession of an offender.[5] The older history of this power and some modern examples of its exercise are discussed in an article by C N Stoddart in 1974 SLT (News) 27.[6] A short, authoritative and much quoted passage on the scope and purpose of this exceptional jurisdiction is contained in the opinion of the court delivered by Lord Emslie in *Anderson v HM Advocate*,[7] which is a leading authority. The *nobile officium* jurisdiction is also discussed in the opinion of the court in *Macpherson, Petitioners*.[8]

1 *Cordiner, Petitioner* 1973 JC 16 at 18.
2 *Alison*, ii, 13, p 23.
3 *Gerrard, Petitioner* 1984 SCCR 1.
4 Cf 5.07 below.
5 *Lloyds and Scottish Finance Ltd v HM Advocate* 1974 JC 24.
6 Cf also, *Alison, ii, 13,* pp 23(5).
7 1974 SLT 239.
8 1989 SCCR 518.

## 5.02 Recent illustrative cases

There have been many recent cases in which the power has been invoked by a petitioner, not always successfully. In the Scottish Criminal Case Reports 1981-90 Index, Sheriff Gordon lists fourteen reported cases under the heading *Nobile Officium*, all reported in SCCR or the SCCR Supplement (1950-80) and there are others. Many reported cases arise out of summary proceedings but examples of petitions to the *nobile officium* arising out of solemn proceedings may be found in *Wylie v HM Advocate*[1] and *Evans, Petitioner*.[2] In *Evans* the petitioner was one of several accused on trial on indictment in the High Court in Aberdeen. On the second day of his trial he tendered certain pleas of guilty through his counsel. These pleas were accepted by the Crown and the jury returned verdicts in accordance with the pleas, as directed by the trial judge. On the following day the accused sought leave of the trial judge to withdraw some of his pleas of guilty on the ground that they had been tendered under a substantial error and misconception. That motion was refused on the next morning (Thursday 1 November 1990) on the ground that it was not competent for the trial judge to annul the jury's verdict after it had been recorded; the accused then intimated his intention to petition the *nobile officium*. The trial was then adjourned until the Monday following. The petition was heard on Friday 2 November 1990 in the High Court sitting in Edinburgh. The prayer of the petition was:

'MAY IT THEREFORE PLEASE YOUR LORDSHIPS to appoint this petition to be intimated to Her Majesty's Advocate and to be intimated on the Walls in common form and thereafter to appoint a diet to allow said plea of guilty *quoad* charge (4) to be withdrawn and *quoad ultra* to do further or otherwise in the premises as your Lordships shall seem proper.'[3]

The court refused the prayer because it considered (1) that there existed another remedy, namely an appeal under section 228(1) to correct any miscarriage of justice, such an appeal being competent even after a plea of guilty;[4] and (2) that to exercise the *nobile officium* in the circumstances of this case would be to override an express provision of the statute (the 1975 Act) and to act in conflict with the statutory intention express or implied. *Evans* illustrates the flexibility of the courts and of the procedure when an extraordinary situation develops and also the speed with which, when necessary, procedural emergencies can be addressed and resolved. It also illustrates that the *nobile officium* will be exercised only when no other remedy exists. In *Black, Petitioner*[5] the court said, 'It is clear . . . that the court will only exercise the *nobile officium* when the circumstances are extraordinary or unforeseen, and where no other remedy or procedure is provided by law.'. Such a situation arose in *Hughes, Petitioner*[6] where the trial judge deserted a diet of trial *pro loco et tempore* after it came to his notice that one juror had spoken to her fellow jurors in a way that could have been prejudicial to one of the accused; the trial judge concluded that he could not solve the problem by discharging all the jurors and empaneling a fresh jury under the provisions of section129. The accused presented a petition to the *nobile officium* and the High Court recalled the desertion *pro loco et tempore*, directed the trial judge to excuse the fifteen empanelled jurors and ordered the trial to proceed with a new jury. This was another case in which the High Court moved with exceptional speed to deal with an emergency situation. The court will not exercise its *nobile officium* to entertain arguments which could have formed good grounds of appeal where it is plain that the statute applicable to the situation deliberately excluded any right of appeal.[7]

1 1966 SLT 149.
2 1991 SCCR 160.
3 Cf 1991 SCCR 160 at 161.
4 *Boyle v HM Advocate* 1976 JC 32; cf also *MacGregor v MacNeil* 1975 JC 57; and *Pirie v McNaughton* 1991 SCCR 483.
5 1991 SCCR 1.
6 1989 SCCR 490.
7 *City of Edinburgh District Council* 1990 SCCR 511.

## 5.03 Where other remedy available

An unusual case in which the court declined to exercise the power because another remedy existed arose in *Clayton, Petitioner*.[1] The petitioner had been sentenced in November 1988 in the High Court to six years' detention and, a week later, by a sheriff to four months' detention, consecutive to the former sentence. The petitioner mistakenly believed that the two sentences would be aggregated for the purpose of allowing his early release on licence under section 25(1) of the Prisons (Scotland) Act 1989. When he discovered, late in 1990, that the effect of the consecutive sentence imposed by the sheriff would be to prevent his release while his six year sentence was being served, he petitioned the *nobile officium* asking the court to quash the sentence of four months detention, on the basis that it was too late to appeal against that sentence as exercised in the circumstances. The court held that his remedy was to apply under sections 453B(6) and 444 for a further period of time to lodge an appeal; the petition to the *nobile officium* was therefore dismissed as incompetent. He later obtained leave to appeal late and his appeal was allowed to the extent of ordering the four months' sentence to run from the date of its being imposed.[2] If, however, a petition to the *nobile officium* falls to be dismissed because the petitioner had a statutory right to seek review by a different procedure and neglected to use it, the court, to avoid further expense and to afford the petitioner a remedy to which he appears to be entitled, may treat the petition as if it were an application of the appropriate kind made in the appropriate way: *Gilchrist, Petitioner*.[3] In that case, in which the Court considered that the petitioner could have used his statutory right under section 299 to have his bail conditions reviewed, the Crown consented to the petition being treated as if it were a bail appeal but it is not clear that the Crown's consent is essential. If, however, there were good grounds for the withholding of consent by the Crown, the court would be unlikely to treat an incompetent petition to the *nobile officium* as if it were a different form of application.

1 1991 SCCR 261.
2 Editor's Note, *Clayton, Petitioner* 1991 SCCR 261 at 265.
3 1991 SCCR 699.

## 5.04 Where remedy excluded by statute

The court will not exercise the *nobile officium* to do that which is clearly prohibited by statute. Accordingly the High Court refused a petition to the *nobile officium* in a case in which the effect of entertaining the petition would have been to bring under review a decision of the High Court itself, sitting as an appeal court, contrary to sections 262 and 281, which provide that 'Interlocutors' (meaning any judgment or order pronounced by the court) are final and conclusive and not subject to review by any court whatsoever.[1] The circumstances were highly unusual in that the ruling which the petitioner sought to challenge was a ruling by an appeal court of three judges holding as incompetent and inadmissible evidence which the petitioner, as an appellant against conviction, was seeking to adduce before that appeal court. The evidence was being tendered to the court following an earlier decision of that court[2] to hear additional evidence relevant to an alleged miscarriage of justice, the character of that proposed evidence having been fully disclosed by the lodging of affidavits. However, despite the terms of sections 262 and 281, the court altered a previous order of the appeal court in *James McLellan, Petitioner*.[3] There the appeal court quashed an earlier decision of the appeal court which was based on an error which the court had made; this was done by an exercise of the *nobile officium*. It was not opposed by the Crown. The Court obviously has power to put right its own typographical or similar errors if it is necessary to do so to remedy an injustice. Very wide powers to excuse compliance with rules, statutory or otherwise, governing appeal procedure are contained in section 277; this section should be consulted before an appellant thinks of petitioning the *nobile officium*. A petition to the *nobile officium* was dismissed as incompetent when it appeared that the petitioner was inviting the court to have the merits of his conviction reviewed, having already proceeded by way of stated case and lost.[4]

1 *Perrie, Petitioner* 1991 SCCR 475.
2 See *Perrie v HM Advocate* 1991 SCCR 255 at 256.
3 Unreported, but mentioned in *Perrie, Petitioner* 1991 SCCR 475 at 481.
4 *Anderson v HM Advocate* 1974 SLT 239.

## 5.05 Failure to comply with timetable

The court refused to exercise the *nobile officium* to allow an appeal by stated case against conviction to proceed after the appeal had been deemed to have been abandoned because the principal copy of the stated case was not lodged timeously, owing to the negligence of the solicitors acting for the appellant.[1] The current position in such cases is discussed in *Berry, Petitioner*[2] and in the Editor's note to the report of that case. The remedy provided by statute is contained in section 448(6) which gives the court power to direct that further time be allowed to an applicant for a stated case who has failed to intimate his adjustments (or that he has none to propose) within the three months allowed by section 445(1) or has failed to cause the stated case to be lodged within the one week prescribed by section 448(4). The power must be exercised with regard to the same considerations (of avoiding injustice or oppression) as in the exercise of the *nobile officium*.[3] As Sheriff Gordon implies it is not easy to envisage a continuing role for the *nobile officium* in such cases. A similar comment can be made about solemn cases, given the terms of section 277.

1 *Brown, Petitioner* (1974) SCCR Supp 71.
2 1985 SCCR 106.
3 1985 SCCR 106 at 112 per Lord Emslie.

## 5.06 Excusing procedural lapse by agent

Generally, the High Court is reluctant to exercise the *nobile officium* to put an appeal process back on the rails if the appeal has been dismissed owing to a failure by the appellant's solicitor to take a mandatory step in the process.[1] In *Fenton, Petitioner*[2] the court declined to grant the prayer of a petition to the *nobile officium* (inviting the court to admit the petitioner to bail) in a case in which the petitioner who was appealing against sentence had omitted to lodge his appeal against the sheriff's refusal of bail within the time prescribed by section 446(2). It was said that the court would not exercise its power under the *nobile officium* simply because an accused or his legal advisers had been 'mindless of a statutory timetable'. If the failure to comply with the mandatory timetable is not mindless, but is explicable and explained the court may, however, exercise the *nobile officium* effectively to allow the time limit to be extended if it is considered to be in the interest of justice to do so.[3] But the circumstances must always be such that something extraordinary or unforeseen has occurred and that the court can properly hold that it is necessary for the proper administration of justice that the *nobile officium* be exercised. So the court refused to exercise it where, an appeal having been dismissed for want of insistence because the appellant did not appear and was not represented when his case was called before the appeal court, he later sought to have the appeal reinstated, explaining that his failure to attend court resulted from his having gone to live at an address different from that of his domicile of citation. A change of address without having the domicile of citation changed provided no basis for an excuse in the circumstances condescended on: *Manson, Petitioner*.[4] Section 446, which *inter alia* prescribes a 24 hour time limit for proceeding by note of appeal in relation to bail, contains no dispensing power such as is found in section 448(6); accordingly it should be competent to petition for the exercise of the *nobile officium* in a case where the failure to adhere to that statutory time limit was excusable and not to entertain the late appeal would result in oppression or injustice. Thus, for example, if because of some emergency such as a riot or a fire, all prisoners were locked in their cells during the 24 hour period, an appellant, who as a result could not have his note of appeal processed timeously would be able to petition for the exercise of the *nobile officium*.

1 *McLeod, Petitioner* (1975) SCCR Supp 93.
2 1981 SCCR 288.
3 *HM Advocate v Wood*; *HM Advocate v Cowie* 1990 SCCR 195.
4 Printed as a note in 1991 SCCR at 472.

## 5.07 *Nobile officium* reviews in respect of legal aid applications

In a number of cases decisions in relation to legal aid applications have been considered by the courts. The varied fates of these applications well illustrate certain of the criteria governing the exercise of this exceptional jurisdiction. In *Rae, Petitioner*[1] the petitioner, a solicitor, invited the court to exercise its *nobile officium* by reviewing the refusal of the trial judge, at a High Court trial, to grant to the petitioner a certificate under paragraph 13(2) of the Act of Adjournal (Criminal Legal Aid Fees) 1964 as amended, which allowed additional remuneration in certain circumstances. (This troublesome provision has now been repealed.) The Court had previously held in *Heslin, Petitioner*[2] that the court would not, in the exercise of its *nobile officium*, entertain an application seeking review of the refusal by a trial judge to grant a paragraph 13(2) certificate, because the Act of Adjournal had not intended that the exercise by a trial judge of his discretion on this matter should be reviewed on appeal. But in *Rae* the court concluded that the trial judge had not exercised his discretion at all and therefore remitted the application with a direction to the trial judge to dispose of the application upon its merits. In *Harper, Petitioner*[3] the court refused to exercise the *nobile officium* in a 13(2) case in which the sheriff declined to consider a 13(2) application on its merits because, in the circumstances disclosed to the sheriff, he decided that 13(2) did not apply. The court agreed with that decision and rejected a submission that there was a *lacuna* or *casus omissus* in the failure of 13(2) to provide for the making of an application in the circumstances which had arisen. In *McLachlan, Petitioner*[4] a stipendiary magistrate had refused legal aid. Although the appeal court considered that the decision was plainly wrong, it refused to intervene in the exercise of the *nobile officium* because it felt obliged to hold that the stipendiary magistrate had in fact exercised his discretion; so the petition had to be dismissed as incompetent. Whether or not that decision will be reconsidered in the light of the ruling of the European Court of Human Rights in *Granger v United Kingdom*[5] remains to be seen.

1 1981 SCCR 356.
2 1973 SLT (Notes) 56 (followed in *Mullane, Petitioner* 1990 SCCR 25).
3 1981 SCCR 363.
4 1987 SCCR 195.
5 (1990) 12 EHRR 469.

### 5.08 Additional inquiry

If on the first hearing of a petition to the *nobile officium* the court considers that it needs additional information in response to averments in the petition or statements made at the bar, the court may continue the case for answers, for some form of investigation or inquiry or for a report from the court in which the proceedings giving rise to the petition took place.[1]

1 *Lau, Petitioner* 1986 SCCR 140.

### 5.09 Crown applications to *nobile officium*

The Lord Advocate may petition the High Court to exercise the *nobile officium*.[1] *Keegan* was a bail case in which the sheriff did not exercise any judgment in relation to a bail application because he believed, wrongly, that the application for bail had not been disposed of within twenty-four hours, as required by section 28(2), and therefore liberated the applicant forthwith. In *MacDougall, Petitioner*[2] the procurator fiscal successfully applied by petition to the *nobile officium* when the sheriff refused the Crown's application to state a case against a decision to uphold a submission of no case to answer;[3] the High Court directed the sheriff to state a case within three weeks, as craved in the petition.

1 *HM Advocate v Keegan* 1981 SLT (Notes) 35; *HM Advocate v Wood, HM Advocate v Cowie* 1990 SCCR 195.
2 1986 SCCR 128.
3 S 345A.

## REFERENCES TO COURT OF JUSTICE OF THE EUROPEAN COMMUNITIES

### 5.10 The nature of a reference

A 'reference' to the Court of Justice of the European Communities (the 'European Court') (not to be confused with the European Court of Human Rights), by means of which a 'preliminary ruling' is sought on a 'question' (as defined in the next paragraph) is not in the strict sense an appeal from a decision of the court which makes the reference. However, despite the possible ambiguity in the term 'preliminary ruling', the judgment of the European Court finally determines the issues raised by the reference; and the Scottish court which has made the reference is obliged to accept the rulings made by the European Court and apply them to the case in respect of which the rulings were sought and made. Such a reference is therefore treated in this book alongside ordinary appeal procedure.

## 5.11 The European Community and the European Court

What is commonly called the European Community consists of three Communities. The first to come into existence was the European Coal and Steel Community [ECSC] created by the Treaty of Paris, which came into force in 1952. The two others, the European Economic Community [EEC] and the European Atomic Energy Community [Euratom], were created by the Treaties of Rome which took effect in 1958. In 1967 the three Communities were merged and, after signing the Treaty of Accession in 1972, the United Kingdom became a member of each of the three merged Communities. The Court of Justice of the European Community (referred to as 'The European Court') is common to all three Communities. The language which is used in Article 31 of the ESCS Treaty to describe the role of the European Court is slightly different from that used in the EEC and Euratom Treaties in Articles 164 and 136 respectively; but the effect is the same: the European Court has the responsibility of ensuring that, in the interpretation and application of the Treaties and of any rules made for their implementation, 'the law' is observed. The jurisdiction of the court in relation to the giving of preliminary rulings is conferred by separate articles in each of the three Treaties. The one most commonly invoked is Article 177 of the EEC Treaty. Detailed consideration of these matters if beyond the scope of this book.[1] All that need be observed for present purposes is that a 'question' which may arise for reference to the European Court means, in the Act of Adjournal (Consolidation) 1988, 'a question within the meaning of Article177 of the Treaty establishing the European Economic Community, Article 150 of the Treaty establishing the European Atomic Energy Community or Article 41 of the Treaty establishing the European Coal and Steel Community': see Rules 63 and 113 of the Act of Adjournal (Consolidation) 1988. As the Treaty texts are able to be altered it will be necessary to consult the current text of the relevant Treaty if a question is thought to be likely to arise.

1 A simple introduction to the European legal order and the institutions will be found in Lord Mackenzie Stuart's 1977 Hamlyn Lectures, 'The European Communities and the Rule of Law'. A fuller, up-to-date introduction is to be found in Edward & Lane *European Community Law – an Introduction* (1991, Butterworths) cf especially paragraph 68 thereof, dealing with references for a preliminary ruling.

## 5.12 European questions — solemn procedure

The rules governing the reference to the European Court of questions arising in solemn cases are contained in Rules 63 to 67 of the Act of Adjournal (Consolidation) 1988. Rule 64 is concerned with proceedings on indictment (other than proceedings on appeal) and deals with the giving of notice of intention to raise a 'question';[1] it also sets forth the functions, powers and duties of the court before which the trial is to take place. The terms of the rule, subject to alteration by amending Act of Adjournal, should be consulted by anyone involved in a case where a question of EC law may arise. In brief, the current procedure specifically prescribed by the Act of Adjournal for disposing of European questions in solemn procedure is as follows.

(1) Notice of intention to raise the question has to be given to the court before which the trial is to take place, and also to any other 'parties' (including co-accused), not later than 15 days[2] after service of the indictment.[3]

(2) The notice has to be recorded on the record copy of the indictment or in the record of proceedings, as the case may be, and the court, in chambers, must reserve consideration of the question to the trial diet.[4]

(3) The court may order that witnesses and jurors are not cited to attend at the trial diet.[5]

(4) At the trial diet, the court, after hearing parties, may determine the question or may decide that a preliminary ruling should be sought.[6]

(5) If the court determines the question without making a reference, and if, following that determination, all or some part of the indictment remains, the accused are then called upon to plead to that indictment; and the court is empowered to prorogate the time for lodging any special defence and to continue the diet to a specified time and place.[7] If witnesses and jurors have not been cited to attend the trial diet, the court must continue the diet and order the citation of witnesses and jurors to attend the continued diet.[8] No period during which the diet is so continued is to be longer than 21 days,[9] but that period can be lengthened by the court, on special cause shown, on the application of any party to the proceedings.[10] Whatever period of continuation is granted under Rule 64(5), the time of that period must be left out of account in determining whether any time limit has expired.[11]

1 As defined in Rule 63.
2 Contrast with '15 clear days' in section 76(7)(a), applicable to preliminary diets.

3 Rule 64(1).
4 Rule 64(2).
5 Rule 64(3).
6 Rule 64(4).
7 See also s 77.
8 Rule 64(5).
9 Rule 64(6).
10 Rule 64(7).
11 Rule 64(6).

## 5.13 Deciding if reference to be made

In terms of rule 64(4), the trial court, after hearing parties, may determine the question or may decide that a preliminary ruling — from the European Court — should be sought. This provision echoes the Treaty provisions which empowers (but does not compel) the court to refer 'if it considers that a decision on the question is necessary to enable it to give judgment'. In an English case in the House of Lords[1] Lord Diplock, with whom all the other judges agreed, stated that 'in a criminal trial on indictment it can seldom be a proper exercise of the presiding judge's discretion to seek a preliminary ruling before the facts of the alleged offence have been ascertained, with the result that the proceedings will be held up for nine months or more . . . It is generally better . . . that the question be decided by [the presiding judge] in the first instance and reviewed thereafter if necessary throughout the hierarchy of the national courts.' Clearly, the considerations that lay behind that statement are also material in Scotland; but there are in Scotland other relevant considerations. The Scottish courts are more accustomed than their English counterparts to deciding questions of law in advance of the determination of the facts: this circumstance is reflected in the existence of the preliminary diet procedure contained in sections 76 to 76A of the 1975 Act and rules 24 to 40 of the Act of Adjournal (Consolidation) 1988.[2] It is not clear how the requirement in section 76(1), paragraph (a) to hold a 'preliminary diet'[3] 'before the trial diet' fits in with rule 64(2), which requires the court to reserve consideration of the question to the trial diet, but this is a small matter. What is more important is that an accused is entitled under the statute[4] to raise a matter relating to the competency or relevancy of the indictment and to obtain a preliminary diet to determine that matter. Most European questions (as defined in rule 63) would relate to the competency or relevancy of the indictment. Accordingly, as rule 64(4) also appears to envisage, the accused is entitled to obtain either a decision on any question raised or a reference for a preliminary ruling by the European Court. For it is clear — although it does not expressly say so in the 1975 Act — that the judge presiding at the preliminary diet must decide the questions properly raised at such a diet before calling upon the accused to plead.[5] The judge's options are to make a reference or to decide the 'question'. Whatever he may do he cannot postpone a decision on any question of relevancy or competency raised at a preliminary diet until after 'the facts of the alleged offence have been ascertained' (as favoured by Lord Diplock); there is no proof before answer on indictment. If he grants leave to appeal under section 76A then the case goes to the High Court on appeal and the High Court must proceed to make a reference if the (European) question is still raised on appeal and has to be decided in order to resolve all issues as to the competency and relevancy of the proceedings. This is the necessary result of rule 64A(1), which in turn flows from Article 177 of the EEC Treaty, making a reference to the European Court mandatory if a European question is raised in a case pending before a court against whose decision there is no judicial remedy. The relevant wording of Article 177 is, 'Where any such question is raised in a case pending before a court or tribunal of a Member State, against whose decisions there is no judicial remedy under national law, that court or tribunal shall bring the matter before the Court of Justice.' The High Court of Justiciary sitting as an appeal court or when exercising the *nobile officium* is such a court: cf sections 262 and 281. Furthermore, even without leave to appeal from a preliminary diet under section 76A, the Crown may appeal by bill of advocation;[6] and, if it does so, there must be a reference of any European question which has to be decided in the appeal. Thus it appears that the only certain way that a reference can be avoided by a judge who has to consider a European question at a preliminary diet (in solemn proceedings) is to decide the question against the accused and refuse leave to appeal under section 76A. This point was not expressly before the court in *Wither v Cowie*; *Wither v Wood*[7] when, in a summary case, the court appeared to suggest that it would have been better for the sheriff to deal with the matter and hear the evidence before before deciding if a preliminary ruling should be sought. That would appear to be the course least likely to lead to long delay; a proof before answer would make sense in this context.

1 *R v Henn* [1981] AC 850.
2 See chapter 2 at 2.03 et seq.
3 Cf s 76(2).
4 s 76.
5 Act of Adjournal (Consolidation) 1988, r 34.
6 s 280A(1) and Rule 64A(2); chapter 4.
7 1990 SCCR 741.

## 5.14 Form of reference

If the trial court decides that a preliminary ruling should be sought,[1] Rule 65 requires that that court shall

(1) give its reasons for so deciding and cause those reasons to be recorded in the record of proceedings; and
(2) continue the proceedings from time to time as necessary for the purposes of the reference.[2] The reference has to be in the form set out in Form 31 of Schedule 1 to the Act of Adjournal, to which reference should be made.

An identical rule, *mutatis mutandis*,[3] applies in summary cases and the form of reference is the same in solemn and summary proceedings. A style may be seen in *Wither v Cowie*; *Wither v Wood*.[4] (Another example, which may serve as a style, is to be found in *Walkingshaw v Marshall*[5] where the reference was made by the appeal court; the procedure for such a reference is now contained in Rule 64A(1), added to the Rules in 1989). It will be seen from a report of earlier proceedings in the *Cowie* and *Wood* cases, *sub nom HM Advocate v Wood*; *HM Advocate v Cowie*[6] that after he decided to seek a preliminary ruling the sheriff ordered the accused, who had raised the question by taking pleas to the competency of the complaints, to prepare a draft reference to be lodged within 21 days, allowed a further 21 days thereafter for adjustment by the parties and the court, and appointed a date thereafter for a hearing for the approval of the reference. This is the procedure contained in Rule 116(2) — and also in Rule 65(2) — in terms of which the court may give directions to the parties as to the manner in which and by whom the case is to be drafted and adjusted and for adjustment at the sight of the court. After approval of the draft reference, the court has to make an appropriate order. (In *HM Advocate v Wood*; *HM Advocate v Cowie*, above, the order was, 'The court having heard parties approved the case for reference and referred the case to the European Court for a preliminary ruling'). The reference is then transmitted by the clerk of the court to the Registrar of the European Court, along with a certified copy of the relative record of proceedings and, where applicable, a certified copy of the relative indictment.[7] The Court of Justice will, eventually, deal with the reference, except in the most exceptional circumstances.[8]

1 Under Rule 64(1).
2 Rule 65(1).
3 Rule 116.
4 1990 SCCR 741 at 743/5.
5 1991 SCCR 397 at 405/7.
6 1990 SCCR 195.

7 Rule 65(2)(c).
8 *Edward and Lane*, para 68.

## 5.15 Appeal against reference order

Where an order making a reference is made under Rule 65, any party to the proceedings who is aggrieved by the order may appeal against the order within 14 days thereafter.[1] The words 'any party to the proceedings' are broad enough to include a co-accused who has raised no European question and objects to the reference, possibly because he is anxious to avoid the inevitable delay in proceeding to trial. The appeal against the making of the order must be taken within 14 days. However, it is clear from *HM Advocate v Wood; HM Advocate v Cowie*[2] (summary proceedings) that the High Court may in the exercise of the *nobile officium* relieve a party from the consequences of an excusable failure to comply with the statutory timetable. The appeal against the order making the reference is made by lodging with the clerk of court that made the order a note of appeal in the form of Form 32 of Schedule I to the Act of Adjournal (Consolidation) 1988. In that form the appellant must set forth details of the order appealed against and grounds for appeal. The form must be signed by the appellant or his solicitor and a copy of the note of appeal must be served by the appellant on each other party to the proceedings. The court which has made the reference order may be the sheriff court or the High Court. If the sheriff court has made the reference, the clerk of that court has to record the lodging of the note in the record of proceedings and forthwith to transmit the note to the Clerk of Justiciary together with the record of proceedings and a certified copy of the relative indictment.[3] If the High Court has made the reference, these steps, apart from making an appropriate entry in the record of proceedings, are, of course, unnecessary.

1 Rule 67.
2 1990 SCCR 195.
3 Rule 67(3).

## 5.16 Grounds of appeal (against reference to Europe)

There is as yet no judicial guidance as to what grounds of appeal may be competent. In *Wither v Cowie; Wither v Wood*[1] (summary cases) grounds of appeal were prepared by the prosecutor;[2] the appeal court refused the appeal without criticising the grounds, which set forth, in some detail, the prosecutor's submissions on the very questions which the sheriff was referring to the European Court; the underlying submission or ground appeared to be that the issues referred were too clear for argument. On one view, such grounds are self-defeating because they raise in the appeal court a question which, in terms of Article 177[3], the appeal court must refer to the European Court: however, it is not clear that in those cases the appeal court looked at the grounds in that light. Grounds of appeal should be brief, comprehensive, accurate and relevant. Ideally they should precis the argument to be presented. As to their content, the possibilities are hardly yet explored. If, as already noted, the European question itself is raised for decision in the appeal court, the effect of Rule 64A and of the preliminary ruling clauses of the Treaties is that the appeal court has no option but to make a reference; so the appeal against the making of the reference is likely to be self-defeating. Accordingly, as Scotland does not have an elaborate 'hierarchy of courts' with one level able (at least in the short term) to refuse leave to appeal to the next level against the making of a reference order, and as the appeal court is, in any event, unlikely to interfere with the exercise of the trial judge's discretion — see *Wither v Cowie*; *Wither v Wood* above — the prospects for a successful appeal against a decision to make a reference do not appear to be good. A co-accused who did not want his trial to be delayed by the need for a reference, where that need did not affect any charge brought against him, or where he did not seek to raise the European issue, would be well advised to move at a preliminary diet for a separation of trials and, if necessary, renew that motion when appealing under Rule 67 against a reference order. That would appear to be a better route for avoiding delay for him in such a case.

1 1990 SCCR 741.
2 See pp 745/6.
3 See 5.13 above.

## 5.17 Disposing of the appeal

Rule 67(4) provides:

'In disposing of an appeal under this section the High Court (sitting as a court of appeal) may—

(a) if the appeal is against an order made in proceedings on indictment in which the accused has been indicted for trial in the High Court, either sustain or dismiss the appeal and in the latter case itself cause the reference to be transmitted to the Registrar of the European Court;

(b) if the appeal is against an order made in any other proceedings, either sustain or dismiss the appeal and in either case remit the proceedings to the court of first instance with instructions to proceed as accords;

(c) in any case, give such directions for other procedure as it thinks fit'.

Rule 67 does not apply to an order made in the High Court sitting as a court of appeal or to *nobile officium* proceedings there.[1] If the court of appeal dismisses the appeal against making the reference, the effect of the rule is clear and the reference is transmitted to the Registrar of the European Court. If the court of appeal sustains the appeal and recalls the order the position is less clear. The effect of recalling the order is that no preliminary ruling can be sought at that stage. Yet neither the appeal court nor the trial judge has yet decided the European question; all the trial judge has decided is to refer it to the European Court. The case would then go back to the trial judge with the European question unresolved. But he cannot leave it unresolved because he must decide all questions of relevancy and competency of the indictment before the trial proper starts. Accordingly, if the appeal court sustains an appeal against making a reference, (and does not itself refer the case to Europe) the trial judge must then rule upon the European question: he must decide it. If he decides against the Crown, the Crown can bring *that* decision to the appeal court by bill of advocation or by an appeal with leave under section 76A. When the appeal court is thus seized of the issue it *must* refer to the European Court because of Rule 64A and Article 177 (*et al*). The same result follows if the trial judge decides the European question against the defence and grants leave to appeal against that decision; if the defence then appeals to the appeal court and raises the question there, that court must refer. Accordingly the only way in which the reference can be prevented (after a successful appeal against the making of a reference) is for the trial judge to decide the European question against the defence *and* to refuse leave to appeal against that decision. This might be thought to be an odd course to follow, given that on his first examination of the problem he concluded that a preliminary ruling was required: *prima facie* therefore the question, however he decides it on the remit back, would be of such a character that he would regard it as appropriate for leave to appeal to be granted. So to refuse leave after deciding the question against the defence would smack of expediency. Of course nothing could prevent the defence seeking and obtaining a 'preliminary' ruling after conviction by including the European question in the grounds of appeal. Presumably an appellant who was in custody would be released on bail lest the final disposal of the appeal should take two more years; it is not clear that the potential problems of references in solemn proceedings have as yet been fully addressed.

1 Rule 67(1): see Rule 64A.

### 5.18 Appeal against a refusal to refer

There is no provision in the rules governing an appeal against a refusal by the trial court to seek a preliminary ruling, apart from the preliminary diet procedure[1] which would appear to govern a case in which the issue has been properly raised under section 76. There seems to be no reason to doubt that if leave to appeal were granted the appellant would be free to seek a reference at the appeal hearing. Even without leave under section 76A, the Crown could effectively take the issue to the appeal court by bill of advocation; but the Crown would be unlikely to wish to raise the issue of reference, or indeed any issue, unless the trial judge had decided the European question itself in favour of the defence. In that event, the Crown would be likely to place the question itself before the appeal court and a reference from that court would become necessary in terms of Rule 64A. If the trial judge decided the European question against the defence and refused leave to appeal under section 76A the defence would have no right of appeal in respect of the European question at that stage. The European issue would then be raised, if necessary, in a section 228 appeal after conviction. The appeal court would at that stage be obliged to refer the question to the European Court and to apply the answer received from the European Court when deciding the section 228 appeal later. 'Later' might mean much later: in *Walkingshaw v Marshall*[2] the European Court received the reference on 21 December 1988 and delivered judgment nearly two years later, on 13 November 1990.

1 s 76A.
2 1991 SCCR 397.

### 5.19 European questions in summary procedure

The principles and procedures governing the ways of handling European questions which are raised in summary cases are effectively the same as those applicable to solemn proceedings, without the precise complications resulting from preliminary diet procedure: but similar procedural issues may arise under section 334 which governs preliminary pleas taken at the first calling of the case. The relevant Rules governing European questions expressly are Rules 113 to 118.

Rule 113 repeats the definitions found in Rule 63. Notice of intention to raise a European question must be given before the accused is called on to plead to the complaint. If such notice is given it has to be entered in the minute of proceedings and the court does not then call on the accused to plead to the complaint. The court may hear parties on the question forthwith or may adjourn the case to a specified date for a hearing. After hearing the parties the court may determine the European question or may decide that a preliminary ruling should be sought. Only if the court determines the European question is the accused called upon to plead to the complaint; unless, of course, the complaint has by then been dismissed or withdrawn. The court has a wide discretion as to whether or not to make a reference[1] and the court's decision is not likely to be reversed unless the appeal court concludes that it was plainly wrong.

1 *Wither v Cowie; Wither v Wood* 1990 SCCR 741.

## 5.20 Reference in summary proceedings

If the court decides that a preliminary ruling should be sought the procedure it must follow is that contained in Rule 116. The court must give reasons for making the reference and record the reasons in the minute of proceedings. The proceedings themselves are continued from time to time as necessary for the purposes of the reference. The form of the reference is that set out in Form 31. As noted at 5.14 above, the form of reference is the same in summary and solemn proceedings, *mutatis mutandis*, and reference should be made both to 5.14 and to the summary cases there referred to. The transmitting of the reference after the court has made the appropriate order is delayed until after the expiry of the appeal period[1] namely 14 days; see Rules 116(2)(c) and 118(5).

1 Rule 116(2)(c).

## 5.21 Appeal against reference (summary)

The procedure for appealing to the High Court against the making of an order for a reference in summary proceedings is that contained in Rule 118. The procedure and the principles involved are effectively the same as in solemn cases: see 5.14 above. However, in disposing of the appeal, whether it sustains or dismisses the appeal, the High Court remits to the court of first instance with instructions to proceed 'as accords' and may give such directions for other procedure as the appeal court thinks fit. There is nothing in the rule to prevent the appeal court's refusing the appeal itself but giving directions to the court of first instance as to incidental matters, such, for example, as the content of the reference as drafted and contained in Form 31. Thus the lower court might be directed to alter some part of the statement or to revise, abandon or add a question.

## 5.22 Appeal against a refusal to refer

If a European question is raised in summary proceeding and the court (sheriff or justices) declines to seek a preliminary ruling, that court will then determine the European question. If the decision goes against the Crown an appeal may be taken by bill of advocation or by note of appeal, as in *Walkingshaw v Marshall.*[1] If the decision goes against the defence the court may grant leave to appeal under section 334(2A) if, prior to pleading, the accused has stated an objection (including one founded upon a European question) under section 334(1) and Rule 128 (as amended). If leave is not obtained the court will go on to hear and decide the case, after which the accused, if convicted, will have all his ordinary rights of appeal and can pursue the European question, if it is still appropriate to do so, in the appeal court. Similarly any other party could raise the European question in the appeal court.

1 1991 SCCR 397.

## 5.23 Proceedings on appeal

If a European question is raised in the High Court, in any proceedings on appeal or on a petition for the exercise of the court's *nobile officium*, the court 'shall proceed to make a reference'.[1] The effect of the Treaty provisions[2] and of this rule is that the appeal court cannot decide questions which are properly European questions as defined in the Act of Adjournal (Consolidation) 1988, as amended.[3] If any such question is raised in the appeal court then, unless it has already been referred to by the court of first instance, as in *Wither v Cowie; Wither v Wood*,[4] the appeal court must refer the question to the European Court.

1 Rule 64A(1) (solemn); 115(1) (summary).
2 See 5.11 et seq.
3 Rules 63 and 113.
4 1990 SCCR 741.

## 5.24 Preliminary ruling — final procedure

When a preliminary ruling has been given by the European Court on a question referred to it and the ruling has been received by the clerk of the referring court, the clerk lays it before that court which then gives directions as to further procedure. These directions will almost invariably be that the case will be put out for (further) hearing. The directions are intimated by the clerk along with a copy of the ruling to each of the parties to the proceedings.[1] If the European Court's ruling exhausts the only live questions remaining in the case the court, after hearing parties, will simply apply the ruling and decide the case in accordance with it. If the ruling is not exhaustive of the issues the court will, after hearing parties, apply the ruling and decide the case in accordance with it and with the findings in fact and the relevant domestic law. Any statement of the relevant law contained in a preliminary ruling is in effect treated as if it were a matter of fact.

1 Rule 66 (solemn); 117 (summary).

## 5.25 Secretary of State's Reference

The Secretary of State may, if he thinks fit, refer to the High Court the case of any conviction of a person or sentence passed upon a person; and the case so referred shall be heard and determined by the High Court, subject to any directions the High Court may make, as if it were an appeal under Part I (solemn procedure) of the 1975 Act.[1] When the Court hears the case, the appellant is not restricted to those questions or matters that have led the Secretary of State to refer the case; fresh grounds of appeal may be allowed to be presented and they may contain additional grounds of appeal, as in *Kilpatrick and McEwan v HM Advocate*.[2] The reference may be made at any time and whether or not an appeal against the conviction or sentence, or both, has previously been heard and determined by the High Court. A sentence of death cannot be made the subject of such a reference. Nothing in section 263, nor elsewhere in Part I of the 1975 Act, affects the prerogative of mercy; and the power of the Secretary of State to make a section 263 reference to the High Court is exercisable whether or not the person convicted has petitioned for the exercise of Her Majesty's Mercy. Few cases have been referred since this power (with some differences) was created by section 16 of the Criminal Appeal (Scotland) Act 1926. The first was the celebrated case of Oscar Slater[3] in which the High Court first allowed additional evidence to be led, then heard the evidence and argument and allowed the appeal (nearly twenty years after the crime) not upon the basis of the additional evidence but upon the basis of a clear and material misdirection in law. Another was the notorious case of *Higgins v HM Advocate*[4] where the Secretary of State referred the whole case to the High Court under section 16(a) of the 1926 Act and it was then said by the High Court to have 'become an ordinary appeal'. The appeal failed because of the narrow view taken by the majority of the court as to the test which fell to be applied in considering whether or not to hear additional evidence. A reference was also made in *John Preece v HM Advocate*.[5] This extraordinary case (which does more credit to the sense of justice of the High Court than does *Higgins*, supra) is nowhere properly reported.[6] It was treated as an ordinary appeal. An earlier appeal had been refused. On the reference, the court of three judges heard substantial additional evidence from experts to contradict expert evidence relied upon by the Crown at the trial and, on the basis of the new evidence, concluded that no reasonable jury would have convicted had the evidence heard by the appeal court been adduced at the trial. The seven year old conviction was quashed. In the 1926 Act which applied only to criminal cases tried on indictment the power was expressly conferred in relation to convictions and sentence on indictment. In the consolidating Act of 1975 the words 'on indictment' were omitted but the new version (section 263) was placed in Part I (solemn procedure). The Criminal Justice (Scotland) Act 1980[7] provided that the provisions of the 1975 Act relating to appeals in solemn proceedings should have effect as amended by Schedule 2; that Schedule (para 22) amended section 263. The section was again amended by the Criminal Justice (Scotland) Act 1987.[8] On a simple reading of the section as it now stands it might be thought that the Secretary of State had power to refer any conviction to the High Court; but in the light of the legislative history and the placing of the section in Part I it appears to confer such a power in relation to convictions and sentences obtained in solemn procedure only. The decision whether or not to operate the provisions of the section is one for the Secretary of State.[9] His discretion in the matter is unfettered.[10]

**1** s 263(1).
**2** 1 November 1991.
**3** *Slater v HM Advocate* 1928 JC 94.
**4** 1956 JC 69.
**5** 19 June 1981: [1981] Crim LR 783.
**6** But cf *Renton & Brown*, para 11-41.
**7** s 33 and Sch 2.
**8** s 70(2), Sch 2.

9 *Moore v Secretary of State for Scotland* 1985 SLT 38.
10 *Leitch v Secretary of State for Scotland* 1983 SLT 394.

## 5.26 Fundamental nullity

In the course of criminal proceedings some of the errors which are perpetrated are of such a character that everything that follows the error is irredeemably flawed. Such errors give rise to fundamental nullity, sometimes described as fundamental irregularity or illegality. For example, if a person is charged with committing a statutory offence on a date before the relevant statutory provision has come into force or after it has been repealed, the charge is fundamentally null and all subsequent proceedings following upon it are fundamentally flawed. So, even if an accused pleads guilty to such a charge, or to one which does not disclose a known crime or offence, the conviction and sentence following the plea are fatally flawed. In *Aitkenhead v Cuthbert*[1] the accused pled guilty and appealed to the High Court against sentence only. In the course of the hearing, however, the appellants argued that the complaint was incompetent because it charged an offence which did not exist.[2] The High Court agreed and, despite recognising that the defect could easily have been remedied had the objection been taken before conviction, concluded that it could not properly allow the accused to stand convicted of a non-existent offence. The convictions were quashed. Similarly if the court which convicted an accused had no jurisdiction to do so, whether the want or defect of jurisdiction was geographical or flowed from the court's lack of statutory power to deal with the crime or offence charged[3] the conviction is fatally flawed. Even in an otherwise straightforward case which starts and proceeds at first in a regular way, some procedural step may be missed or some positive procedural blunder perpetrated, with the result that all that follows it is vitiated. Thus, for example, failure to serve an indictment upon an accused was fatal to all the proceedings which purportedly followed against him upon that indictment;[4] though failure to serve a complaint did not result in a fundamental nullity in *Scott v Annan*.[5] The error will usually be made by the prosecutor; but it may be made by the court. Thus, for example, because all criminal diets are peremptory and all cases which are called have to be adjourned by the court to a specified time and place, if a case is called but not adjourned to a fixed diet then, in the absence of any saving statutory provision, the instance dies at midnight of the day on which the case has been called; any proceedings following thereon are fatally flawed and fundamentally inept or illegal.[6] See also *Hull v HM Advocate*[7] where, in solemn proceedings, the court failed to deal at all with the case at a peremptory diet; that was a fundamental nullity which rendered all subsequent proceedings *funditus* null and void. *Heywood v Stewart*[8] is a striking case of fundamental irregularity. In that case the accused pled guilty, the Crown accepted the plea and the court adjourned the case for three weeks for preparation of a social inquiry report; but the court failed to minute the adjournment of the diet. Even although both the accused's agent and the Crown were prepared to overlook the absence of the minute, the sheriff held that the failure to sign a minute adjourning the diet was a fundamental defect which was incapable of being cured. The High Court, after discussing the relevant authorities, agreed. There are, of course, many errors that may be perpetrated in the bringing or handling of a case which are capable of being remedied by amendment,[9] or by correcting the official record under section 439; there are other procedural errors or omissions which are not challengeable after a certain stage in the proceedings has been passed. Thus, for example, a defect in the name or designation of an accused person may sometimes be cured by amendment if the court in the exercise of its discretion decides to allow amendment of the complaint or indictment.[10] If a remediable defect is not in fact remedied before conviction the conviction may (or may not) be treated as *funditus* null and void. There is statutory provision[11] cutting off the right to object (except by leave) after a specified preliminary stage in the proceedings. The question of what is or is not a fundamental nullity can be a difficult one. This is well illustrated by *HM Advocate v McDonald*[12] where the accused were indicted for trial on 18 June 1984 without having been given the minimum statutory induciae of twenty-nine 'clear days' between the service of the indictment and the trial diet, as required by section 75 of the 1975 Act. When the trial diet was called each of the accused took objection to the competency of the proceedings as being fundamentally flawed by the failure to give the requisite induciae. The trial judge, and two consulted judges, concluded that the events which had happened disclosed a fundamental nullity, and that the trial could not proceed even although the accused could point to no prejudice. An appeal court of five judges took the opposite view, holding that no fundamental irregularity was disclosed but a mere defect in citation which, not having been objected to at a preliminary diet, could not be raised later without leave. See also *Rendle v Muir*[13] where nice distinctions were drawn between fundamental nullity and mere irrelevancy. Similar difficulties of analysis and classification have emerged in other cases concerned with procedure. Contrast eg *Beattie v McKinnon*[14] with *Scott v Annan*;[15] cf the editorial discussion of the two cases in 1981 SCCR at page 176. Nice distinctions between procedural blunders which are fatal and others which are not also emerge in the discussion in *Heywood v Stewart* above of *Pettigrew v Ingram*.[16] These cases also illustrate that in giving effect to a plea of fundamental nullity the High Court is not applying the miscarriage of justice test.[17]

1 1962 JC 12.
2 Illegal fishing for salmon on a Sunday by persons acting together.
3 *Gallaghan v HM Advocate* 1937 JC 27.
4 *Hester v MacDonald* 1961 SC 370.
5 1981 SCCR 172.
6 *Lafferty v Jessop*1989 SCCR 451.
7 1945 JC 83.
8 1992 SCCR 42.
9 Cf ss 123(2) and 335.
10 Cf *Hoyers (UK) Limited v PF Lanark* 1991 SCCR 919. See also the article by Gerald H Gordon 'Fundamental nullity and the power of amendment' 1974 SLT (News) 154.
11 ss 108, 334.
12 1984 SCCR 229.
13 1952 JC 115.
14 1977 JC 64.
15 1981 SCCR 172.
16 1982 SCCR 259.
17 Chapter 7 at 7.01–7.05.

## 5.27 Raising fundamental nullity on appeal

It is not within the scope of this book to examine all the defects that may in certain circumstances be regarded by the court as giving rise to a fundamental irregularity or to attempt to produce a rationale for distinguishing between borderline cases. Many of the cases illustrating such distinctions are referred to and discussed in *Renton and Brown* in various paragraphs, indexed under 'fundamental nullity'. It is, however, important to note that any error that produces what is truly a fundamental nullity can be raised on appeal and dealt with by the High Court even although the issue has not been raised or even foreshadowed in the grounds of appeal, the questions in the stated case or the averments or the pleas in the bill of suspension or of advocation.[1] The High Court will itself raise any issue of fundamental irregularity that is discovered whether by itself, as in *Hull v HM Advocate*[2], or by a reporting judge. The court has an inherent power to consider such a matter[3] even if review is expressly excluded or is permitted only by means of a prescribed procedure which the appellant has not invoked. It is obvious, however, as some of the preceding cases illustrate, that, although the court will always take note of a true fundamental nullity, it can be difficult to predict whether or not any particular irregularity will be treated as fundamental — unless there is a clear precedent for so treating it. Thus any point of relevancy or competency or any irregularity should be raised and made the subject of objection or submission as early as the procedure allows.

1 *Christie v Barclay* 1974 JC 68; *Robertson v Aitchison* 1981 SCCR 149.
2 1945 JC 83.
3 *O'Malley v Strathern* 1920 JC 74.

# 6. Powers of the court

## SOLEMN



## SUMMARY

## ADDITIONAL EVIDENCE

## SOLEMN

### 6.01 Disposal of preliminary diet appeal

This matter is dealt with in chapter 2, at 2.09. In brief, in disposing of an appeal under section 76A(1)[1] the High Court (ie a quorum of three or more judges) may affirm the decision appealed against or may remit the case to the court of first instance with such directions in the matter as the High Court thinks fit. If the court of first instance has dismissed the indictment or any part of it, the High Court has power to reverse that decision and to direct the court below to fix a trial diet (if necessary).[2]

1 Cf chapter 2, at 2.03 to 2.09.
2 s 76A(3).

### 6.02 Powers incidental to an appeal hearing

Section 252, which is without prejudice to any existing power of the High Court,[1] enables the court to employ various methods for the purpose of enabling it properly to determine an appeal under section 228(1), ie any appeal against conviction or sentence or both. The court may order the production of any document or other thing connected with the proceedings.[2] This provision would, for example, allow the appeal court to order the production of an article which should have been produced at the trial but was not[3] because it had been temporarily mislaid; if it later appears to be of materiality the court may order its production. The court may hear additional evidence relevant to any alleged miscarriage of justice or order such evidence to be heard by a judge of the High Court or by such other person as it may appoint for that purpose:[4] see Additional Evidence, at 6.26 et seq. The appeal court may take account of any circumstances relevant to the case which were not before the trial judge.[5] This is an obscure provision the full effect of which is as yet not clear. In *Rubin v HM Advocate*[6] its meaning was discussed but not decided. Section 252 applies expressly to all appeals under section 228(1), and, therefore, to appeals against conviction as well as to appeals against sentence; but paragraph (c) refers to 'any circumstances . . . which were not before *the trial judge*' (as distinct from the jury or the trial court). On that basis Lord Justice General Emslie expressed the opinion *obiter* that this power was designed for use only in appeals against sentence. Lord Cameron was not, without fuller argument and consideration, prepared so to restrict its application. It is submitted that the power is available in all appeals and is deliberately provided in addition to the 'additional evidence' power in paragraph (b); see the comments by the Lord Justice Clerk in *Marshall v MacDougall*[7] on the identically worded provision in section 452(4), which applies to summary proceedings. It would be difficult to give the same words wholly different meanings or applications simply because one section is in Part I and the other in Part II of the 1975 Act. This provision could cover, for example, those cases in which material is put before the appeal court either by the Crown or by the appellant, but which is not put forward as evidence. In *McDonald v HM Advocate*[8] the court, though without reference to any statutory power under section 252(c), took account of circumstances highly relevant to the case which were not before the trial judge or the jury, principally the fact that in the course of the trial, and while a witness (McLeod) was giving evidence, he was charged with perjury during an adjournment; but the defence and the trial judge (and the jury) were not told of this off-scene development. The Crown continued to present the witness to the trial jury as worthy of credit and to assert to the jury that statements which the witness had made were true, although in the perjury proceedings the same statements were averred to be false. The appeal court's knowledge of these circumstances came not from the evidence or from the presenting of additional evidence but to some extent from assertions and explanations by Crown counsel. In *McColl v HM Advocate*[9] the appeal court took account of representations as to matters of fact, made to the appeal court by counsel for the appellant, as to what had happened between the clerk of court and the jury in the course of the jury's deliberations and also of statements by the clerk of court and the trial judge on the same events. On that basis the appeal court concluded that there had been a miscarriage of justice in that part of the trial had taken place outwith the presence of the accused, contrary to section 145(1).[10] In *McCadden v HM Advocate*[11] the court, again without reference to paragraph(c), took account of precognitions from persons bearing upon a juror's alleged prejudical statements about an appellant during the trial; the appellant's motion (which was refused) was to order an inquiry into the matter by a suitable person in terms of paragraph (d). It may well be, however, that the High Court does not need the statutory authority which paragraph (c) of section 252 confers as the High Court's 'existing power' is extremely wide and constantly finds new expression. The power to remit to any fit person to inquire and report in regard to any matter or circumstance affecting the appeal is contained in paragraph (d) of section 252. The competency of such a proceeding was affirmed in *McCadden* (above, at p 289). In a summary case, *Bradford v McLeod*[12] the appeal court remitted to the Sheriff Principal to inquire and report in relation to the conduct of the sheriff who, it was said, had on a social occasion made remarks about miners in a context which disqualified him from sitting as the trial judge in relation to certain charges brought against miners shortly thereafter. The report was fully taken into account by the appeal court.

Finally, the court may appoint a person with expert knowledge to act as assessor to the High Court in any case where it appears to the court that such express knowledge is required for the proper determination of the case. In *Carraher v HM Advocate*[13] Lord Justice General Cooper said that this power (then contained in section 6 of the Criminal Appeal (Scotland) Act 1926) had never been exercised and was one which should be used with the greatest reserve.[14] That remains the position. If additional expert evidence is needed the court can obtain it, as in *Duff v HM Advocate*,[15] where the court did not explain the source of its power to call upon the psychiatrists who had submitted written reports to the trial court to give oral evidence to the appeal court, which was considering an appeal against sentence only.

**1** See 6.03 below.
**2** s 252, para (a).
**3** As in *MacNeil v HM Advocate* 1986 SCCR 288.
**4** s 252, para (b).
**5** s 252, para (c).
**6** 1984 SCCR 96.
**7** 1986 SCCR 376 at 380.
**8** 1987 SCCR 153.
**9** 1989 SCCR 229.
**10** See also *Cunningham v HM Advocate* 1984 SCCR 40.
**11** 1985 SCCR 282.
**12** 1985 SCCR 379.
**13** 1946 JC 108.
**14** That case concerned medico-legal questions of responsibility.
**15** 1983 SCCR 461.

## 6.03 Other routine incidental powers

The High Court sitting as a court of appeal makes such orders or gives such directions as are reasonably incidental to and necessary for determining any appeal. It may decide to remit to the judge in the inferior court for clarification of some matter which has not been adequately dealt with in any report or case that he may have prepared. If the Court decides to allow additional or amended grounds of appeal it may remit to the inferior court for an additional report. It may allow the Crown to amend the indictment in an appeal being heard by the court if that is appropriate. It may order a transcript of any part of the proceedings[1] including proceedings at a preliminary diet. It has power to require the judge who presided at the trial to produce his trial notes.[2] The court can adjourn an appeal to await the result of other proceedings, as happened in *Mitchell v HM Advocate*;[3] in that case the appellant lodged as additional evidence[4] an affidavit of another man, Chapman, to the effect that it was he, not the appellant (Mitchell) who had carried out the crime of which Mitchell had been convicted; learning from the Crown that Chapman was to be tried on a charge of attempting to pervert the course of justice by swearing a false affidavit (the one being relied upon by Mitchell), the court postponed any further hearing of the appeal until after the trial.[5] The court may, as an exceptional indulgence, permit part of an appeal to be presented by counsel and part by the appellant himself.[6] When the appeal court continues[7] or adjourns a case for what is likely to be a long period it may grant bail.[8] The court can also call for reports, such as social inquiry reports, community service reports or medical or psychiatric reports. Where the court below has failed in its statutory duty to obtain some such report the appeal court can quash the sentence, call for the necessary report and, at a later date, consider what sentence to impose in the light of the report. As noted elsewhere, the court has discretionary power to extend time limits or to excuse non-compliance with them with most rules of practice for the time being in force under Part I of the 1975 Act; the exception relates to rules under section 280 (Appeals against Hospital Orders, etc).[9] It has no power to award expenses (in solemn appeals).[10]

**1** ss 274(1) and 275.
**2** s 237.
**3** 1989 SCCR 502.
**4** s 228(2).
**5** See 1989 SCCR 502 at 510A-E.
**6** *Montgomery v HM Advocate* 1987 SCCR 264.
**7** s 259.

8 s 238(1).
9 ss 247, 277 and chapter 2, at 2.32.
10 s 266.

## 6.04 Frivolous appeals

If on any note of appeal against a conviction purporting to be on a ground of appeal which introduces a question of law alone it appears to the High Court that the appeal is frivolous or vexatious, and that it can be determined without adjourning it for a full hearing, the Court has power to dismiss the appeal summarily without calling on any persons to attend the hearing or to appear for the Crown.[1]

1 s 256.

## 6.05 Disposal of appeal against conviction

The leading section regulating the powers of the High Court in disposing of an appeal against conviction in solemn proceedings is section 254. This section empowers the High Court to dispose of the appeal by affirming the verdict, by setting it aside and quashing the conviction, by setting it aside and substituting an amended verdict of guilty or by setting aside the verdict and granting authority to bring a new prosecution. If the Court sets aside a verdict but the appellant still stands convicted — whether because the Court has substituted an amended verdict of guilty, or because he remains convicted on other charges on the same indictment and in respect of which the verdict was not set aside (or for both these reasons) — the Court may pass another, but not more severe, sentence. The Court has 'an entirely free hand' to reduce or effectively to re-impose the original sentence(s), though it may not increase any sentence when exercising the relevant power under section 254(2).[1] If, in relation to any appeal,[2] it appears to the High Court that the appellant committed the act(s) charged against him but was insane when he did so, the Court is obliged to act in accordance with section 254(4). It must, therefore, (a) set aside the verdict of the trial court and substitute therefor a verdict of acquittal on the ground of insanity,[3] and (b) quash any sentence imposed on the appellant as respects the indictment and order his detention in a state hospital or such other hospital as for special reasons the court may specify: the provisions of section 174(4) apply to such an order.

1 *Caringi v HM Advocate* 1989 SCCR 223.
2 Ie against conviction, sentence or both.
3 Cf s 174(2).

## 6.06 Setting aside the verdict

If the High Court sets aside the verdict it may simply quash the conviction. If the convictions on all charges are set aside all the sentences must be quashed. If the appellant was convicted on several charges but is successful in his appeal against some only of the convictions, the court is entitled to reconsider and may alter the sentences imposed in respect of the convictions which still remain standing.[1] Such sentence or sentences can therefore be reconsidered whether the trial court imposed discrete sentences for each charge in respect of which the appellant was found guilty or one cumulo sentence, or some mixture of separate and cumulo sentences. In no case, when dealing with an appeal against conviction alone,[2] has the court power to increase the sentences imposed in the trial court. The court may quash a conviction and substitute therefor an amended verdict of guilty provided that the amended verdict is one which the trial court jury could have returned on the indictment before them: see sections 44 to 67 of the 1975 Act. The appeal court may, for example, substitute a verdict of culpable homicide for one of murder, or of reset for one of theft or of a statutory offence for a common law crime, if that could have been done on the trial indictment, as in *McKenzie v HM Advocate*.[3] In *Salmond v HM Advocate*[4] the court substituted a verdict of 'guilty of assault under extreme provocation' for a verdict held to be incompetent, viz. 'guilty (of attempted murder) by reason of reckless indifference with extreme provocation'; the sentence was then reduced from five years imprisonment to three years. As the amended verdict must be one that could competently have been returned on the indictment before the trial court,[5] it follows that if after a partly successful appeal the appellant stands convicted of some of the charges of which he was convicted in the trial court, and is newly convicted by the appeal court of amended offences in relation to other charges of which he was convicted in the trial court, (but in respect of which he has been acquitted on appeal), the appeal court will then have a completely free hand to reconsider all questions of sentence in relation to the actual convictions which are recorded against the appellant at the conclusion of the appeal. The appeal court is not bound by the trial judge's view; the only formal limitation upon its power is the statutory requirement not to impose a more severe sentence than those quashed.[6] The High Court may impose a probation order or a community service order; the appellant then remains subject to the jurisdiction of the High Court and if he transgresses the conditions can be brought back before that court to be dealt with. The Court may issue a warrant for the arrest of a person it decides should appear before it again or issue a citation to such a person to appear. The appeal court can also defer sentence and it not infrequently does. There is no appeal against any sentence imposed by the appeal court: sections 262 and 281; cf *Perrie, Petitioner*.[7] It does appear, however, that a technical error by the court can be remedied.[8]

1 *Caringi v HM Advocate* 1989 SCCR 223 at 225B, per Lord Justice Clerk Ross, delivering the opinion of the Court.
2 But see s 254(3)(b), appeals against sentence.
3 1959 JC 32.
4 1991 SCCR 43.
5 s 254(1)(b).
6 See s 254(2).
7 1991 SCCR 475.
8 See *Perrie* above at 481A, and the case of *James McLellan* there referred to.

## 6.07 Authority for new prosecution

If the High Court, in disposing of an appeal against conviction, sets aside a verdict of a trial court, it may grant authority to bring a new prosecution in accordance with section 255 of the Act (added by 1980 Act).[1] Exactly similar provisions confer the same power on the High Court in relation to appeals in summary proceedings.[2] In either case (solemn or summary), if authority is granted, the accused may be prosecuted in respect of the same or any similar offence arising out of the same facts which gave rise to the conviction which the court has set aside. If he is later convicted in the new proceedings which have taken place under such authority no sentence may be passed on conviction unless it could have been passed on conviction under the earlier proceedings. If new prosecution proceedings are to be brought they must be commenced within two months of the date on which authority to bring the new prosecution was granted. If the two months pass and no new prosecution has been brought the order setting aside the verdict has the effect, for all purposes, of an acquittal.[3] The new proceedings are deemed to be commenced on the date on which a warrant to apprehend or cite the accused is granted, provided such warrant is executed without unreasonable delay; in any other case the proceedings are deemed to be commenced on the date on which the warrant is executed. There is no power to extend the two months limit. The subject of 'unreasonable delay' in the execution of warrants is much litigated, but it lies outwith the scope of this book.[4] A new prosecution may be brought (both under section 255 and under section 452B) notwithstanding that any other time limit for the commencement of the proceedings in question has elapsed.[5]

1 s 254(1)(c).
2 ss 452A(1)(d), 452B, 453A(2); see 6.18 below.
3 ss 255(3) and (4); and 452B(3) and (4).
4 Cf *Renton and Brown*, 13-05 and 13-08.
5 ss 255(2) and 452B(2).

## 6.08 New prosecutions: the practice

The first case in which the High Court granted authority to bring a new prosecution was *Mackenzie v HM Advocate*.[1] The trial judge had misdirected the jury (in a case of alleged murder by stabbing) by erroneously withdrawing the defence of accident. Lord Justice Clerk Wheatley observed that the new statutory provisions left the matter of granting authority for a new prosecution to the discretion of the court without specifying any grounds on which that course was warranted.

'Each case will require to be dealt with on its own facts. Where it is not suggested that there was not sufficient evidence to warrant the conviction, or any fault on the part of the Crown, and the one thing which has led to the setting aside of the verdict is a material misdirection in law by the trial judge, that is something which, in the interests of justice and the public interest, must be seriously taken into account when deciding whether to grant authority to bring a new prosecution instead of simply quashing the conviction.'[2]

*Mackenzie* had originally been charged with murder; the Crown brought a new prosecution charging him with culpable homicide, which charge was found not proven.[3] Lord Wheatley's phrase, 'Where it is not *suggested*...' is less accurate than it should be: what matters, it is submitted, is the view formed by the appeal court as to any such suggestion. The phrase would be better worded if those words were replaced by, 'Where it does not appear to the appeal court...'. In *King v HM Advocate*,[4] where the one successful ground was a material misdirection for which the trial judge alone was responsible, authority was granted for a new prosecution: one was successfully taken. In *Cunningham v HM Advocate*[5] the trial judge erred in giving instructions to the jury outwith the presence of the accused, in contravention of section 145. A new prosecution was authorised because the error was purely that of the judge and was 'procedural in character'.[6] The new prosecution resulted in a verdict of not proven (some five months after the appeal). In *McGhee v HM Advocate*[7] the trial judge's error consisted of making improper comments on the appellant's answers at judicial examination; but, as there was adequate evidence, authority was granted, and the new prosecution resulted in a conviction. The fault which warranted the setting aside of the verdict of *Slater v HM Advocate*[8] was purely procedural: the jury, under direction, returned an ambiguous verdict to an ambiguous partial plea of guilty. The Crown successfully moved the appeal court to grant authority under section 254(1)(c). In *Sinclair v HM Advocate*,[9] a misdirection case, the court granted authority to the Lord Advocate to bring a new prosecution despite a 'suggestion' of fault on the part of the Crown, any such fault being described as 'not of great significance'. In the event, no new prosecution was taken.[10] No new prosecution was taken in *Mitchell v HM Advocate*[11] a highly unusual case where fresh evidence was presented to the appeal court and cast doubt upon the truthfulness of important police evidence. The Lord Advocate does not publicly explain or justify such decisions. The approach of the court in additional evidence cases is explained in *Cameron v HM Advocate*;[12] and see Additional Evidence at 6.26 et seq below. '[If] the court is to find that a miscarriage of justice had occurred in an appeal such as this, it must be satisfied that the additional evidence is at least capable of being described as important and reliable evidence which would have been bound, or at least likely, to have had a material bearing upon, or a material part to play in, the jury's determination of a critical issue at the trial. If the court is so satisfied, it will be open to it to hold that a conviction returned in ignorance of the existence of that evidence represents a miscarriage of justice and may exercise its power to authorise the bringing of a new prosecution.'[13]

1 1982 SCCR 499.
2 1982 SCCR 499 at 505-6.
3 See Sheriff Gordon's editorial note, 1982 SCCR at 508.
4 1985 SCCR 322.
5 1984 SCCR 40.
6 1984 SCCR 40 at 57, per Lord Hunter.
7 1991 SCCR 510.
8 1987 SCCR 745.
9 1990 SCCR 412.
10 Ibid, Editor's note at 416.
11 1989 SCCR 502.
12 1987 SCCR 608.
13 1987 SCCR 608 at 619, opinion of the court.

## 6.09 New prosecutions: refusal of authority

There are no cases in which the court has authorised a new prosecution after upholding an appeal on the ground that the evidence adduced at the trial was insufficient in law to warrant conviction. To allow a new prosecution in any such case would be to allow the Crown two bites at the cherry. Nor does this course appear to have been considered in *McGeary v HM Advocate*[1] when the trial jury had deleted all the specification in the libel but nonetheless convicted the appellant. That was properly a verdict of acquittal in respect of the facts libelled and it would be inconsistent with such a verdict to allow a new prosecution.[2] Authority was refused in a summary case, *Kelly v Docherty*:[3] that was a case in which the sheriff was held not to have taken the correct and necessary steps to satisfy himself as to the capacity of a child witness, aged seven, to distinguish between telling lies and telling the truth. Although this was a technical judicial error (especially in a summary case) authority for a new prosecution was refused, having regard to the young age of the child — who was an essential corroborating witness — the lapse of time which might affect his evidence and the possibility of distress to the child if he were to be required to give evidence again. It thus appears that if the admissible evidence has been ruled to be insufficient or if the evidence is likely to have degraded because of the passage of time and the age of important witnesses or other reasons (eg death or disappearance since trial of vital witnesses) or if the error that resulted in the quashing of the conviction is a material one for which the Crown must bear the responsibility, then the court will be slow to allow a fresh prosecution.

It is possible to think of other factors which would militate against granting authority for a new prosecution, such as wide adverse publicity for the appellant after the conviction, or the character of the evidence, eg identification depending on momentary glimpse by a stranger, or the fact that the appellant had substantially served the sentence imposed or was terminally ill; but as more cases are decided the relevant criteria will emerge and be more clearly defined. As noted elsewhere, the existence of this relatively new power probably has an important bearing upon the appeal court's interpretation of the term 'alleged miscarriage of justice' in sections 228 and 442.[4]

1 1991 SCCR 203.
2 The trial judge should have invited the jury to reconsider their verdict.
3 1991 SCCR 312.
4 See Miscarriage of justice, chapter 7, at 7.01 et seq.

## 6.10 Disposal of appeal against sentence

The powers of the High Court in relation to disposal of an appeal against sentence[1] are available to the court both when disposing of an appeal against sentence alone, under section 228(1), paragraph (b), and also when disposing of an appeal against both conviction and sentence, under section 228(1), paragraph (c).The same powers are available in a case in which the appellant, having brought an appeal against both conviction and sentence, abandons the appeal in so far as it is against conviction but proceeds with it against sentence alone, under section 244(2). If, however, an appellant appeals against both conviction and sentence but, before the hearing, abandons the appeal against sentence and proceeds with his appeal against conviction alone, the appeal court, though it may substitute a different sentence for the one imposed in the trial court, cannot impose a more severe sentence. The Court has power to defer sentence and, additionally, to call for reports to be made available to the Court at the next diet; the membership (ie the composition) of the Court at the next diet need not be the same as it was at the diet when sentence was deferred.

1 s 254(3).

## 6.11 Power to increase sentence

Accordingly, in disposing of any appeal in which the appellant has put sentence in issue and has not timeously abandoned his appeal against sentence, the High Court has power, in terms of section 254(3), not only to affirm the sentence but also 'if the court thinks that having regard to all the circumstances, including any additional evidence such as is mentioned in section 228(1) of this Act, a different sentence should have been passed' to quash the sentence and pass another sentence 'whether *more* or less severe' in its place.[1] The court may choose to defer sentence and to call for reports available to the court at the next diet; the membership of the court at the second diet need not be the same as at the diet when sentence was deferred. The power to increase a sentence is used when the court, after the appeal hearing has started, concludes that the sentence appealed against is inadequate. If the appeal is against conviction and sentence the court may dismiss the appeal against conviction and reconsider the sentence. Examples of the exercise of the power to increase a sentence appealed against include *O'Neil v HM Advocate*[2] where a party appellant argued that a two year sentence (then the sheriff court maximum) imposed in the sheriff court, for masked armed robbery at a station book office, was excessive: the High Court described that sentence as 'grossly inadequate' and increased it to five years.[3] *Connolly v HM Advocate*,[3] though partly overruled in effect by section 254, is still authority for the rule that the High Court can impose a sentence greater than any sentence that could competently have been imposed by the sheriff, if the sheriff could have remitted for sentence. In *Grant v HM Advocate*[4] two appellants (represented by counsel and agents) submitted that their consecutive sentences of three years' imprisonment in respect of (1) a counterfeiting charge and (2) a Firearms Act charge were excessive. A vain attempt was made to abandon one of the appeals during the course of the hearing; but the appeal court refused to allow it to be abandoned. The sentences were described as 'inadequate' and the court increased each sentence from three years' to five years' imprisonment, the sentences to run consecutively. In *Walker v HM Advocate*[5] a woman appealed against two sentences, each of one year's imprisonment, for possession of drugs contrary to sections 5(2) and 5(3) of the Misuse of Drugs Act 1971; the trial judge had ordered that the two sentences should run concurrently. The appeal was persisted in despite the trial judge's statement in his report that 'it would be easier to criticise my sentences as too light rather than excessive'. The appeal court considered both sentences to be inadequate and doubled each to two years, but ordered the two sentences to run concurrently: what was lost on the swings was gained on the roundabout. The appeal court may choose to make even a modest increase in a sentence: in *Donnelly v HM Advocate*[6] a sixteen year old first offender who appealed against a sentence of eighteen months' detention for possessing a C5 gas grenade at a football match had his sentence increased to two years'. The power of the High Court to pass any sentence under Part I of the 1975 Act (solemn procedure) can be exercised in relation to an appellant even if he is absent.[7]

1 s 254(3), para (b).
2 1976 SLT (Notes) 7.
3 1954 JC 90.
4 1985 SCCR 431.
5 1987 SCCR 379.
6 1988 SCCR 386.
7 s 258.

## 6.12 Time pending appeal

Where an appellant has been admitted to bail pending determination of his appeal, under section 238, the period beginning with the date of his admission to bail and ending on the date of his re-admission to prison in consequence of the determination or abandonment of his appeal is not to be reckoned as part of any term of imprisonment under his sentence, in so far as he was not in custody during that period.[1] If, however, the appellant was in custody for any part of the time pending the determination of his appeal, whether because he was not admitted to bail or because his bail was recalled and he was, in consequence of that recall, returned to custody, the time actually spent in custody is reckoned as part of any term of imprisonment under his sentence, although the High Court may give a direction to the contrary.[2] The power of the High Court to give a direction that any time spent in custody pending appeal is *not* to be reckoned as part of the sentence of imprisonment is rarely used, but is available and may be used in respect of appeals considered to be frivolous. In *Scott (J N) v HM Advocate*,[3] this was the test applied in relation to the exercise of a similar power in section 9(4) of the Criminal Appeal (Scotland) Act 1926.

1 s 268(1).
2 s 268(2).
3 1946 JC 68.

## 6.13 Finality of proceedings

Subject to the provisions of section 263 (reference by the Secretary of State), section 262 (effectively duplicated by section 281) provides that 'all interlocutors and sentences pronounced by the High Court under this Part [solemn procedure] of this Act shall be final and conclusive and not subject to review by any court whatsoever and it shall be incompetent to stay or suspend any execution or diligence issuing from the High Court under this Part of this Act.' It is, however, clear that the High Court in the exercise of its *nobile officium* can, in very special circumstances, alter or correct an order pronounced by the Court in exercise of its appellate jurisdiction. It could correct a clear error, as in *James McLellan, Petitioner*, referred to in *Perrie, Petitioner*.[1]

1 1991 SCCR 475 at 481.

# SUMMARY

## 6.14 Disposal of pre-trial appeals

Appeals may be taken pre-trial in certain circumstances: see chapter

3, at 3.01 et seq. Certain objections if not taken timeously cannot be competently taken on appeal.[1] The High Court may affirm the decision of the court of first instance or may remit the case to it with such directions as the High Court thinks fit:[2] see chapter 3 at 3.04.

1 s 454.
2 s 334(2D).

## 6.15 Powers incidental to an appeal hearing

Section 452(4), which is without prejudice to any existing power of the High Court, enables the court to employ various methods for the purpose of enabling it to determine properly an appeal by way of stated case. The character of the 'existing power of the High Court' is discussed in 6.03 above. The powers which are contained in paragraphs (a), (b), (c), (d) and (e) of section 452(4) are identical to those conferred upon the court in solemn proceedings; but see the observations of the Lord Justice Clerk in *Marshall v MacDougall*.[1] The powers are listed and discussed in 6.02 above. Both the 'existing powers' and these statutory powers are available to the High Court in dealing with summary appeals by bill of suspension or by advocation as well as with stated cases.[2] Additionally, the High Court may at the hearing remit the stated case back to the inferior court to be amended and returned. It should also be noted that the High Court may at the hearing of an appeal take into account an allegation relating to an alleged miscarriage of justice which has been made by the appellant in his application for a stated case or in any duly made amendment or addition to that application, even although the inferior court itself was unable to take the allegation into account in preparing the stated case.[3] There may be circumstances relevant to an alleged miscarriage of justice of which the trial judge knows nothing and upon which he is therefore unable to comment, as in *McDonald v HM Advocate*.[4]

1 1986 SCCR 376 at 380.
2 s 453A(2).
3 s 452(2).
4 1987 SCCR 153; cf p159 (ground 5).

## 6.16 Stated case: special powers

In terms of paragraphs (f) and (g) of section 452(4) the High Court has certain powers exercisable in hearing a stated case which are related to the modern statutory provisions for the proposing of adjustments and the treatment of rejected adjustments:[1] see chapter 3 at 3.30. The appeal court can take account of any matter proposed in any adjustment rejected by the trial judge and of the reasons for such rejection. It can also take account of any evidence contained in a note of evidence appended to the case by the trial judge, in terms of section 448(2D). That subsection requires the trial judge to append to the signed case *inter alia* a note of any evidence which he has rejected, and which a party in the course of the adjustment process alleged supported any proposed adjustment rejected by the trial judge, and of any evidence upon which he has based any finding in fact which is challenged (as unsupported by the evidence) by any party who attended a subsection (2A) hearing and made his challenge there. The cases referred to in paragraph 3.30 illustrate how the High Court exercises these powers.

1 s 448(1) and (2A), (2B), (2C) and (2D).

## 6.17 Disposal of appeals against conviction by stated case

The principal statutory provisions regulating the powers of the High Court in disposing of an appeal by way of stated case (unless the High Court considers that the appellant was insane at the material time[1]) are those contained in section 452A (not all of these powers are available in relation to bills of suspension and advocation[2]). The appeal court may remit the cause to the inferior court with their opinion and any direction thereon.[3] In *Aitchison v Rizza*[4] where the sheriff declined to admit evidence tendered by the Crown the High Court upheld the Crown's appeal and remitted to the sheriff to proceed as accords, making it plain to him that that meant he had to hear the evidence he had previously refused to hear. Thus where, for example, the sheriff upon a mistaken view of the law of corroboration has acquitted, the court may answer the appropriate questions and remit the case to the sheriff with a direction to convict, as in *Tudhope v Smellie*[5] or in *McLeod v Mason*.[6] If the inferior court improperly sustains an accused's submission of no case to answer the court will deliver an opinion on the points at issue and remit the case to the sheriff to proceed as accords with the trial, as in *Galt v Goodsir*.[7] The appeal court may affirm the verdict of the inferior court.[8] Although it is not necessary in terms of the statute for the court to deliver an opinion in this or various other types of disposal, it has become the practice for the appeal court to deliver an opinion setting out its reasoning in almost all appeals which are finally disposed of at a hearing. Paragraph (c) of section

452A(1) empowers the court to set aside the verdict of the inferior court and either quash the conviction or substitute for that conviction an amended verdict of guilty, provided that such amended guilty verdict could have been returned on the same complaint in the inferior court: these powers are conferred in the same terms as the powers exercisable in solemn appeals: reference should therefore be made to 6.05 and 6.06 above. Similarly, the powers of the High Court in relation to dealing with sentences when any verdict of the inferior court is set aside or amended, contained in section 452A(3), are in the same terms as those exercisable in solemn appeals.[9] The discussion in 6.06 applies to those powers, except that section 312 governs the form of complaints in the way that sections 41 to 67 govern the form of the indictment.

1 See 6.25 below.
2 s 453A(2).
3 s 452A(1), para (a).
4 1985 SCCR 297.
5 (1977) SCCR Supp 186.
6 1981 SCCR 75.
7 1981 SCCR 225.
8 s 452A(1), para (b).
9 See 6.10 and 6.11 above.

## 6.18 Authority to bring new prosecution

If the High Court, in disposing of an appeal by stated case, or an appeal by bill of suspension or by bill of advocation,[1] sets aside the verdict of the inferior court, it may grant authority to bring a new prosecution in accordance with section 452B.[2] The relevant provisions governing the powers of the court in this regard are effectively in the same terms as those applicable to solemn appeals. Reference should therefore be made to 6.07 to 6.09 above.

1 s 453A(2).
2 s 452A(1)(d).

## 6.19 Appeal against acquittal

The provisions governing the powers of the High Court when an appeal against acquittal is sustained are specified in section 452A(4). Where an appeal against acquittal is sustained, the High Court may convict and sentence the respondent (ie the accused in the complaint). If the High Court itself proceeds to sentence it cannot impose a sentence on the respondent beyond the maximum which could have been passed by the inferior court from which the prosecutor has successfully appealed. Alternatively, the High Court may remit the case to the inferior court with instructions to convict and sentence the respondent: in that event, the respondent must attend any diet fixed by the inferior court for that purpose (convicting and sentencing). Its third option is to remit the case to the inferior court along with the opinion of the High Court: this would be the appropriate course to follow when further evidence (eg evidence wrongfully excluded at the trial) might be placed before the inferior court, or when the case cannot be decided without some step or decision which only that court can make.

## 6.20 Disposal of appeal against sentence

Whether the appeal against sentence is taken as an appeal against sentence alone or is combined with an appeal against conviction the disposal of the appeal against sentence is regulated by section 453C(1).[1] In a summary appeal the appeal court cannot increase the sentence beyond the maximum sentence that could have been passed in the inferior court.[2] In other respects the considerations discussed in relation to the similarly worded statutory provisions governing solemn appeals apply also to summary appeals against sentence: see 6.10 and 6.11 above.

1 By virtue of s 452A(2).
2 Proviso to s 453C(1).

## 6.21 Disposal of bills

If the appeal has come before the High Court by way of bill of suspension the court has the incidental powers already noted in 6.15. Under section 453A(2) the High Court has power to set aside the verdict of the inferior court and grant authority for a new prosecution, as in an appeal by stated case: see 6.17.[1] In setting aside a verdict the High Court may quash any sentence and proceed as in a stated case hearing: cf 6.06 above. The Court has power to pass the bill and to suspend any sentence, order, judgment or proceeding to which it relates *simpliciter* and to order repayment of any fine, penalty or expenses paid in terms of the findings and orders of the inferior court. The court may suspend the proceedings in part and sustain them in part or amend or alter or vary them provided the good and the bad portions are distinctly separable.[2] If the court refuses the bill it may re-commit the appellant (the suspender) to prison if that is appropriate. The court has powers to remit the case to the inferior court with specific instructions as to how to proceed or with instructions to proceed 'as accords'. In that event the High Court will make it clear in an accompanying opinion just what that entails. The court may both alter the conviction and/or sentence and remit to the inferior court with instructions. The foregoing powers are available to the court not only in bills of suspension but also in bills of advocation. Such a bill may be passed in whole or in part and the subject matter of the inferior court's decision may be dealt with by the High Court; the case may be remitted to the inferior court with instructions as to how to proceed in relation to that subject matter.

1 ss 453A(2) and 452A(1)(d).
2 *Moncrieff*, chapter III, section II, p178.

## 6.22 Expenses

The High Court has power in an appeal arising out of summary proceeding whether by stated case or by bill to award such expenses both in the High Court and in the inferior court as it may think fit.[1] The power is discretionary and the conduct of the parties to the appeal is relevant. Expenses usually follow success and are almost always modified by the High Court in proceedings for review: cf *Gallacher, Petitioner*.[2] The same practice of modification obtains when the parties before the High Court are private parties. The sum to which any expenses are modified tends to be one of several standard sums which increase over time: currently (since 1 May 1987) the sums awarded in stated cases (not legally-aided) are usually modified as follows:

(1) a wholly successful appellant (accused) who has printed the stated case: £200;
(2) a wholly successful respondent (accused) who has not printed: £100;
(3) a partly successful appellant (accused) who has printed: £100;
(4) a partly successful respondent (accused) who has not printed: nil.

An accused who successfully appeals against sentence alone can expect an award modified to £75. An appellant may get an award of expenses (currently £60) if the prosecution consents to set aside the conviction: see chapter 4 at 4.15 to 4.16. The Crown will be awarded modified expenses of £50 against an appellant (accused) who has printed but has been wholly unsuccessful, or £100 against an unsuccessful appellant (accused) who has not printed. Awards in bills of suspension or advocation tend to follow the same guidelines although the sum awarded may be less because the printing costs tend to be less. In legally-aided cases it is not the practice to make any awards, irrespective of the result. The older authorities are mentioned in *Renton and Brown*, paragraphs 17-88 and 17-90. In theory, if awards of expenses are not modified to stated sums, accounts may be remitted to the Auditor of the Court of Session for taxation. But in practice this never happens nowadays.

1 s 452A(5).
2 1990 SCCR 492 at 496 per Lord Justice General Hope.

## 6.23 Warrants or sentence orders

Where, following an appeal, the appellant remains liable to imprisonment or detention under the sentence of the inferior court, or is so liable under a sentence passed in the appeal proceedings, the High Court has power, where at the time of disposal of the appeal the appellant was at liberty on bail, to grant warrant to apprehend and imprison (or detain) the appellant for a term. The term of imprisonment or detention, which is to run from the date of his apprehension under the warrant, can not be longer than that part of the term or terms of imprisonment (or detention) specified in the sentence brought under review which remained unexpired at the date of liberation. The Crown will formally move the court to grant any necessary warrant. If at the time of disposal the appellant was in custody serving one or more terms of imprisonment in detention imposed in relation to a conviction subsequent to the conviction appealed against, the High Court has power to exercise the like powers in regard to him as may be exercised, in relation to an appeal abandoned, under section 446(5) by a court of summary jurisdiction: see chapter 3 at 3.32 and *Proudfoot v Wither*.[1] If disqualification for driving has been suspended pending the outcome of an appeal and at the hearing the appeal court refuses to suspend the disqualification or imposes a sentence of disqualification, the Crown moves the court to recall the interim suspension, and any unexpired portion of the disqualification starts to run from the date of the hearing. If the appeal court quashes an order for disqualification but exercises some other penalty power it may need to consider if an order should be made in respect of penalty points. If the appeal court interferes with a sentence involving disqualification or endorsation or recalls an interim suspension of disqualification the High Court will direct the clerk of the sentencing court to intimate the result of the appeal to the police and driving licence authorities.

1 1990 SCCR 96.

## 6.24 Limitations upon the powers of the court

The High Court cannot quash proceedings in an inferior court on certain grounds unless the point has been raised timeously in the inferior court. This matter is discussed in chapter 3 at 3.47. An incidental limitation upon the power of the court came to light in *Farmer v Guild*[1] where it was observed that neither the inferior court exercising powers of interim regulation nor the appeal court had any power to suspend a community service order.

1 1991 SCCR 174.

## 6.25 Disposal of appeal where appellant insane

The governing statutory provisions, in section 453D, relate to any appeal by a convicted person in respect of whom it appears to the High Court that the appellant committed the act charged against him but that he was insane when he did so.[1] They are in the same terms and have the same effects as the powers available to the court in appeals for solemn proceedings;[2] see 6.05 above.

1 s 442(1)(a).
2 ss 254(4) and (5)

# ADDITIONAL EVIDENCE

## 6.26 The new (post-1980) law

The present law relating to the use that may be made of additional evidence in an appeal was introduced by the Criminal Justice (Scotland) Act 1980, by amendment to the 1975 Act. For solemn procedure, the important statutory provisions are those contained in sections 228(2), 252 and 253. For summary procedure the important statutory provisions are those contained in sections 442(2), 452(4) (stated case) and 453A(2) (bill of suspension or advocation). These provisions, as explained and applied by the High Court in a number of recent cases, taken along with the replacing of the former grounds of appeal by one new ground, 'alleged miscarriage of justice in the proceedings'[1] and the newly created right of the court to authorise the bringing of a new prosecution,[2] are so different in their character and effect from the former law that, except in so far as the High Court has expressly adopted criteria from the pre-1980 authorities, those authorities are now of little value for the purpose of ascertaining how the High Court deals with this special type of appeal. The pre-1980 history of additional evidence as a ground of appeal in Scotland is summarised in *Renton and Brown*, chapter 11-41.

1 ss 228(2) and 442(2).
2 ss 254(1)(c), 452A(1)(d).

## 6.27 Additional evidence not previously available

The appellant must satisfy the High Court that 'additional' evidence — namely evidence which was not heard at the trial — was 'not available and could not reasonably have been made available at the trial'.[1] There are thus two different characteristics of the evidence which have to be considered; namely: (a) whether or not it is additional; (b) its previous availability. In principle, the High Court will not hear the evidence unless it passes the tests (sometimes closely connected) derived from both considerations. It may be, however, that the evidence may have to be heard before a final decision can be made as to whether or not it passes both tests.[2]

1 ss 228(2) and 442(2).
2 *Morland v HM Advocate* 1985 SCCR 316; see 6.30 below.

## 6.28 Meaning of 'additional'

In solemn proceedings 'additional evidence' comprises any evidence not laid before the jury. In a solemn trial, evidence might be adduced in a so-called 'trial within a trial'[1] and not then adduced before the jury. That would not be evidence which was 'heard at the trial' because, in this context, 'trial' means the proceedings which take place in the presence of the jury sworn to try the case. Such evidence would, it is submitted, be 'additional'. In short, 'additional' evidence is evidence which the jury did not hear. But that is perhaps a misleadingly wide description, because the reason why a jury might not hear certain evidence could be that the trial judge deliberately excluded it, as in *Sandlan v HM Advocate*[2] or in *Bates v HM Advocate*.[3] In that situation the evidence might properly be described as 'additional'; however, if the exclusion of the evidence were to be attacked as wrongful, the ground of appeal would be the more familiar one — as in *Sandlan* or in *Bates* — that the trial judge erred in excluding the evidence. Furthermore, it would obviously be difficult for such evidence to pass the 'non-availability' test. Evidence might be said to be additional, in the sense of 'not heard by the jury' if it were the evidence of a potential witness who, at the time of the trial, could not be traced or who was then out of the country or incapacitated by illness (or something else) from giving evidence. In any such case, the evidence is likely to pass the 'additional' test, though it would then have to pass the 'non-availability' test. In some cases, no doubt, the appellant might adopt the alternative approach of appealing on the ground that the trial judge wrongfully refused a motion for adjournment or failed to desert *pro loco et tempore*[4] in circumstances in which, in the interests of justice, he should have done, and so prevented the appellant from putting the desired evidence before the jury (or another jury) when the witness became available. Such an approach might be combined with advancing another ground of appeal asking the High Court to hear additional evidence. The evidence that might be obtained for the purposes of an appeal by an appellant from a person who was a co-accused at the trial but who did not give evidence at the trial would also pass the 'additional' test as being evidence not heard by the jury which convicted the appellant. The appellant might, in some such cases, be able to appeal on the ground that he made a motion for separation of trials[5] in order to be able to adduce the co-accused's evidence and that the trial judge refused the motion; but appeals in relation to such matters are notoriously difficult because of the large measure of discretion enjoyed by the trial judge.[6] In any event, such a ground of appeal could be advanced at the same time as a separate ground of appeal based on the existence and significance of additional evidence. The fact that one accused desires to lead (or to leave open the possibility of leading) the evidence of a co-accused in presenting his defence at the trial does not in itself necessarily mean that a motion by him for separation of trials for that purpose will succeed: cf the full discussion in *Renton and Brown*, 9-40.[7] If such a motion is made and refused then the appellant would be able to submit that the evidence was not heard, was 'additional', and he would then require to show that it passed the 'non- availability' test.

1 Renton and Brown, 10-15, 10-18.
2 1983 SCCR 71.
3 1989 SCCR 338.
4 *Aitchison v Rizza* 1985 SCCR 297.
5 Cf *Renton and Brown*, paras 9.37 et seq.
6 Cf *Reid v HM Advocate* 1984 SCCR 153.
7 Cf also *HM Advocate v Granger* 1985 SCCR 4 at 8 per Lord Hunter.

## 6.29 Non-availability

The words of the statute which place the non-availability limit on the introduction of fresh evidence are, 'which was not available and could not reasonably have been made available at the trial'. At first sight actual non-availability raises a simple question of fact: either it was available or it was not. But one must also ask: 'available to whom?'. In the case of several co-accused, A, B and C, all of whom maintain pleas of not guilty, the evidence of A is available to A but not to B or to C, in the sense that A has a choice as to whether or not he enters the witness box.[1] He is a competent witness, provided he consents, for a co-accused.[2] If he chooses not to enter the witness box then his evidence will not be 'heard at the trial' and it can hardly be said to have been 'available' at the trial, so far as the co-accused are concerned. The spouse of a person charged with an offence is a competent but not a compellable witness; accordingly B can not adduce A's wife or C's husband as a witness, unless that spouse chooses to give evidence.[3] It could hardly be said that the evidence of these spouses was 'available' to B at the trial of B if in fact the spouses declined to answer all questions. An accused person may lodge a special defence of incrimination of X. If X is sworn as a witness, having been adduced by the accused, but thereafter declines to answer any questions because he has been given no immunity from prosecution and exercises his right not to incriminate himself, his evidence, or some of it, is not heard at the trial nor can it be said to have been available to the accused person at that person's trial. If the incriminee thereafter acquires immunity,[4] but only after the trial has been concluded, his evidence can then be said to have become available and to be 'additional' evidence which was not heard at the trial'. These examples serve to illustrate that the additional evidence provisions introduced by the 1980 Act to replace those originally contained in the 1926 Act deserve, and will no doubt be given, more searching scrutiny than has been necessitated by the cases so far decided in the High Court. It appears, however, that 'availability' must be considered from the standpoint of the appellant, taking full account of what was practicable to him at the trial.

**1** s 141(1)(a), but see s 141(2) and (3).
**2** s 141(2)(a).
**3** Cf *Bates v HM Advocate* 1989 SCCR 338.
**4** Cf *Thom v HM Advocate* 1976 JC 48.

## 6.30 Reasonable availability

If an accused person elects not to give evidence at his trial he will not be able to persuade the High Court that evidence which he could have given was not reasonably available at the trial.[1] Evidence tendered as additional evidence to be given by a person to contradict evidence given at the trial by that person, will not be regarded as evidence which could not reasonably have been made available at the trial, whether the reason for tendering it is that, since his trial, the witness claims to have remembered something which he had not remembered at the trial,[2] or that he now claims that he committed perjury at the trial.[3] If evidence which is tendered as additional evidence would have been discoverable by more careful investigation, such as by consulting experts, the appellant is likely to have difficulty persuading the court that such evidence was not reasonably available at the trial.[4] In this respect at least — discoverability by more careful investigation — the appellant will not easily escape responsibility by blaming his lawyers for failure to investigate properly. This is the effect of the observations of Lord Wheatley LJC in *Moffat v HM Advocate*,[5] not overruled on this point by *Cameron v HM Advocate*.[6] It was also an important factor in *Williamson v HM Advocate*[7] where the court said 'his [the appellant's] real complaint is that his defence at the trial was conducted on the wrong lines'.[8] In *Grimes v HM Advocate*[9] the appellant was effectively held responsible for the failure of counsel at the trial to ask questions that would have elicited the evidence now claimed to be additional. If an accused asserts that he did not in fact know of the existence of the fresh evidence and persuades the court that he had no reason to know of it, then it seems unlikely that the court will refuse to entertain the additional evidence if it passes the other statutory tests: *Mitchell v HM Advocate*[10] relating to the party appellant's earlier ignorance of the possibility of there being such evidence as he now sought to introduce. Mitchell had no counsel after the first day or two of his trial and thenceforward conducted his own defence; it is clear that the court did not apply to his appeal too stringent a test in relation to reasonable availability.

The word 'reasonable' is notoriously elastic and it remains to be seen how severely the High Court will apply this test where the appellant was in fact ignorant of the existence or potential of the additional evidence but could have learned of it if, by harder work or better detection work, he or his advisors might have discovered it. In *Cameron v HM Advocate*[11] the High Court had considerable doubt about the alleged non-availability of one of the witnesses tendered (Mrs Steed) who had given statements to the police, but took a lenient view, no doubt partly because of the seriousness of the convictions (two murders); but no explanation was given for the lenient approach. An indulgent approach appears to have been taken at the preliminary stage in *Morland v HM Advocate*,[12] perhaps because everyone, including the trial judge, regarded the conviction as unsafe and unsatisfactory. It is thus clear that the evidence might have to be heard before it could properly be said to pass the availability test.[13] Also, if some of the fresh evidence tendered passed all the tests and so should be heard, it might well be necessary also to hear some other evidence which, on its own, could not pass the availability tests, because such evidence might, in the particular circumstances, be necessary to provide the context for the proper evaluation of the other additional evidence.[14] Thus evidence might be judged to be evidence 'which was not available and could not reasonably have been made available at the trial' if it was evidence which was omitted because, in the context of the trial as it was in fact conducted, it had no apparent relevance or significance.

1 *McDonald v HM Advocate* 1987 SCCR 153; cf p 158.
2 *Jones v HM Advocate* 1989 SCCR 726.
3 *Mitchell v HM Advocate* 1989 SCCR 502.
4 *Salusbury-Hughes v HM Advocate* 1987 SCCR 38.
5 1983 SCCR 121 at 129.
6 1987 SCCR 608.
7 1988 SCCR 56
8 Ibid, at 59.
9 1988 SCCR 580.
10 1989 SCCR 502; see p 512D/F.
11 1987 SCCR 608.
12 1985 SCCR 316.
13 Ibid, at 320.
14 See Editor's Notes to *Stillie v HM Advocate* 1990 SCCR 719 at 736/7.

## 6.31 Significance of additional evidence

The question of the significance of the additional evidence placed or to be placed before the court arises at two stages: (1) when the court is invited to exercise the power conferred upon it by section 252(b) to hear the additional evidence, or to order it to be heard by a judge or by some other person appointed for the purpose; and (2) when the court having the evidence, or a full report of the evidence, before it decides how to dispose of the related ground of appeal. The court may decide that on the basis of precognitions or affidavits alone it can decide the ground of appeal against the appellant, as in *Stillie v HM Advocate*[1] or *Moffat v HM Advocate*.[2] The application to hear additional evidence may be refused by the

High Court on the basis that a jury in another trial has rejected the 'additional' evidence as untrue (as in *Mitchell v HM Advocate*).[3] If it does not decide to refuse the application at stage (1) the court can at that stage go no further than to conclude that such additional evidence may be of significance ('whether the alleged additional evidence was *prima facie* of materiality').[4] In *Mitchell v HM Advocate* (above) the court said of the additional evidence tendered (or precognition) '... since the trial judge felt that there was a question mark hanging over the credibility and reliability of the police officers ... we cannot at this stage be certain that the evidence of Mr Stalker and Miss Fair could not have had a material part to play in the jury's deliberations upon the issue of whether it accepts the evidence of the police officers, which the appellant challenged at the trial.'[5] Apart, however, from the fact that at stage (1) the court is looking merely at the potential significance of the additional evidence but at stage (2) is deciding if a miscarriage of justice has been established on the basis that the jury's verdict was delivered in ignorance of evidence which would have been likely to have had a material bearing on the jury's determination, the underlying notion of the significance of the evidence is the same; this is discussed in the following paragraph.

1 1990 SCCR 719.
2 1983 SCCR 121.
3 1989 SCCR 502 at 510B/E.
4 *Cameron v HM Advocate* 1987 SCCR 608 at 611.
5 1989 SCCR 502 at 512F.

## 6.32 The approach of the court

Initially, the court seemed uncertain about the extent to which the new (1980) statutory provisions altered the law related to the old (1926) provisions, which had been consolidated into the Criminal Procedure (Scotland) Act 1975 as enacted in 1975: *Moffat v HM Advocate*[1] is in sharp contrast to *Green v HM Advocate*.[2] However, the conflict was finally resolved in *Cameron v HM Advocate*[3] which is the leading authority; but it must be read with *Mitchell v HM Advocate*[4] in which the appeal succeeded: the appeal failed in *Cameron*. These cases make it clear that the current statutory provisions fall to be interpreted on their own and that the pre-1980 cases interpreting and applying the repealed provisions are not authoritative in relation to the new provisions; that the underlying notion is of 'miscarriage of justice'; and that the court, being free to uphold the conviction or quash it *simpliciter*, or to quash it and grant authority for a new prosecution, must interpret and apply the statute in the light of the court's new enlarged powers. If it concludes, on the basis of the new evidence, that the jury would have been bound to acquit, the conviction will be quashed, as in *Morland v HM Advocate*.[5] If it does not so conclude but is persuaded that the additional evidence is 'relevant evidence of such significance that it will be reasonable to conclude that the verdict of the jury, reached in ignorance of its existence, must be regarded as a miscarriage of justice'[6] the court will set aside the verdict of the trial court and, unless there are compelling reasons to the contrary, authorise a new prosecution as in *Mitchell*, above. Thus the court has to assess the credibility of the witnesses (if it can) and the reliability and materiality of the additional evidence in the light of what the High Court considers to have been the critical issues at the trial. These were the tests applied and developed in *Mitchell* above. In particular, the 'materiality' test was re-examined; the court obtained a concession from the Crown and proceeded upon the basis of that concession, viz that 'it was sufficient to consider whether the evidence would have been likely to have had a material bearing on the jury's determination'. It is evident from the reported cases that the views of the trial judge, the importance or seriousness of the case itself and the High Court's sense of whether or not justice may have miscarried are all factors that have a bearing upon how the various tests are applied in the circumstances of any particular case. Thus 'significance' in section 228(2) is a synonym for materiality, judged in the context of both the evidence placed before the jury and the whole evidence available to the Appeal Court, and related to the judgmental concept of 'miscarriage of justice': see chapter 7 at 7.01 *et seq*.

1 1983 SCCR 121.
2 1983 SCCR 42.
3 1987 SCCR 608.
4 1989 SCCR 502.
5 1985 SCCR 316.
6 1987 SCCR 608 at 618.

## 6.33 Presentation of new evidence

The proper practice is to tender to the court, in support of an explicit ground of appeal, which condescends upon the additional evidence, its earlier non-availability and its significance, precognitions taken by a qualified person.[1] In *Stillie v HM Advocate*[2] affidavits were placed before the court, but properly taken precognitions are all that is necessary. In *Salusbury-Hughes v HM Advocate*[3] an expert report by an engineer was produced to indicate the (additional) evidence that its author would give if the court decided to hear the additional evidence; that was clearly treated as satisfactory although the application was refused on its merits.

1 *Allison v HM Advocate* 1985 SCCR 408.
2 1990 SCCR 719.
3 1987 SCCR 38.

## 6.34 Sentence

The additional evidence provision in the 1975 Act can be used in support of an appeal against sentence, though this would be a highly unusual course to take, because the sentencing judge does not usually impose sentence upon the express basis of parts of the evidence, but upon the basis of the verdict or the plea. It is, however, competent to submit that additional evidence is available to show that a miscarriage of justice has occurred in relation to the sentencing; so it is possible to conceive of circumstances in which such evidence might be tendered. The court's powers under section 252 are such that it should not be necessary to invoke the additional evidence ground of appeal in appeals against sentence; cf *Duff v HM Advocate*[1] this was not, strictly speaking, an additional evidence case because the appellant presented no ground of appeal asking the appeal court to hear additional evidence; however, the appeal court itself decided to hear additional psychiatric evidence as to the likelihood of repetition of the violent behaviour of the appellant. The appellant had pled guilty to the culpable homicide, by assault, of his elderly aunt; the appeal court, after hearing the additional evidence, declined to quash the sentence of imprisonment for life.

1 1983 SCCR 461.

# 7. Miscarriage of justice and grounds of appeal

## MISCARRIAGE OF JUSTICE



## PARTICULAR GROUNDS OF APPEAL

## MISCARRIAGE OF JUSTICE

### 7.01 The new law (post 1980)

Section 228(1), as enacted in 1980,[1] confers upon a person convicted on indictment the right to appeal to the High Court in accordance with the provisions of Part I of the Act. Section 228(2) enables a convicted person to bring under review of the High Court any alleged miscarriage of justice in the proceedings in which he was convicted, including any alleged miscarriage of justice on the basis of the existence and significance of additional evidence which was not heard at the trial and which was not available and could not reasonably have been made available at the trial. (Additional evidence is discussed above; cf chapter 6, at 6.24 et seq.) Section 254(1)[2] provides:

'The High Court may, subject to subsection (4) below,[3] dispose of an appeal against conviction by —
(a) affirming the verdict of the trial court;
(b) setting aside the verdict of the trial court and either quashing the conviction or substituting therefor an amended verdict of guilty; Provided that an amended verdict of guilty must be one which could have been returned on the indictment before the trial court; or
(c) setting aside the verdict of the trial court and granting authority to bring a new prosecution in accordance with section 255 of this Act.'

Section 254(3) has appropriately similar wording in relation to the disposal of an appeal against sentence:

'The High Court may . . . dispose of an appeal against sentence by—
(a) affirming such sentence; or
(b) if the court thinks that, having regard to all the circumstances, including any additional evidence such as is mentioned in section 228(2) of this Act, a different sentence should have been passed, quashing the sentence and passing another sentence whether more or less severe in substitution therefor'.

These provisions were entirely new, although the concept of miscarriage of justice itself was not new; indeed the words 'miscarriage of justice' appeared in the Criminal Appeal (Scotland) Act 1926, section 2(1), and were construed and applied in numerous cases for the next fifty-five years. The application of the 1926 provisions is discussed in *Renton and Brown* paragraphs 11-33 et seq where it is suggested that 'circumstances which formerly were classified as miscarriages of justice will continue to be so classified'. The High Court has not chosen to approach the interpretation of those words in quite that way, although the older cases on 'miscarriage of justice' are not entirely superseded.

1 Criminal Justice (Scotland) Act 1980, s 33 and Sch 2.
2 Also inserted into the 1975 Act by the 1980 Act.
3 Disposal when High Court concludes that appellant committed act charged while insane.

## 7.02 Miscarriage of justice and discretion of High Court

The effect to be given to the provisions inserted into the 1975 Act by the 1980 Act in place of provisions derived from the 1926 Act was the subject of the opinion of the Lord Justice Clerk (Wheatley) in *McCuaig v HM Advocate*,[1] an opinion with which the other judges agreed. In that case there was undeniably a breach of section 160(1) of the 1975 Act which provides that the jury is not to be informed of the accused's previous convictions. It had previously been held, in *Cordiner v HM Advocate*[2] that a breach of section 160(1) of the [1975] Act amounted to a 'miscarriage of justice' within the meaning of section 254(1)[3] though it would not necessarily amount in all cases to a 'substantial' miscarriage of justice. In *McCuaig* the Lord Justice Clerk held that under the newly enacted provisions, 'The matter in my view is now entirely one for the *discretion* of the Court' [emphasis added]. That opinion was delivered extempore and it appears that there was no argument submitted to the High Court (other than by the reporting sheriff) as to the true import of the newly enacted sections 228(2) and 254. The reasoning in support of the conclusion which Lord Wheatley reached there has been described as involving 'an exercise in statutory interpretation which, in the weight it places on the single word 'may',[4] might be described as almost rabbinic in its boldness'.[5] The true function and purpose of the word 'may' in section 254(1), it is submitted, is not to confer an unfettered discretion on the High Court to 'dispose' (ie finally dispose) of an appeal by doing whichever one or other of the things specified in paragraphs (a), (b) and (c) it chooses. On the contrary, because the High Court is not empowered to do anything other than those things authorised by paragraphs (a), (b) and (c), the effect is that the High Court is *required* to do one or other of these things. On this reading there is no 'discretion' conferred by the word 'may', although there may well be some flexibility in the construction and application of the words 'miscarriage of justice' in section 228. By drawing a distinction, nowhere to be found in the statute, between, on the one hand, a miscarriage of justice and, on the other, a miscarriage of justice *sufficient to warrant the setting aside of the verdict*, the court in *McCuaig* held that, even if a miscarriage of justice occurred, the court could nonetheless uphold the conviction. The effect was tantamount to reading the words 'miscarriage of justice' as if they meant *any* flaw or error in the proceedings, and then holding that once such flaw were discovered the High Court was free to decide whether or not to allow the appeal.

In *Sandlan v HM Advocate*[6] it was argued by the appellant that *McCuaig* was wrongly decided and that if there was any miscarriage of justice, *properly so called*, the appeal had to be allowed. However, *Sandlan* was decided in favour of the appellant upon the ground that the exclusion by the trial judge of certain evidence had resulted in 'a *serious* [my emphasis] miscarriage of justice' (per Lord Hunter). Thus there was no need for any reconsideration of *McCuaig* and the opinion of the judges did not deal with the argument that *McCuaig* was wrongly decided. *McCuaig* was followed in *McAvoy v HM Advocate*[7] in which Lord Wheatley spoke of the absence in that case of 'a miscarriage of justice of such *materiality* [emphasis added] as to warrant the setting aside of the verdict'. Lord Dunpark there observed that in the new section 254 (1980 version):

'All reference to miscarriage of justice has disappeared, and with it the distinction between miscarriage of justice and substantial miscarriage of justice. Instead . . . the High Court is given, as your Lordship in the chair [Lord Wheatley] has pointed out, a discretionary power to affirm the verdict or to set it aside. While the power to affirm a verdict is *ex facie* unfettered, it must, in my opinion, be qualified by certain implied limitations. Obviously a court would not affirm a verdict which seemed to the court to be perverse or not supported by the evidence. The old provision required the court to allow the appeal on either of these grounds. But if the appeal is based, for example, upon a misdirection by the trial judge or the admission by the judge of inadmissible evidence and either of these grounds is established, then I am of opinion that the court is empowered to consider the materiality of that misdirection, or of the evidence which ought not to have been admitted, in relation to all the other factors relevant to the verdict of guilty. If, having done that, the court is satisfied that neither the misdirection nor the admission of the inadmissible evidence, whatever it may be, was sufficiently material to cast doubt upon the guilty verdict, then the appeal should be dismissed'. (p 274)

Precisely what is embraced in Lord Dunpark's phrase 'qualified by certain implied limitations' is not clear nor is any specific consideration given to the central fact that the only *ground* of appeal is 'any alleged miscarriage of justice',[8] words which seem to put the concept of 'miscarriage of justice' at the very heart of the appeal, and to provide the true measure of the court's duty and discretion. Nor does Lord Dunpark really seem to be giving examples of a 'discretionary' power, despite his use of that word. Making a judgment as to the materiality, significance and likely consequence of an error is not, it is submitted, an exercise of 'discretionary power'. However, in *McAvoy* (above), Lord Dunpark did not seem to be confidently adopting the *McCuaig* position, that the court can say, 'Yes, there has been a miscarriage of justice, but we will exercise our statutorily unfettered discretion to uphold the conviction anyway'.

1 1982 SCCR 125.
2 1978 JC 64, (opinion of the Court delivered by Lord Justice Clerk Wheatley).
3 Which re-enacted section 2(1) of the 1926 Act.
4 In s 254(1) as amended.
5 Sheriff Gordon, editor, in 1982 SCCR at p 129.
6 1983 SCCR 71.
7 1982 SCCR 263 at 271.
8 s 228(2).

## 7.03 Developments since 1982

In later cases the court has tended either to hold that there has been a miscarriage of justice and so to allow the appeal[1] or that there has not, and, therefore, to refuse it.[2] In *Hunter v The Lord Advocate*[3] the court (opinion of the court delivered by Lord Justice Clerk Wheatley) held that the trial judge had fallen into error by excluding certain evidence that he should have admitted. The opinion included the passage, 'An error in law by the trial judge in regard to the evidence of a witness does not *eo facto* [ie by reason of that fact alone] necessarily lead to a granting of an appeal. By the terms of section 228 of the said (1975) Act the appellant has to show that the error resulted in a miscarriage of justice... In all the circumstances... while we are of the opinion that the trial judge erred in law in the manner complained of, we are also of the opinion that no miscarriage of justice resulted from it. We accordingly refuse his appeal.'

1 *Cordiner v HM Advocate* 1991 SCCR 652.
2 *Binks v HM Advocate* 1984 SCCR 335.
3 1984 SCCR 306.

## 7.04 Current understanding of miscarriage of justice

The final position may therefore be that the court will cease to look for supposed degrees of miscarriage of justice. The High Court now tends to look rather at the seriousness, importance and materiality of the error that the appeal brings to light. Whatever the character of the error (misdirection, wrongful exclusion of evidence, misconduct by the prosecution, etc), the High Court, in the light of its judgment about the importance of that error in the context of the whole trial, goes on to make the further judgment as to whether or not what went wrong may have affected the understanding and the deliberations of the jury in such a way as to lead them to draw an important inference or inferences adverse to the appellant. If the judgment is that the error was likely to have influenced the jury to reach a material judgment adverse to the appellant it will hold that the ground of appeal has been made out, that the 'alleged' miscarriage of justice was a true miscarriage of justice, and, a miscarriage of justice having occurred, the conviction appealed against must be quashed.[1] In the recent case of *McGougan v HM Advocate*[2] in which the trial judge misdirected the jury as to what circumstances could be treated as corroborative of guilt, the Lord Justice Clerk, delivering his opinion of that court, said:

'Whether or not a misdirection produces a miscarriage of justice must depend upon the circumstances and we readily accept that there may be cases where there is no miscarriage of justice despite the fact that there has been a misdirection by the trial judge'.

The case of *Mumraiz Khan and Aman Khan v HM Advocate*[3] is a striking example of how the same error by the trial judge in relation to each of two accused in one trial was held to have led to a miscarriage of justice in one case, but not in the other. The final decision rests upon the court's assessment of the gravity and possible results of the error seen in the context of the whole circumstances.

1 Cf *Renton and Brown* para 11–44.
2 1991 SCCR 49.
3 1992 SCCR 146.

## 7.05 Miscarriage and incorrect rejection of section 140A submission

That way of putting the matter, however, does not help to solve the related question[1] as to whether or not a miscarriage of justice has occurred if the trial judge has incorrectly refused a section 140A submission (no case to answer) and the accused then gives evidence which fills the 'fatal gaps', as they were described by Lord Emslie in *Little*. In that case the Lord Justice General said:

'In refusing both appeals we wish to observe that in the course of the hearing it appeared that we might require to consider the implications of section 140A of the Criminal Procedure (Scotland) Act 1975, if we had been satisfied that the trial judge had erred in rejecting the submissions of no case to answer made on behalf of the appellants. As we have pointed out, counsel for Mrs Little accepted that in asking ourselves if there had been a miscarriage of justice we were quite entitled to have regard to the evidence which Mrs Little herself elected to give and lead but, ignoring that concession, the problem would have been how to deal with convictions, fully justified by the whole evidence before the jury, on the assumption that there were fatal gaps in the Crown evidence which were only filled by the evidence given by and on behalf of the first appellant and by the evidence given by MacKenzie [a witness led for the defence].. In view of the conclusions at which we have arrived we are fortunate that we do not have to resolve this problem in these appeals without the advantage of much more comprehensive exploration of the proper interpretation to be placed on section 140A than was presented on behalf of the appellants. That section, which is entirely novel to our accustomed and well-tried procedure, would appear to echo rules of law long familiar to other jurisdictions, and the problem to which we have referred has, we apprehend, been examined in the courts of England and in courts of the Commonwealth, including the Supreme Court of Victoria, in relation to their own systems of prosecution and criminal procedure. No relevant decisions in these other jurisdictions were cited to us and when the problem requires to be resolved in a criminal appeal in Scotland we would expect to have full discussion of relevant foreign decisions to assist us to appreciate clearly the full implications of the new factor which has been introduced by Parliament into the law of Scotland in the shape of section 140A of the Act of 1975.'.

That question still remains to be answered by the High Court. It is tentatively suggested that, whatever assistance may be found in the jurisprudence of England and the Commonwealth, the answer for Scotland must be found in the 1975 Act. Because section 228 provides for only one ground of appeal, namely 'alleged miscarriage of justice', and because errors by the judge who presides at the trial do not necessarily[2] constitute or result in a 'miscarriage of justice' within the meaning of section 228, the fact that the trial judge has fallen into error by not upholding the section 140A submission does not appear *eo facto* to compel the court to conclude that a miscarriage of justice has occurred. So, for example, if the real issue in a culpable homicide trial, resulting from a traffic accident death, is the quality of the accused's driving, but the prosecution evidence falls marginally short of what is necessary to corroborate that the accused was driving the car, the accused's advocate will quite properly make a section 140A motion. If the trial judge wrongly rejects it and the accused, acting on legal advice, decides not to rest upon the hope of establishing on appeal that the trial judge was wrong, enters the witness box, admits he was the driver and gives evidence which fails to convince the jury that his driving was such as to warrant his acquittal, it appears unlikely that the High Court will conclude that a miscarriage of justice has taken place. Of course, procedurally, things have gone wrong; but a finding that a procedural blunder has occurred, including one that may have adversely affected the interests of an accused, has never been enough, on its own, to warrant the quashing of a conviction, unless it has been of such a character that it may well have brought about injustice. The High Court would be acting in accordance with its pragmatic, non-technical traditions if in this type of case it looked behind the procedural forms to judge the reality. Such an approach, though it might well lead to a reconsideration of *McCuaig v HM Advocate*[3] (cf 7.02 above), would not, of course, exclude the possibility of a finding that a miscarriage of justice had occurred even in a case where the accused, acting on legal advice, has entered the witness box and while there has filled the fatal gap in the prosecution evidence. The court's understanding of the justice of the case would, on this approach, always be more important than any merely procedural or technical consideration. Accordingly, it is suggested that the solution to the problem of the course to be adopted when the issue highlighted in *Little* (above) comes before the High Court is to be found within the 1975 Act, as amended, and especially in the words 'miscarriage of justice' in their true context in section 228, without the *McCuaig* gloss.

1 Cf *Little v HM Advocate* 1983 SCCR 56.
2 *McGougan v HM Advocate* 1991 SCCR 49.
3 1982 SCCR 125.

## PARTICULAR GROUNDS OF APPEAL

### 7.06 Examples of common grounds

Although there is only one ground of appeal, 'alleged miscarriage of justice . . . including any alleged miscarriage of justice on the basis of the existence and significance of the additional evidence'[1] there are various particular grounds of appeal which are commonly advanced as a basis for the conclusion that there has been a miscarriage of justice in the proceedings brought under review of the High Court in the appeal. 'Additional evidence' as a particular ground has already been discussed in chapter 6 at 6.26 to 6.34. The grounds which are discussed in the rest of this chapter are not exhaustive of the possible types or categories of appeal. Some examples are given, or suggestions are made, in this chapter as to how particular grounds may be formulated; but there are no set forms. Clarity, accuracy, brevity and comprehensiveness are the features of a well-formulated ground.

1 ss 228(2) and 442(2).

## 7.07 Misdirection

Any alleged misdirection by the trial judge which is to be founded upon must be specifically identified and highlighted in the grounds of appeal. A judge may misdirect a jury by omitting to give a direction that he ought to have given, by giving a direction that he ought not to have given or by giving a direction that is likely to mislead the jury. Some examples are given below, purely for the purpose of illustrating how to formulate the ground of appeal. However, the capacity for error in a charge is unbounded; accordingly, the practitioner who listens to or subsequently scrutinises the judge's charge to the jury must ask himself when considering the statement of grounds of appeal:

(1) What was the law applicable to the case on which the jury needed directions?
(2) Was the jury given all the directions that were necessary, and given them accurately, fully and clearly?
(3) Was any important direction omitted?
(4) If the trial judge gave examples to the jury to illustrate the way the law fell to be applied did he do so in a way that was unhelpful, contradictory of his more general statements as to the law, or simply confusing?
(5) In dealing with the evidence, did the trial judge refer to it accurately or misleadingly?
(6) Did the trial judge deal with the evidence fairly or did he give undue weight to certain evidence or insufficient attention to other evidence?
(7) Did the trial judge seek to appear to impose his own views on matters properly with the jury's province?
(8) Did the trial judge express opinions, however qualified, upon matters not properly falling within his province?

If the practitioner asks himself the right questions the answers should reveal the flaws in a defective charge. The task is then to articulate the answers as grounds of appeal, as coherent criticisms of the charge as printed. Some examples of grounds of appeal related to alleged misdirection follow. It is, however, essential to bear in mind that the appeal court will read the charge as a whole in the light of what were the real issues in dispute: 'The court is not disposed to examine with niceness isolated sentences in the charge of a judge who presides at a criminal trial'.[1] The issue is not whether or not the directions given might have been better expressed; the issue is whether or not there has been a miscarriage of justice.

1 *Wilkie v HM Advocate* 1938 JC 128 at 131, per Lord Justice Normand. Cf *McPhelim v HM Advocate* 1960 JC 17.

## 7.08 Misdirection by omission

In *McTavish v HM Advocate*[1] a conviction of murder was quashed because, although the presiding judge in his charge to the jury reminded the jury of an incriminating reply allegedly made by the accused to the murder charge preferred by the police, he omitted to make specific reference to the fact that the accused in evidence had denied making the alleged reply at all. The successful ground of appeal was framed thus:

'The presiding judge misdirected the jury in regard to the police evidence concerning the events in the police station and the panel's alleged replies to said charge in that he referred the jury to the replies only in the context of whether they had been elicited fairly and failed to put to the jury the fact that the panel denied altogether having made the replies'.

In *McKenzie v HM Advocate*[2] where the presiding judge omitted to give the standard and elementary directions on onus and reasonable doubt the successful grounds were framed as follows:

'The presiding judge misdirected the jury in respect that: (1) He failed to direct the jury that the onus of proof of the accused's guilt rested on the Crown; (2) he failed to direct the jury that the Crown had to prove the accused's guilt beyond all reasonable doubt; (3) he failed to direct the jury that, in the event of their having any reasonable doubt as to the accused's guilt, the accused should have the benefit of such doubt'.

1 1975 SLT (Notes) 27.
2 1959 JC 32.

## 7.09 Misdirection — error of law

In *Macdonald v HM Advocate*,[1] where the presiding judge misdirected the jury in reference to the 'not proven' verdict, the successful ground of appeal was in these terms:

'3. The sheriff misdirected the jury in relation to the not proven verdict. He states that if the not proven verdict did not exist the jury's verdict would almost certainly be that of guilty. This could clearly have been taken by the jury as a judicial indication that the not guilty verdict was not appropriate to this case'.

In *Sinclair v HM Advocate*[2] the sheriff directed the jury that the charges were linked in time, character and circumstances, so that the *Moorov*[3] doctrine could apply. The successful ground of appeal, which made the correct criticism, viz. that it was for the jury to resolve that issue, being essentially an issue of fact, was couched in these words:

'The trial sheriff misdirected the jury in that he (a) failed to give adequate and proper directions in relation to the application of the *Moorov* doctrine. In particular, he failed to leave it to the jury to decide whether the connection which the application of the rule requires was proved to their satisfaction (*HM Advocate v Stewart*, 19 March 1981, unreported, Crown Office Circular A7(81)'.

This ground discloses with great clarity that the complaint is of misdirection, that it relates to the *Moorov* direction given and precisely what was wrong with the direction given in the charge. It does not quote in full the passage containing the faulty direction; and such full quotation is seldom necessary because the High Court has a full transcript of the charge and has to examine the criticised direction in its full context. The ground in *Sinclair* also helpfully refers to a relevant authority.

1 1989 SCCR 29.
2 1990 SCCR 412.
3 *Moorov v HM Advocate* 1930 JC 68.

## 7.10 Misdirection regarding corroboration

No person can be convicted of a crime or of a statutory offence, except where the legislature otherwise directs, unless there is evidence of at least two witnesses implicating the person accused with the commission of the crime or offence with which he is charged: *Morton v HM Advocate*.[1] In that case, in which only one witness, the victim, identified the accused as the assailant, it appears that the ground of appeal was that 'the verdict was contrary to the evidence'. That would not be regarded as a sufficiently specific ground today; nowadays, in a case such as *Morton*, it would be necessary to say something such as: 'The trial judge misdirected the jury by saying that there was evidence sufficient to identify the appellant as the person who assaulted Miss X. There was no evidence of identification to corroborate that given by Miss X herself'. The first ground of appeal would be, 'There was insufficient evidence to identify the appellant as the person who assaulted Miss X. There was no evidence from any other witness pointing to the appellant as Miss X's assailant.'

In *Cordiner v HM Advocate*[2] a conviction of rape was quashed because the trial judge directed the jury that they could find corroboration of the complainer's evidence in a possible connection between the accused and an article of the complainer's clothing; the clothing, however, was connected with the crime only by the evidence of the complainer herself. The successful ground of appeal was, 'The Crown sought to rely for corroboration on the identification of a jersey (label number 16) as being the property of the appellant. The jersey was identified by the complainer only and accordingly could not form a separate, independent source as is required to constitute corroborative evidence. The learned trial judge failed to direct the jury that it would not be open to them to rely on such evidence for corroboration. Such failure to give appropriate directions resulted in a miscarriage of justice'.

Another example of fully stated, well-expressed cogent grounds of appeal may be seen in *McGougan v HM Advocate*[3] in which the appellant was charged with using lewd practices towards a very young girl; the trial judge had instructed the jury that they could hold that the appellant's reactions and demeanour could corroborate incriminating admissions made by him. That was held to be a material misdirection. The ground stated was: 'The jury were not directed by the learned trial judge to any relevant elements of evidence which could be taken to corroborate the appellant's statement. This was a material misdirection which led to a miscarriage of justice'. The particular ground of appeal upon which the successful submission was based was slightly less specific than it might have been because it did not specifically mention the trial judge's reference to the evidence about the appellant's reactions and demeanour. It would have been better had it done so.

1 1938 JC 50, per Lord Justice Clerk Aitchison delivering the Full Bench opinion.
2 1991 SCCR 652.
3 1991 SCCR 49 at 51/52.

## 7.11 Misdirection by withdrawing defence

It is a misdirection to withdraw a plea of self-defence in circumstances in which there is evidence which would entitle the jury to conclude that the accused had been acting in self-defence. In *Surman v HM*

*Advocate*[1] where the ground of appeal was upheld the ground was stated simply, clearly and without elaboration:

'The learned trial judge erred in law and misdirected the jury by withdrawing consideration of the special defence of self-defence from the jury in so far as it relates to the fatal wound.'

Similar grounds of appeal would exist if the trial judge erroneously withdrew any line of defence, such as provocation or accident or diminished responsibility or involuntary intoxication.[2]

1 1988 SCCR 93.
2 Cf *Ross v HM Advocate* 1991 SCCR 823.

## 7.12 Conduct of the trial

There are numerous examples of grounds of appeal in which the alleged miscarriage of justice is said to have resulted from some circumstance related to the conduct of the trial. Some examples are given to illustrate how grounds of appeal may be framed to give adequate notice of what is complained of.

## 7.13 Conduct by the trial judge

In *Tallis v HM Advocate*[1] the sheriff took over the role of cross-examiner of the accused, and, both in that way and by the terms of his charge to the jury, conspicuously failed to demonstrate and maintain his complete impartiality upon the vital issue of the credibility of the accused. The successful ground of appeal was in these terms: 'The sheriff interrupted the cross-examination of the procurator fiscal and proceeded to cross-examine the panel. After the conclusion of the speeches the sheriff adjourned for one and a quarter hours before charging the jury and thereafter the terms of his charge were such as to show a bias and may have constituted a miscarriage of justice resulting in the panel being convicted by a majority of the jurors.'. Though this formulation could have been improved, it gave clear notice of the points to be made and therefore achieved its purpose as a ground of appeal. In *Hutchison v HM Advocate*[2] a witness prevaricated and denied having made a prior statement to the police. The trial judge, in the presence of the jury and on the motion of the advocate depute, ordered the witness to be detained and to be brought before the court at the end of the trial; the witness was taken into police custody in court before the eyes of the jury. Similar treatment was meted out to a second witness who was also taken into custody but only after a courtroom struggle with the police. The detailed grounds of appeal may be seen in 1983 SCCR at 505; they merit study as an example of full, clear and coherent grounds of appeal which focus the issue well. They contain a full narrative of events and assertions as to the likely consequences of such events upon the minds of the jurors, concluding:

'In the foregoing circumstances the jury were precluded from fairly assessing the credibility of the said . . . witnesses and the proper weight to be placed upon their evidence in particular in so far as the said evidence exculpated the appellant; accordingly the appellant has been subjected to a miscarriage of justice.'

On this basis the court was given full notice of the criticisms to be advanced and was invited to consider the likely impact of these events upon the verdicts. In the event, the court, though agreeing with the criticisms made, felt able, on the basis of the strength of the evidence and of certain saving directions in the judge's charge, to conclude that no miscarriage of justice had occurred. Reference should also be made, both for entertainment and enlightenment, to the fourth ground of appeal in *Macdonald v HM Advocate*[3] where the complaint was of oppression by the sheriff who, it was said, sought to rush the trial through and expressed the wish that he would be spared 'the usual counsel's disease' of 'long-winded speeches'. Alas, the High Court chose to decide the case upon another ground and offered no guidance on the proper conduct of trials in the Western Isles; but the ground of appeal is a model of clarity.

1 1982 SCCR 91.
2 1983 SCCR 504.
3 1989 SCCR 29.

## 7.14 Conduct of the prosecutor

The prosecutor's conduct may afford a good ground of appeal. So where a prosecutor in his address to the jury commented adversely on the accused's failure to give evidence the ground of appeal was, 'There was a miscarriage of justice under section 228 of the Criminal Procedure (Scotland) Act 1975 in respect that the procurator fiscal depute, in contravention of the terms of section 141(1)(b) of said Act, commented at length on the accused's failure to give evidence to support his special defence on one charge and on his withdrawal of his special defence on the other charge. Although the sheriff directed the jury to disregard these remarks, it was not possible for them not to be influenced by them'.[1] At the hearing, although the ground of appeal was largely accepted by the High Court, it was concluded that the evidence and the sheriff's charge were such as to warrant the conclusion that no miscarriage of justice had occurred.

1 *Upton v HM Advocate* 1986 SCCR 188.

## 7.15 Conduct by defence advocate

Misconduct by counsel acting for an appellant's co-accused, eg by making improper and prejudicial remarks to the jury about the appellant in the course of his address, could give rise to a good ground of appeal. An example of how such a ground may be worded is to be found in *Pike v HM Advocate*.[1] The relevant ground for the appellant, Mrs Pike, was:

'That a miscarriage of justice may have occurred by reason of the remarks made by counsel for the fifth-named panel Mrs Finlay . . . in his address to the jury and in the absence of any evidence to support the said remarks (or notice of intention to lead such evidence) to the effect that:

(i) the evidence indicated a scheme of deception played upon the fifth-named panel by her co-accused, including the appellant;

(ii) the statement to the police by the fifth-named panel could be compared with that of the appellant to show the lack of guilty knowledge on the part of the fifth-named panel and, by inference, the existence of such knowledge in the appellant.'.

If there was substance in such a ground of appeal one would expect the ground of appeal to be associated with, a complaint that the trial judge had failed to give adequate directions to the jury in connection with the matter (as it was in *Pike*). It is not uncommon or improper for the same underlying point to figure more than once in distinct grounds of appeal.

1 1987 SCCR 163.

## 7.16 Incompetent proceedings

In *Gallagher v HM Advocate*[1] the Crown brought a charge against the accused under the Coinage Offences Act 1936, section 9(1) and indicted the accused in the sheriff court where he was convicted. No objection was taken by the panel to the competency of the trial although the statutory penalty was penal servitude, a penalty that could not be imposed in the sheriff court. The sheriff remitted the panel to the High Court for sentence and a sentence of three years' penal servitude was imposed, despite a plea that the whole proceedings were fundamentally null. The High Court of Justiciary upheld an appeal against conviction and sentence upon grounds stated as follows:

'(1) That the sheriff and jury had no jurisdiction to try the indictment on which the appellant was convicted, in respect that the minimum sentence which could be imposed by the court on conviction was, under section 9(1) of the Coinage Offences Act 1936, three years penal servitude. (2) That, in view of a fundamental nullity in the proceedings in the sheriff court, it was incompetent for the High Court to impose any sentence on the appellant . . .'

It should be noted, however, that although an issue of fundamental nullity may be raised at any time, or noticed *ex proprio motu* by the court itself, questions of the competency or relevancy of the indictment itself must be raised at a preliminary diet and may not be raised later except by leave of the court on cause shown.[2] But if such a point is raised at a preliminary diet, and repelled, it may be raised again on appeal without leave.[3]

1 1937 JC 27.
2 s 108(2).
3 *Renton and Brown* para 11-35.

## 7.17 Evidence: wrongful admission or exclusion

There are numerous examples of appeals taken against convictions on the ground that evidence which should have been excluded was admitted or that evidence which should have been admitted was excluded. *Brady v HM Advocate*[1] is an example of an (unsuccessful) appeal against a refusal to admit evidence which, it was argued, should have been admitted. The ground was 'After debate outwith the presence of the jury, the presiding judge refused to allow evidence to be led of earlier specific incidents of violence by the victim or other person and/or property. In the circumstances of the case and in the interest of justice, it was appropriate that an exercise of discretion by allowing said evidence should have been made in favour of the accused.'. *Tonge v HM Advocate*[2] provides examples of grounds in a successful appeal relating to the wrongful admission of evidence, the evidence consisting of a response by a detained suspect made in reply to a police accusation which had not been preceded by a common law caution. The grounds were:

'1. That the trial judge misdirected the jury in that he did not direct them that on the evidence the statement alleged to have been made by the applicant [sic, should be "appellant"] to the investigating police officers was made in circumstances which rendered the statement inadmissible as evidence. 2. That the trial judge erred in not sustaining the objection made on behalf of the applicant to the statement made by the applicant to the investigating police officers.'.[3]

In effect the same point (no common law caution) lay behind both grounds and number 2 fell to be considered first. It was that ground upon which the appeal was allowed. In *Sandlan v HM Advocate*[4] various grounds of appeal were taken relating to alleged misdirections by the trial judge as to the evidence, the wrongful admission of evidence over objection, and the trial judge's failure to afford counsel for one of the accused an opportunity to cross-examine witnesses on matters on which they had given evidence incriminatory of the appellant. *Bates v HM Advocate*[5] also contains (at p 341) fully stated grounds of appeal in relation to the admission of evidence and includes a statement as to the course that the trial judge should have followed.

1 1986 SCCR 191.
2 1982 SCCR 313.
3 1982 SCCR 313 at 336.
4 1983 SCCR 71.
5 1989 SCCR 338.

## 7.18 Irregularities affecting the proceedings

There are many examples of improprieties occurring in the course of proceedings and giving rise to appeals.[1] Of their nature they are usually unprecedented and not repeated; so there is no regular style or form for writing a ground of appeal based on some such incident. The ground must simply narrate succinctly what it was that occurred, why it was, or might have been, prejudicial to the interests of the accused or of justice and, usually, its context. So where the trial judge communicated with the jury after they had retired to consider their verdict, by sending them messages via the clerk of court about important matters which should have been the subject of direction given in open court, the High Court held that a miscarriage of justice had resulted: *Cunningham v HM Advocate*;[2] the grounds of appeal in *Cunningham* were very detailed and should be studied in full[3] but two of them are quoted here to illustrate how to frame grounds of appeal to fit the circumstances.

'1. It is contended that a miscarriage of justice occurred in the proceedings at the appellant's trial in each of the following respects:

(a) After the conclusion of the judge's charge to the jury, and during the course of their deliberations, they received advice or instructions as to their powers and obligations, not directly from the judge, by way of any further charge delivered in court and in the presence of the accused in response to issues there raised by the jury, but indirectly from or through the clerk of court, outwith the presence of any person other than the clerk and the jury, or one or more of them, in response to questions raised by the jury (or one or more of them) with the said clerk; the said questions being conveyed by the clerk to the judge,and the judge's response being likewise conveyed to the jury (or one or more of them) in terms verbatim or otherwise to the appellant unknown. It is respectfully submitted that the said procedures constitute a miscarriage of justice; that the verdict of the trial court should be set aside; and that the convictions following thereon should upon review be quashed.'

The second, a supplementary ground of appeal, read:

'In any event, as narrated in the foregoing grounds of appeal, the clerk of court was on more than one occasion present with the jury after they had been enclosed, contrary to section 153(2) of the Criminal Procedure (Scotland) Act 1975; and visited the jury, contrary to section 153(3) thereof. He also communicated with the jury, not or not only in giving a direction or in response to a request under section 153(3)(b thereof on behalf and with authority of the presiding judge, contrary to the said section 153(3). These circumstances constituted a material breach of said section 153 and accordingly the appellant should be acquitted in terms of section 153(4) of said Act and his conviction should be quashed.'

Another case which gave rise to a successful appeal on a similar ground was *McColl v HM Advocate*[4] where the ground was: 'There was a miscarriage of justice in that the clerk of court communicated with the jury and gave the jury certain advice outwith the presence of any other person in breach of both sections 145 and 153 of the Criminal Procedure (Scotland) Act 1975 (as amended).' This was an interesting case because, in effect, counsel for the appellant gave the High Court his own account of what had transpired. The whole matter was investigated by obtaining reports from the clerk and the trial judge and even a precognition of the clerk of court. This process left several matters unclear but disclosed enough to enable the court to find that a miscarriage of justice had occurred and to quash the conviction.

In *W v HM Advocate*[5] the trial judge, before pronouncing sentence, interviewed alone a social worker who had prepared a report on the appellant. That gave rise to a ground of appeal in the following terms:

'There was a miscarriage of justice in that, having heard the plea in mitigation which sought disposal by way of a probation order, the presiding judge adjourned the case in order to speak in chambers with the social worker who had prepared the social enquiry report. Said meeting took place outwith the presence of the appellant, defence counsel and the advocate-depute. On his return to the bench the presiding judge made no reference to what had been discussed in chambers but proceeded to sentence the appellant. Said conduct by the presiding judge was improper and oppressive.'

The court stated that it was not appropriate or desirable for a judge to interview a social worker in private when considering sentence; but the sentence imposed was quashed upon a different ground.

1 Cf *Renton and Brown*, para 11–40.
2 *Cunningham v HM Advocate* 1984 SCCR 40.
3 1984 SCCR 40 at 43/4.
4 1989 SCCR 229.
5 1989 SCCR 461.

## 7.19 Verdict — unreasonable or ambiguous

It is a good ground of appeal that the recorded verdict is incompetent[1] or does not make sense because it is self-contradictory or incomprehensible or ambiguous[2] and confused or that it does not disclose a crime known to the law of Scotland.[3] Similarly, if a verdict goes beyond the terms of the indictment that will afford a good ground of appeal. A verdict given in defiance of a direction by the trial judge may be appealed. It is, of course, open to the trial judge to take whatever steps are appropriate in open court to discover if the patent flaw reflects some superficial error which can be put right before the verdict is recorded[4] or if it discloses some irremediable confusion which is fatal to the verdict: cf *White v HM Advocate*[5] where the relevant ground of appeal was: 'That the trial judge erred in law in allowing to be recorded a verdict from the jury that was in direct conflict with directions he had given to them'. The High Court said that the trial judge should have reminded the jury of his original directions and sent them out again to consider their verdict. The convictions were quashed.

See also *McGeary v HM Advocate*[6] where it was said that the proper course to take is to draw the jury's attention to the defect in the verdict which they have returned before it is recorded and to provide them with an opportunity of reconsidering it. *Salmond v HM Advocate*, where the jury in an attempted murder case returned a verdict of 'guilty by reason of reckless indifference, with extreme provocation', provides a good example of a ground of appeal fully stated but with commendable brevity. 'The jury's verdict of guilty of attempted murder under provocation being incompetent, a miscarriage of justice has resulted'. The court set aside the conviction and substituted an amended verdict, holding the appellant guilty of assault (to the danger of life etc) under extreme provocation.

1 *Salmond v HM Advocate* 1991 SCCR 43.
2 *Hamilton v HM Advocate* 1991 SCCR 282.
3 *Sayers v HM Advocate* 1981 SCCR 312.
4 Cf *Took v HM Advocate*1988 SCCR 495.
5 1989 SCCR 553.
6 1991 SCCR 203.
7 1991 SCCR 43.

## 7.20 Conviction — perverse and unreasonable

Because an appeal may bring under review 'any alleged miscarriage of justice'[1] it must be open to an accused to argue that, even although the evidence was sufficient in law to warrant conviction and there was no irregularity in the conduct of the proceedings, the verdict was so unreasonable as to be perverse: cf. the reservation by Lord Keith in *Dow v MacKnight*.[2] Such a ground of appeal was advanced in *Rubin v HM Advocate*:[3] 'The quality, character and strength of the evidence against the pannel when viewed as a whole was insufficient to justify the conviction of the pannel'. The particular appeal was dismissed, despite the gravest doubts about the reliability of a principal witness for the Crown, but the Lord Justice General said, 'I do not, however, bearing in mind Lord Keith's reservation of opinion in *Dow v MacKnight* 1949 JC 38 [at 56], require to consider and decide whether there could ever be circumstances sufficiently exceptional in which an appellate court might properly quash a conviction upon that ground'. Given that now it is possible to hear additional fresh evidence[4] and to grant authority to bring a new prosecution,[5] and given the growing familiarity of the civil courts in judicial review cases with the concept of a decision so unreasonable that no reasonable person called upon to decide it could have decided it in the way it was decided[6] it is at least conceivable that the High Court of Justiciary may find it possible in a suitable case to retreat from the notion, hitherto underlying the consideration of solemn appeals, that the conclusions, or supposed conclusions, of the jury on each and every issue of fact are sacrosanct and inviolable whatever the weight and coherence of the evidence. All that can properly be said at present is that the door is not necessarily finally closed.

1 ss 228(2) and 442(2).
2 1949 JC 38 at 56.
3 1984 SCCR 96.

4 ss 228(2) and 252.
5 ss 254, 255.
6 Cf Lord President Emslie in *Wordie Property Co Ltd v Secretary of State for Scotland* 1984 SLT 345, cp. p 347.

## 7.21 Sentence — grounds of appeal, examples

There are many possible grounds of appeal against sentence. They include incompetency,[1] excessiveness, inappropriateness,[2] failure to back-date or to take account of the so-called comparative principle,[3] taking account of irrelevant matters.[4] The practice note of 29 March 1985[5] applies to grounds of appeal against sentence. Accordingly it is not enough just to say in the ground of appeal, 'The sentence imposed was excessive in all the circumstances'. In a recent summary appeal against sentence[6] the court declined to entertain an appeal where the stated ground was 'The sentence is excessive. No previous convictions libelled'. The circumstances must be set forth in the ground of appeal. If the ground is incompetency the character of the alleged incompetency must be spelled out. The test of adequacy will be whether or not the grounds of appeal have given sufficient notice to enable the sentencing judge to understand the complaint made and to comment fully upon it. But even in the unusual type of case where the substantial ground of appeal (permitted by sections 252(c) and 452(4)(c)) is that since the conviction and sentence there has been such a marked improvement in the appellant's behaviour that the court should give him an opportunity to maintain the improvement[7] — a matter upon which the sentencing judge may well be unable to comment — it is still necessary to condescend upon the alleged new circumstances, if only to allow the Crown an opportunity to seek information about them to place before the court if asked to do so, or the court to order further inquiry under section 252 or section 452(4).

1 Cf *Noble v Guild* 1987 SCCR 518 (summary).
2 *McRae v HM Advocate* 1987 SCCR 36.
3 *Bates v HM Advocate* 1989 SCCR 338; *Allan v HM Advocate* 1990 SCCR 226.
4 *Khaliq v HM Advocate* 1984 SCCR 212.
5 Cf 2.27 above.
6 *Campbell v MacDougall* 1991 SCCR 218.
7 As in *Rennie v MacNeill* 1984 SCCR 11.

## 7.22 Sentence — deportation etc

The same considerations as to the giving of adequate notice and specification apply in respect of grounds of appeal relating to incidental orders or penalties such as deportation, forfeiture, disqualification or the like. Thus in a summary case, *Willms v Smith*,[1] where the sheriff recommended deportation of a German who pleaded guilty to an assault of punching and admitted one minor previous conviction the successful grounds of appeal which stated the circumstances briefly but fully were: 'The decision of the sheriff to recommend deportation to Her Majesty's Government is harsh and oppressive[2] for the following reasons:

(1) The offence in itself did not merit such a recommendation.
(2) The appellant is married to a British citizen, who is unwilling to live in West Germany because of language difficulties. If the appellant were to be deported, the parties would therefore be separated.
(3) The social inquiry report available to the court when sentence was imposed showed the appellant to be both a caring and educated person who had given his wife much assistance and support in her attempts to overcome problems which she had encountered.

1 1981 SCCR 257.
2 The test since 1981 has been not whether the sentence was 'harsh and oppressive' but whether it was excessive.

# 8. Legal aid

8.01 Introductory
8.02 Advice and assistance
8.03 Assistance by way of representation (ABWOR)
8.04 Tests of eligibility: all appeals under section 25 of 1986 Act
8.05 Urgent stops in appeals: 'regulation 15' cover
8.06 Appeals arising from preliminary matters — solemn proceedings
8.07 Appeals arising from preliminary matters — summary proceedings
8.08 Appeals arising from proceedings on indictment
8.09 Appeals arising from summary trial proceedings
8.10 Petitions to the *nobile officium*
8.11 Miscellaneous other appeals
8.12 Appeals in respect of bail
8.13 What happens if legal aid is refused?
8.14 Duties of solicitor and counsel
8.15 Withdrawal of legal aid
8.16 Payment of fees from the Fund

## 8.01 Introductory

This chapter deals with various legal aid matters which arise when an appeal is taken to the High Court of Justiciary.[1] Most such appeals operate within strict time limits[2] and accordingly the busy practitioner may easily overlook the necessity of ensuring payment for the steps he is instructed to take on behalf of his client. Since the vast majority of appeal proceedings before the High Court are wholly funded by the state, it is vitally important for the practitioner to be aware of the relative provisions of the Legal Aid (Scotland) Act 1986 and the potential pitfalls in the legislation.

1 In this chapter statutory references are to the Legal Aid (Scotland) Act 1986, unless otherwise indicated.
2 See chapters 2 and 3.

## 8.02 Advice and assistance distinguished from legal aid

Under the 1986 Act 'advice and assistance'[1] is quite separate from criminal legal aid. The former is the subject of Part II of the Act, while the latter is covered by Part IV. Appellants frequently qualify on financial grounds for preliminary advice and assistance on the courses open to them by way of appeal: such advice is quite separate from any action taken to lodge appeal documents, to carry out steps of process or to provide representation before the High Court. Any solicitor can provide advice and assistance provided certain financial criteria are met;[2] the appellant may have to pay a contribution to the cost of such advice, depending on his circumstances;[3] this is collected by the solicitor.[4] No application requires to be made to the Legal Aid Board (referred to hereafter as 'the Board'); the solicitor is empowered to give advice immediately up to an initial limit of the cost of such advice, currently £80.00.[5] If he thinks the advice is likely to cost more than that, he must apply to the Board for prior authority to exceed that limit.[6] In relation to advice on criminal appeals, these provisions are widely used.

1 Defined in s 6(1) of the 1986 Act.
2 1986 Act, ss 6(1), 8.
3 1986 Act, s 11.
4 Advice and Assistance (Scotland) Regulations 1987, reg 8.
5 1986 Act, s 10(2), as modified under s 9(2)(e).
6 *Drummond & Co WS v Scottish Legal Aid Board* 1991 SCLR 540, affd 1992 SLT 337, HL.

## 8.03 Assistance by way of representation (ABWOR)

One particular form of advice and assistance under Part II of the 1986 Act is advice by way of representation (ABWOR).[1] This means *inter alia* advice and assistance provided to a person by taking on his behalf any step in instituting, conducting or defending any proceedings or by otherwise taking any step on his behalf.[2] ABWOR, being a form of advice and assistance, is available subject to the same tests of eligibility and in the same way. It is likewise subject to the same rules as to the limit of expenditure and increases thereon.

The only relevance of ABWOR in criminal appeals is that it is available in restricted circumstances to an accused in summary proceedings who wishes to appeal or resist an appeal under section 334(2A) of the Criminal Procedure (Scotland) Act 1975 in the High Court against a decision on a preliminary plea.[3]

1 1986 Act, s 6(1), para (b).
2 1986 Act, s 6(1).
3 See 8.07 below.

## 8.04 Tests of eligibility: all appeals under section 25 of 1986 Act

Section 25 of the Legal Aid (Scotland) Act 1986 applies to criminal legal aid in connection with an appeal against conviction, sentence or acquittal, including also a petition to the *nobile officium* of the High Court of Justiciary, and a reference to the High Court by the Secretary of State under section 263 of the Criminal Procedure (Scotland) Act 1975. Such legal aid is available on application made to the Board if the Board is satisfied:

(1) after consideration of the financial circumstances of the applicant, that the expenses of the appeal cannot be met without undue hardship to the applicant or his dependants (but this does not apply where criminal legal aid was made available under section 23 or 24 of the 1986 Act in connection with the proceedings at first instance in respect of which the appeal is being made); and

(2) where the applicant is the appellant, that he has substantial grounds for making the appeal and that it is reasonable, in the particular circumstances of the case, that legal aid should be made available to him.[1]

Accordingly, the double test, of financial eligibility and eligibility on the merits, requires to be satisfied in all cases, subject only to the proviso that if legal aid was made available in the court of first instance, then the applicant for legal aid in respect of an appeal does not again have to satisfy any test of financially eligibility for criminal legal aid for his appeal; he is deemed to be still financially eligible for legal aid for the appeal stage just as he was assessed as financially eligible for the proceedings at first instance. It is for this reason that financial eligibility for legal aid for an appeal is not often a problem; those who are legally aided at first instance do not have to pass any such test for an appeal and very few accused persons who are not financially eligible at first instance become financially eligible when the appeal stage is reached. For the small number of cases in the latter category an appellant's means require to be assessed before he can receive legal aid for his appeal; this also requires to be done where the only legal aid he received at the court of first instance was from the duty solicitor under section 22 of the 1986 Act.[2]

Where it is necessary to pass the financial test, the application form for criminal legal aid for the appeal contains an annexation where the applicant is required to give full details of his financial position. His income and capital (if any) require to be vouched and indeed the fullest documentation available should be lodged with the Board so that it can assess whether the financial test is met.[3] The Board is given no statutory guidance in assessing what constitutes undue hardship but it will take into account the likely costs of appeal proceedings, including the costs of counsel's fees and any necessary printing cost. In considering his financial eligibility, the applicant may be required by the Board to attend for interview by its representative or to supply such further information or such documents as it may require to enable it to determine his application.[4]

The tests of 'substantial grounds' and 'reasonableness' also require to be met; and again the Board is given no guidance in the legislation as to what these terms mean. Obviously it will proceed on the basis of its experience in such matters and in the light of previous decisions of the High Court and trends of authority as they appear. The views of the solicitor or counsel who conducted the proceedings at first instance are of great importance and often a note by counsel will assist the Board on any legal matters that arise. Frivolous appeals at the public expense will not be encouraged by the Board. Any views of the judge at first instance expressed in any report prepared for the appeal court will also be of great importance, since he will normally outline in his report the submissions or points made before him and why he disposed of them as he did.

Where the applicant has available to him rights and facilities making it unnecessary for him to obtain legal aid, or has a reasonable expectation of receiving financial or other help from a body of which he is a member, the Board cannot grant him legal aid for a criminal appeal in the absence of special reasons.[5]

1 s 25(2)(b).
2 1986 Act, s 25(4).
3 At the very least, the Board would require to see recent wage slips or proof of state benefit.
4 Criminal Legal Aid (Scotland) Regulations 1987, reg 13(2).
5 Ibid, reg 10.

## 8.05 Urgent steps in appeals: 'regulation 15 cover'

Almost all steps in criminal appeals have to be taken within strict timetables and certain steps have to be taken as a matter of urgency in order to preserve the right of appeal for a prospective appellant.[1] Such steps may be taken without prejudice to the decision as to whether the appeal will actually proceed or not, but unless certain urgent steps are taken the right of appeal is likely to be lost. Legal aid for these urgent steps is provided under regulation 15 of the Criminal Legal Aid (Scotland) Regulations 1987. The regulation provides that where an applicant seeks legal aid for an appeal in a matter of special urgency, the Board may, if it thinks fit, make criminal legal aid available to him notwithstanding that it has not been satisfied that he is financially eligible or that he has substantial grounds for making the appeal and that it is reasonable, in the particular circumstances of the case, that legal aid should be made available to him. The regulation goes on to provide that in the event that the Board does make criminal legal aid available as a matter of special urgency, it must also (a) specify that criminal legal aid is available only for such limited purposes as it thinks appropriate in the circumstances; (b) require the assisted person as soon as practicable to satisfy it that the financial and other tests are met; and (c) in the event that it is not so satisfied, cease to make criminal legal aid available to him.[2]

It will thus be apparent that 'regulation 15 cover' is often an essential prerequisite to a grant of legal aid for the full appeal itself. Its availability is unrestricted both in relation to the steps that may be taken and because the normal tests of financial and other eligibility do not require to be satisfied at the time that it is applied for. The sole question which the Board is obliged to consider is whether the steps which are proposed are steps which require to be taken as a matter of special urgency. The commonest situations in which regulation 15 cover is encountered are as follows:

**(1) In appeals arising out of solemn proceedings:**

(a) framing and lodging the intimation of intention to appeal under section 231 of the 1975 Act;

(b) framing and lodging a note of appeal against conviction and/or sentence under section 233 of the 1975 Act;

(c) applying for an extension of time under section 236(B) of the 1975 Act to take the foregoing steps; and

(d) applying for bail under section 238 of the 1975 Act pending the appeal against conviction and/or sentence; and

**(2) In appeals arising from summary proceedings:**

(a) framing, lodging and intimating, or later altering, an application for a stated case under section 444 of the 1975 Act, including an application for interim liberation or interim suspension of driving disqualification;

(b) perusing and adjusting a draft stated case including attendance at a hearing on adjustments;

(c) framing, lodging and intimating a note of appeal against sentence under section 453(B) of the 1975 Act, again including an application for interim liberation or suspension of a driving disqualification; and

(d) making an appeal by note of appeal to the High Court against the refusal by the sheriff or district court to grant bail pending an appeal against conviction or sentence in a summary case.

While these are the situations often encountered there are others which are encountered from time to time; if the Board is satisfied that the step requires to be taken as a matter of special urgency then regulation 15 cover can be provided.

Since time is usually of the essence, regulation 15 cover can be obtained by telephone from the Edinburgh office of the Board provided it is followed up by a written request setting out the full position.[3] There is no prescribed form of application but a request for regulation 15 cover should at the very least give details of (1) the method of appeal; (2) the grounds of appeal; (3) the solicitor's views on the prospects of the appeal, and (4) the date of the appeal if this is known. If the Board decides that regulation 15 cover is to be provided it simply sends out a letter giving details of the cover that it is providing and reminding the solicitor that a full application for legal aid for the appeal itself requires to be made. Currently the Board requires this to be lodged within fourteen days.

One matter often overlooked or misunderstood about regulation 15 cover is that it is the provision of legal aid only for those steps of court process which require to be taken to protect the appellant's position. Not only is it not a grant of criminal legal aid to cover the full appeal itself it does not constitute legal aid for the purposes of matters ancillary to the urgent steps of process, such as correspondence with the appellant, other interested parties and the Board. All of the latter steps require to be done under advice and assistance, so it is essential that the solicitor should keep track of the work he is doing and ensure that he also has adequate advice and assistance authorisation for whatever ancillary steps he is instructed to take.[4]

1 See chap 2, at 2.31; chap 3 at 3.35.
2 Criminal Legal Aid (Scotland) Regulations 1987, reg 15(2).
3 See (1988) 33 JLSS 147.
4 See 8.02, above.

## 8.06 Appeals arising from preliminary matters — solemn proceedings

In solemn procedure it may be necessary to appeal to the High Court against a decision made at a preliminary diet under section 76A of the Criminal Procedure (Scotland) Act 1975, or to appeal to the High Court against a decision made by the court of first instance to extend the time limits within which cases can be brought to trial.[1] In both such situations the decisions which may be appealed against are usually made once solemn proceedings are well under way and in that situation no separate application for criminal legal aid is required if it is sought to appeal to the High Court against a decision made on such preliminary points. Such appeals are regarded for legal aid purposes as part of the trial proceedings themselves and any grant of legal aid for those proceedings will be effective without further assessment of resources. Nonetheless, sanction for the employment of counsel to conduct all such appeals will usually be required, since such sanction will not normally have been obtained at an earlier stage. The Board should be advised of the situation and a request made for sanction to employ counsel to represent the appellant before the High Court.[2]

1 See 2.01 and 3.01 above.
2 Criminal Legal Aid (Scotland) Regulations 1987, reg 14.

## 8.07 Appeals arising from preliminary matters — summary proceedings

In summary criminal proceedings, preliminary matters such as objections to relevancy or competency are dealt with before the accused pleads to the charge or charges set out in the complaint.[1] Criminal legal aid for summary proceedings is available under section 24 of the 1986 Act but this applies only to cases where the accused has pled not guilty and seeks legal aid for the costs of his defence. Neither section 24 nor section 23 (which deals with the power of the court to grant legal aid in certain criminal proceedings) has any application to the situation where a person appearing on summary complaint wishes to appeal to the High Court on a preliminary point. Legal aid for such appeals is available from the duty solicitor under section 22 of the 1986 Act or, where the accused is not in custody and is not therefore entitled to the services of the duty solicitor, by the provision of assistance by way of representation (ABWOR) under Part II of the 1986 Act. In the former case, if the duty solicitor is employed, his duties include acting until the conclusion of the first diet at which the accused tenders a plea of guilty or not guilty.[2] Accordingly, if it is necessary to take a preliminary appeal prior to that point, then the duty solicitor's services are available to the prospective appellant automatically without any tests of eligibility requiring to be met. The duty solicitor would be obliged to take the necessary appeal under section 334(2A) of the Criminal Procedure (Scotland) Act 1975 and arrange for the representation of the appellant at all diets before the High Court. In the latter situation, where the duty solicitor is not acting for whatever reason, ABWOR is available both for the purpose of an appeal by the accused against the decision of the lower court on the preliminary plea, or to resist a Crown appeal against such a decision.[3] In such cases, however, ABWOR can be provided only where the accused is not in custody, and where the solicitor is satisfied (1) that the offence is such that it is likely that the court will impose a sentence which would deprive the applicant of his liberty or lead to loss of his livelihood; (2) that there are substantial grounds for tendering the plea; and (3) that it is reasonable in the particular circumstances that assistance by way of representation be made available.[4] The normal authorised expenditure under ABWOR (currently £80) will rarely be enough to cover the cost of more than the simplest preliminary plea, far less an appeal against the decision on that plea to the High Court. A sufficient authorised increase in expenditure is immediately essential, for the appeal will involve the instruction of counsel and Edinburgh agents, if the case originates outside Edinburgh.[5]

1 See 3.02 above.
2 1986 Act, s 22(1)(c); Criminal Legal Aid (Scotland) Regulations 1987, reg 5(1)(d).
3 Advice and Assistance (Assistance by Way of Representation) (Scotland) Regulations 1988, reg 4(a).
4 Ibid, reg 5(1).
5 On increases in authorised expenditure, see Advice and Assistance (Scotland) Regulations 1987, reg 11(1): see also *Drummond & Co WS v Scottish Legal Aid Board* 1991 SCLR 540; affd 1992 SLT 337, HL.

## 8.08 Appeals arising from proceedings on indictment

*Appeals against conviction, or conviction and sentence*

Initial work for appeals against conviction or conviction and sentence in indictment cases requires to be done under regulation 15 of the Criminal Legal Aid (Scotland) Regulations 1987 since again there are strict time limits[1] within which a prospective appellant requires to lodge an intimation of intention to appeal (where the appeal is against conviction) or a note of appeal against the sentence imposed (where only the sentence is being challenged). Any necessary application for bail at this stage will also require to be covered under regulation 15.

Once initial steps are taken, then a full application for legal aid must be made. The documents which are required are the application form itself with the solicitor's views on the merits of the appeal, the indictment to which the appeal relates, the note of appeal itself, the judge's report and certified copies of the proceedings and of the charge to the jury. If any question of sentence is dealt with a note of any previous convictions should also be enclosed. In the case of sheriff court trials the Justiciary Office supplies the Board direct with the note of appeal, indictment, certified proceedings and charge to the jury; in High Court trials only the note of appeal and the judge's charge to the jury are supplied by the Justiciary Office. Any other documents which the solicitor feels would assist the Board in considering the application, such as a note from counsel, should also be provided. If counsel conducted the trial, then his views in the form of a note will be of considerable assistance to the Board. Likewise, if the trial was conducted by a solicitor his views should be given fully as to proposed appeal points.

Since a note of appeal against conviction should not be lodged except on the basis of proper information and after scrutiny of the judge's charge, the solicitor will require to state fully on or with the application form the reasons why he believes the grounds of appeal to be substantial and why he thinks that it is reasonable that legal aid should be made available.

*Appeals against sentence alone*
Initial work is done under regulation 15 and, in this case, extends to the framing and lodging of the note of appeal against sentence and any related application for bail pending the appeal. The initial work must be followed up by a full application for legal aid, accompanied in this case by a copy of the note of appeal itself, the previous convictions (if any), the judge's report and a statement as to the nature of the grounds which the solicitor maintains are substantial grounds for taking an appeal.[2]

1 Chapter 2 at 2.31.
2 Criminal Legal Aid (Scotland) Regulations 1987, reg 5(2).

## 8.09 Appeals arising from summary trial proceedings

*Appeals by stated case against conviction or acquittal*
Where it is intended to appeal by stated case then criminal legal aid is available both to an appellant who wishes to pursue an appeal by this method or to the respondent to such an appeal taken by the Crown. In the former case, the appellant must satisfy the normal financial and other tests of eligibility, but in the latter, only the financial test must be satisfied; in Crown appeals by stated case where the respondent wishes to apply for legal aid there is no requirement that the Board be satisfied that there are substantial grounds for resisting the appeal or that to do so would be reasonable.[1]

Whether the person who applies for legal aid is the appellant or the respondent to the appeal, initial work is likely to require to be done under regulation 15. This includes, as previously indicated,[2] the framing, lodging and altering of the application for the stated case (where the applicant is the appellant) and all work done in relation to perusing the draft stated case; framing and lodging adjustments thereto and attending any hearing on adjustments, right up to the point where the final stated case is issued and has to be lodged in the Justiciary Office. Only when the signed stated case is available can any application for criminal legal aid for the appeal itself be considered finally by the Board. All that the Board requires to see is the application form itself including, where it is necessary, the solicitor's views on the substantiality of the grounds of appeal and why he thinks it reasonable that legal aid should be granted, together also with a copy of the final adjusted stated case. The application, if not made earlier, ought to be made no later than the day on which the principal stated case is lodged in the Justiciary Office so that delays may be avoided. Under Rule 136 of the Act of Adjournal (Consolidation) 1988, as amended,[3] the solicitor for the appellant has the duty of arranging printing of the stated case but this is usually delayed until the result of any legal aid application is known.

*Appeals by bill of suspension*
An appellant proceeding by way of bill of suspension arising from his conviction in a summary case may obtain regulation 15 cover for the initial steps in that process and also criminal legal aid for the appeal itself. While there is no time limit prescribed for bringing a bill of suspension, the bill should be lodged as soon as possible after the making of the order sought to be suspended.[4] Accordingly, initial work in having the bill drafted, lodged and served can be done under regulation 15 and thereafter an application for criminal legal aid for the appeal itself must be made. The Board again requires to see (1) the application form with the views of the solicitor on the merits of the proposed appeal; (2) a statement of the grounds of appeal, unless a copy of the bill itself is by then available, in which case a copy should be lodged instead; and (3) a copy of the complaint on which the appellant went to trial and out of which the appeal arises.

It is particularly important not to delay applying for legal aid until after the bill itself is lodged in the Justiciary Office. The application for legal aid should be made at that point and not delayed until after any interim orders on the bill have been dealt with. Criticism has been levelled in the past at practitioners who lodge a bill of suspension in respect of an appellant who is in custody, obtain interim liberation and then much later apply for legal aid which is subsequently refused. As a result of such a delay the court can be left with no one to whom it can look for performance of the complainer's obligations in relating to printing and instructing counsel for the appeal itself.[5]

*Notes of appeal against sentence*
A great many appeals coming before the High Court are restricted to the question of sentence. Here again initial work in framing and lodging the note of appeal can be done under regulation 15. Once this is done an application for criminal legal aid for the appeal itself must be lodged with the Board.[6] In addition to the application form with the usual information, the Board requires to see a copy of

the complaint, a copy of the note of appeal setting forth the grounds of appeal, and the judge's report which should be available very soon after the note of appeal is lodged.

1 1986 Act, s 25(2).
2 See 8.05 above.
3 Act of Adjournal (Consolidation Amendment No 3) 1991, SI 1991/2676.
4 See chapter 3 at 3.09 above.
5 See Act of Adjournal (Consolidation) 1988, Rules 135, 136 and 138, as amended by SI 1991/2676.
6 Criminal Legal Aid (Scotland) Regulations 1987, reg 15(2).

## 8.10 Petitions to the *nobile officium*

Legal aid is available to petitions in the High Court to exercise the *nobile officium* whether the need to do so arises in the course of proceedings or otherwise. The same tests of eligibility apply to such petitions as they do to appeals against conviction or sentence: the applicant must be financially eligible; there must be substantial grounds for making the appeal; and it must be reasonable, in the particular circumstances of the case, that legal aid should be made available to the applicant.[1] The Board requires to see:

(1) the application form with the views of the solicitor on the merits of the petition;
(2) a copy of the draft petition, if it is available;
(3) a copy of the originating petition, complaint or indictment out ofwhich there arises the proposed petition to the *nobile officium*, if any such document is available.

It is to be stressed that petitions to the *nobile officium* are 'distinct proceedings' for the purposes of legal aid;[2] this means that a separate application is required where is is intended to proceed with such a petition. Accordingly any legal aid granted for other type of criminal proceedings out of which the petition to the *nobile officium* arises does not automatically extend to proceedings by way of such petition.

1 1986 Act, s 25(5).
2 Criminal Legal Aid (Scotland) Regulations 1987, reg 4(1)(g).

## 8.11 Miscellaneous other appeals

*Bill of advocation*

An appeal by an accused person by bill of advocation is never against 'conviction, sentence or acquittal' and accordingly section 25 of the 1986 Act has no application to legal aid for such appeals, nor have any of the criminal regulations which refer to section 25.[1] Appeals by advocation are almost invariably taken by the Crown before a trial is concluded but occasionally are also open to an accused.[2] If a bill is brought while there is in existence legal aid for the trial proceedings, that grant of legal aid will cover opposition to a Crown bill, or the bringing of a bill by the accused. It does not appear that any other statutory tests of eligibility apply, whether financial or otherwise. Nonetheless, since the bill brings the proceedings to the notice of the High Court the solicitor for the accused should advise the Board that the appeal is being taken and ask for approval to employ counsel, if it is a case where counsel has neither been previously sanctioned for the trial proceedings or is employed in a case at first instance where sanction is not required.[3] If a copy of the bill is available then that will assist the Board.

*Suspension of a warrant*

An improper warrant can be brought under appeal to the High Court by way of bill of suspension[4] but it will be evident that in the normal case such an appeal is not an appeal against 'conviction, sentence or acquittal', so section 25 of the 1986 Act has no application. The point has not yet arisen in practice but legal aid for such a bill of suspension would probably be regarded as part of any legal aid which covers the proceedings at first instance. Cases have arisen where suspension of a warrant has been sought before proceedings have started.[4] In that situation the legal aid position is not clear.

*Suspension of driving disqualification*

It is competent to appeal to the High Court under section 41(2) of the Road Traffic Offenders Act 1988 against a decision by a sheriff not to suspend a driving disqualification pending an appeal to the High Court.[5] The legal aid implications of such appeals have not been judicially considered but is is suggested that any initial work is competent under regulation 15 as being incidental to a full appeal against the driving disqualification itself and that legal aid granted for the latter kind of appeal covers the petition under section 41(2). As it is probable that the whole work in relation to the petition will require to be done under regulation 15, the Board should be advised accordingly.

1 See Criminal Legal Aid (Scotland) Regulations 1987, reg 13(1) which is restricted to appeals under s 25 of the 1986 Act.
2 See chapter 3 at 3.13 above.
3 Criminal Legal Aid (Scotland) Regulations 1987, reg 14.
4 See, for example, *Morris v MacNeill* 1991 SCCR 722.
5 Cf chapter 9 at 9.11.

## 8.12 Appeals in respect of bail

The vast majority of bail appeals arise after the accused has been remanded in custody following his initial appearances in court either under summary or solemn proceedings. In such cases no separate application for legal aid is required for the purposes of either making or resisting an appeal in respect of bail to the High Court. Such an appeal is regarded for legal aid purposes as part of the proceedings in the court of first instance; accordingly, any legal aid cover which applies there will also apply for the appeal to the High Court in respect of bail.[1] In solemn or summary proceedings, an accused person appearing from custody is entitled to criminal legal aid from the duty solicitor whose duties extend to advising and acting for any such person on the day when he is brought before a court to answer to any petition or complaint and thereafter *inter alia* in connection with any application for liberation following upon that diet.[2] That includes appeals in respect of bail and applications for review of the bail conditions, which themselves may be made the subject of an appeal to the High Court. In solemn proceedings, where criminal legal aid is usually granted by the sheriff at or shortly after the first appearance of the accused on petition, any such grant of legal aid covers an appeal to the High Court in respect of bail whether that appeal is made by the accused or for the purposes of resisting a Crown appeal against the grant of bail.[3]

Bail appeals also sometimes arise subsequent to the conviction of the accused and against his remand in custody pending sentence, for example, where social inquiry or other reports are ordered. Again, any grant of criminal legal aid for the trial proceedings includes a bail appeal to the High Court without further application to the High Court.[3]

Lastly, an appellant to the High Court may himself seek bail pending his appeal if he has received a custodial sentence. Here, however, application to the Board is necessary; regulation 15 cover is necessary and this has already been considered.[4]

1 Criminal Legal Aid (Scotland) Regulations 1987, reg 4(2)(a).
2 Ibid, reg 5(1). In summary cases, representation under legal aid can be given only by the duty solicitor: reg 5(2).
3 Ibid, reg 4(2).
4 See 8.05 above.

## 8.13 What happens if legal aid is refused?

If legal aid is refused by the Board, then, unlike the position in civil proceedings, there is no procedure whereby the applicant can have the decision to refuse legal aid reviewed by the Board itself. However, it may be possible to proceed by way of judicial review, although there are so far no cases on this particular point. Several petitions for judicial review of decisions of the Scottish Legal Aid Board have been presented, but none has sought to review a decision to refuse legal aid for an appeal. The test for judicial review is hard to meet: see eg *K v Scottish Legal Aid Board*.[1] Following the decision of the European Court of Human Rights in *Granger v United Kingdom*[2] the Lord Justice General issued a Practice Note dated 4 December 1990 to All Appeal Court Chairmen and Appeal Court clerks. It was later decided to bring the Practice Note to the attention of the profession at large. The Practice Note and parts of the related circular by the Deputy Principal Clerk of Justiciary dated 19 June 1991 are printed in the Appendix to this book (with the permission of the Lord Justice General). Accordingly, in a situation in which legal aid has been refused but the High Court considers that an appellant may have substantial appeal grounds, and that it is in the interests of justice that the appellant should have legal representation at the High Court hearing the court may be invited to adjourn the hearing of the appeal and to request the Board to carry out a reconsideration of the appellant's application for legal aid. Such a reconsideration procedure would accordingly have no statutory basis and would not be a 'review' by the Board in the normal sense of the word. Finally, even if legal aid is refused it is open to counsel and solicitors to represent the appellant before the High Court without fee or on the speculative basis that, if the appeal is ultimately successful, they will be able to claim payment from the legal aid Fund under the terms of a determination made by the Secretary of State under section 4(2)(c) of the 1986 Act. The effect of this determination is discussed later,[3] but it is mentioned here simply for the purpose of illustrating that the refusal of legal aid for a criminal appeal may not in fact mean that even the most impecunious appellant cannot be represented in the High Court when his appeal is being argued.

1 1989 SLT 617.
2 (1990) 12 EHHR 469.
3 See 8.21 below.

## 8.14 Duties of solicitor and counsel

The 1986 Act and regulations are silent as to the exact duties incumbent on solicitors and counsel acting in an appeal funded by legal aid. It is thought, however, that they are required to provide the normal services provided by legal representatives in such a case; and this includes a duty on the solicitor to make satisfactory arrangements for the representation of the assisted person at all diets in the appeal. Hitherto, only counsel had rights of audience before the High Court of Justiciary in appeal proceedings, although this is changing as certain solicitors acquire rights of audience.[1] Solicitors already have limited rights of audience in relation to certain incidental matters.[2] Sanction of the Board is not generally required for instructing counsel, but representation is restricted to that provided by one junior counsel, except in relation to appeal proceedings relating to a conviction for murder, where the solicitor acting may, without prior approval, instruct senior counsel alone, or senior and junior, or more than one junior.[3] In all other appeals senior counsel or additional counsel (either senior or junior), may be instructed only with the prior approval of the Board.[3] Retrospective approval for the employment of counsel may be applied for and will be granted where the Board considers that sanction would have been approved by them and that there was a special reason why prior approval was not applied for.[4]

A legal aid certificate may be transferred from one solicitor to another if the Board is satisfied there is good reason and it is reasonable for the applicant to continue to receive legal aid.[5]

1 Law Reform (Miscellaneous Provisions) (Scotland) Act 1990, ss 24 et seq.
2 1975 Act, s 250.
3 Ibid, regs 17(1) and (2).
4 Ibid, reg 14(2).
5 Ibid, regs 17(1) and (2).

## 8.15 Withdrawal of legal aid

Criminal legal aid granted for the purpose of appeal proceedings can be withdrawn by the Board if it is satisfied that the assisted person has wilfully failed to comply with the provisions of the regulations as to the information to be furnished by him or, in furnishing such information he has knowingly made a false statement or false representation.[1] If the Board takes this step then it has the right to recover from the assisted person the amount paid out of the Fund in respect of the fees and outlays of his solicitor and counsel and the solicitor who acted for the assisted person has the right to receive from him the difference between the amount payable out of the Fund and the full amount which would be payable to him on a solicitor and client basis in respect of fees and outlays.[2]

Legal aid may also be withdrawn by the High Court itself where, after hearing the appellant, it is satisfied

(1) that the appellant
 (a) has without reasonable cause failed to comply with a proper request made to him by the solicitor acting for him to supply any information relevant to the proceedings;
 (b) has delayed unreasonably in complying with any such request as is mentioned in heading (a);
 (c) has without reasonable cause failed to attend at a diet of the court at which he has been required to attend or at a meeting with the solicitor or counsel acting for him under the Act of 1986 at which he has reasonably and properly been required to attend;
 (d) has conducted himself in connection with the proceedings in such a way as to make it appear to the court unreasonable that he should continue to receive criminal legal aid;
 (e) has wilfully or deliberately given false information for the purpose of misleading the court in considering his financial circumstances under section 23(1)of the Act of 1986;
 (f) has without reasonable cause failed to comply with the requirement of the regulations; or

(2) that it is otherwise unreasonable for the solicitor to continue to act on behalf of the assisted person in the proceedings.[3]

In such a case the High Court may direct that the appellant shall cease to be entitled to criminal legal aid in connection with the appeal.[3] These provisions are rarely invoked in practice. It should, however, be noted that the same provisions apply in connection with proceedings at first instance; if the court of first instance has withdrawn legal aid for any of the reasons under paragraph 1(a) above it must instruct its own clerk to report the terms of its finding to the Board for its consideration in any application for criminal legal aid in an appeal in connection with the proceedings in that court.[4] A prospective appellant whose legal aid has been withdrawn for the original proceedings may therefore find it somewhat harder to obtain criminal legal aid for any appeal.

1 Criminal Legal Aid (Scotland) Regulations 1987, reg 18(1).
2 Ibid, reg 18(2).
3 Act of Adjournal (Consolidation) 1988, para 164(1).
4 Ibid, para 164(4).

## 8.16 Payment of fees from the fund

On the completion of the appeal the solicitor acting for the appellant must lodge an account of expenses with the Legal Aid Board not later than six months after the date of conclusion of the proceedings, although late accounts may be accepted if the Board considers there is a special reason for late submission.[1] The fees chargeable are set by regulation and are usually amended annually. There are now no maximum fees chargeable for appeal proceedings and those which will be allowed are those which are determined to be reasonable renumeration for the work actually and reasonably done, and travel and waiting time actually and reasonably undertaken or incurred, due regard being had to economy.[2] Fees for work done as a matter of urgency under regulation 15 are chargeable on the same basis. The actual fees payable to solicitors for the steps taken in the course of a criminal appeal are set out in a table of fees annexed to the relative regulations; a separate table in a separate schedule sets out the fees chargeable by counsel.[3]

Once the account is lodged it is then adjusted between the Board and the solicitor concerned, subject to a right of taxation in the event that the account cannot be agreed.[4] Counsel's fees are adjusted with his clerk.

Counsel can obtain payment from the Board slightly more quickly than his instructing solicitor by producing to the Board Form CR/33, which he can request the solicitor to obtain in advance of the appeal. The solicitor has the form certified by the Board at an early stage and simply passes it to counsel so that the latter can submit it to the Board for payment along with his own fee note. This avoids the necessity of waiting until the solicitor's account is drawn up and adjusted with the Board, which process frequently takes some months.

In cases where legal aid has been refused for the appeal but nonetheless solicitor and counsel continue to act and subsequently wish to claim payment if the appeal is successful notwithstanding the refusal of legal aid, then payment can be made under a determination by the Secretary of State under section 4(2)(c) of the 1986 Act. Such payment can be made only where legal aid was refused under section 25(2)(b) of the 1986 Act which relates to the merits and reasonableness of an appeal; the determination has no application where legal aid is refused on financial grounds. Before making payment under the determination the Board must be satisfied:

(1) After consideration of the financial circumstances of the applicant at the time of the initial application for criminal legal aid in connection with the appeal, that the expenses of the appeal could not have been met without undue hardship to the applicant or his dependants; and

(2) that it is reasonable, in particular circumstances of the case, that payment should be made.[5]

If it is intended to proceed under the determination the solicitor should advise the Board immediately after the appeal has been heard quoting details of the earlier refusal of legal aid. The Board then sends him a voucher[6] for submission with his account and counsel's fee notes.

Where ABWOR fees are claimed, payment is made under the provisions of Part I of Schedule 3 of the Advice and Assistance (Scotland) Regulations 1987.[7]

1 Criminal Legal Aid (Scotland) (Fees) Regulations 1989, SI 1989/1491, reg 9(1).
2 Ibid, reg 7(1).
3 The provisions of Schedule 1 to the 1989 Regulations apply to solicitors; Schedule 21 applies to counsel.
4 Criminal Legal Aid (Scotland) (Fees) Regulations 1989, regs 11(1) and (2).
5 Determination dated 21 March 1990.
6 Form ACC/CRIM/DET.
7 These regulations provide for an initial block fee and detailed charges. All are subject to adjustment between the solicitor and the Board, with an ultimate right of taxation: see reg 16.

# 9. Bail



**INCIDENTAL PROCEDURES AND INTERIM REGULATION**

## 9.01 Bailable crimes and offences

All crimes and offences, except murder and treason, are bailable.[1] The Lord Advocate and the High Court have the right to admit to bail any person charged with any crime or offence, including murder and treason. These rights are preserved by section 35.[2] The extra-statutory right of the High Court preserved by section 35 cannot be exercised by a single judge of the High Court.[3]

1 ss 26(1) and 298(1); but see *Welsh, Petitioner* 1990 SCCR 763.
2 *Welsh, Petitioner* 1990 SCCR 763.
3 *Milne v McNicol* 1944 JC 151.

## 9.02 First instance applications for bail

*Solemn*

In solemn proceedings, applications for bail are usually presented in the form of a printed petition either before or after full committal and the court's decision is recorded on the application.[1]

*Summary*

In summary proceedings applications for bail are made orally to the court when the complaint calls before the court. The court's decision is recorded in the minute of proceedings. After the initial stages, the rules and procedures for bail in summary procedure are virtually the same as for solemn procedure.[2]

1 See *Renton and Brown*, para 5–77.
2 See *Renton and Brown*, para 14–08.

## 9.03 Appeal in respect of bail: solemn

Where an application for bail is made after committal until liberation in due course of law and is refused by any sheriff, or where the applicant is dissatisfied with the conditions of bail, he may appeal to the High Court, and the High Court may, in its discretion, order intimation to the Lord Advocate.[1] If, however, bail is refused before committal until liberation in due course of law[2] the accused person has no right of appeal against that refusal but may renew the application after such committal.[3] The court which has refused bail or granted bail on conditions has power to review its decision, including the conditions of bail: see section 30 and *Gilchrist, Petitioner*.[4] If an application for bail is granted by the sheriff, whether before or after commitment until liberation in due course of law, the public prosecutor has the right to appeal to the High Court against the decision or the conditions.[5] If the prosecutor appeals, the accused is not liberated until the Crown appeal has been disposed of,[6] except as provided by section 33, which provides for liberation after seventy-two hours from the granting of bail (or ninety-six hours if the application for bail was made in the Outer Hebrides or in Orkney or Zetland) if the appeal is not disposed of and the court has not granted an order for the applicant's further detention in custody. Sundays and public holidays do not count in computing these time limits. If the prosecutor's appeal is refused the High Court may, but rarely does, award expenses against him.[7]

1 s 31(1) has to be construed as indicated by s 1(4) of the Bail etc. (Scotland) Act 1980: viz. 'bail' means 'release on conditions'.
2 s 26(3).
3 ss 26(3), 27, 31(1).
4 1991 SCCR 699, a summary case under the similarly worded s 299.
5 s 31(2) and Bail etc (Scotland) Act 1980, s 1(4).
6 s 31(2).
7 s 31(5).

## 9.04 Appeal in respect of bail: summary

Similarly, in summary proceedings, when a court has refused to admit a person to bail or has admitted to bail on conditions, it has power on an application by that person to review its decision and to alter it on cause shown.[1] This provision does not affect a person's right of appeal in relation to the refusal of bail or the conditions.[2] The right to appeal against a refusal of bail in summary proceedings, or against the bail conditions, is contained in section 300(1). An appeal lies to the High Court which may in its discretion order intimation to the prosecutor. The prosecutor also has a right of appeal to the High Court against a bail decision by the court of summary jurisdiction or an order by such a court ordaining an accused person to appear; if the prosecutor appeals, the accused is not liberated at once; the provisions regarding his release if the appeal is not disposed of within seventy-two or ninety-six hours from the granting of bail are the same as those applicable in solemn proceedings: see paragraph 9.03 above.[3] If the prosecutor's appeal is refused the High Court may, but rarely does, award expenses against him; but otherwise no fees or expenses are awarded or exigible in respect of any appeal regarding bail or ordaining to appear.[4] Section 300(4) also applies when an appeal is taken by the prosecutor against the fact that a person has been ordained to appear.[5]

1 s 299(2); cf. *Gilchrist, Petitioner,* at 9.03 above.
2 s 299(4), and Bail Etc (Scotland) Act 1980, s 1(4).
3 s 300(4).
4 s 300(6).
5 s 300(4A).

## 9.05 Bail appeal pending sentence or disposal

Both in solemn (s 179) and in summary (s 380) proceedings the court has power to adjourn the hearing for the purpose of enabling inquiries to be made or of determining the most suitable method of dealing with the case and the court has power to remand the accused in custody or on bail. The court has similar remand powers under sections 180 and 381 in respect of a person about whose physical or mental condition the court wants inquiry made. The remanding court cannot review its own decision;[1] but the decision can be appealed. The accused who is so remanded may appeal against a refusal of bail or against the conditions imposed; any appeal must be made within twenty-four hours of his remand by presenting a note of appeal to the High Court. There is no form prescribed for such a note of appeal. The High Court, either in court or in chambers (but almost invariably in chambers), may after hearing parties (1) review the order appealed against, and either grant bail on such conditions as it thinks fit or (in s 179 and s 380 cases only) ordain the accused to appear at the adjourned diet; or (2) confirm the order of the inferior court.[2]

1 *Long v HM Advocate* 1984 SCCR 161.
2 s 179(2), and s 380(2); and s 180(5) and s 381(5).

## 9.06 Procedure in bail appeals

In practice, all bail appeals to the High Court in respect of the grant or refusal of bail, or the conditions, or an order ordaining an accused to appear (all referred to as 'bail appeals') are dealt with in the same way by the High Court. A diet for the hearing of an appeal is normally fixed within two working days of the receipt by the Clerk of Justiciary of the necessary papers. When the bail appeal is marked, the clerk of the court of first instance should obtain from the local solicitor acting for the accused the particulars of that solicitor's Edinburgh solicitor, if he has one.[1] If the appeal is marked by the Crown, the clerk of the inferior court should note the exact time of the marking of the appeal and telephone the Clerk of Justiciary to intimate the necessary details (these steps are necessary because of the strict time limits applicable). All bail appeals, including applications for interim liberation pending determination of an appeal and Crown appeals, are put out before a single judge in chambers at 9.45 am or before the vacation judge while the Court of Session is in vacation. They are usually disposed of at once and without any reasons being given in writing but after parties have been heard. If further information is required by either party or by the judge the case will usually be continued for twenty-four hours to allow the information to be obtained. Those appearing are expected to be brief and to the point but ready to answer relevant questions about the accused person's criminal record and personal circumstances.

1 Cf rule 135, as amended by Act of Adjournal (Consolidation Amendment No 3) 1991, SI 1991/2676.

## 9.07 Later review of a bail decision

The High Court can review its earlier decision on a question of bail: section 30(2); and cf *Shanley v HM Advocate*;[1] but, in so far as the parts of a decision on bail are separable, if the High Court has dealt with one part only, eg whether or not to grant bail, or whether or not to impose a particular condition, other parts, eg different conditions, may be reviewed by the court to which application was first made.[2]

1 1946 JC 150.
2 *Ward v HM Advocate* 1972 SLT (Notes) 22; commenting on *HM Advocate v Jones* 1964 SLT (Sh Ct) 50.

## 9.08 Applying for bail pending determination of appeal (solemn procedure)

It is very common to apply for *interim* liberation, ie bail (since 1980) pending determination of an appeal. The High Court may, if it seems fit, admit the appellant to bail pending the determination of his appeal; but only on his application.[1] All crimes and offences are bailable as of right except murder and treason.[2] The Lord Advocate has the right to admit to bail any person charged with any offence, including murder and treason.[3] The High Court in the exercise of its *nobile officium*[4] may also admit to bail a person charged with murder or treason.[5] Only a quorum of three or more judges of the High Court may exercise this power. Any application for bail following conviction is made on Form 40 and it must narrate *inter alia* that on a date specified the applicant lodged an intimation of intention to appeal, or a note of appeal, to the High Court of Justiciary. The application may well be refused before such lodging.[6] However, the observations on this matter in *Smith v McC* are *obiter* of a single judge and are not binding on the bail judge.

The relevant facts in support of grant of bail must be set forth in Form 40. These will be the usual facts relevant to grant of bail, such as having a fixed address, a supportive family, a job, a modest criminal record, no or few contraventions of section 3 of the Bail (Scotland) Act 1980, plus, in addition, assertions that there are substantial grounds for the appeal, that there is a likelihood that if the appellant remains in custody he will have served much of his sentence before his appeal is determined. The application is heard and determined along with the ordinary bail appeals, etc, usually in chambers at 9.45am in the Supreme Court, Edinburgh, by the bail judge (who may be the vacation judge).[7] The appellant may make the application personally or through counsel.[8] The Crown commonly makes no representations to the bail judge in respect of applications for interim liberation. If the application cannot for some administrative reason be properly dealt with at once it is normally continued or re-heard later the same day or on the next lawful day. The decision of the court is usually given at once orally by the judge; but the Clerk of Justiciary sends a notification under section 251, ie Form 42. This tells the appellant the result of the application. If the bail judge has refused the application the Clerk of Justiciary also sends, with Form 42, Form 43. By completing this form and returning it within five days to the Clerk of Justiciary the appellant can appeal against the refusal of bail. If he does not do so within the five days the refusal by the single judge is final.[9] An appeal court, consisting of three judges, who may include the judge who refused bail,[10] will hear and determine this appeal. If he is not legally represented, the appellant has the right to appear personally at the appeal hearing. If he is legally represented then technically he needs leave of the court to be present but in practice the appellant is always brought to attend the appeal. The Clerk of Justiciary has the responsibility of placing the application before the court and of notifying the applicant if his application to be present has been granted or refused. If it is granted the Clerk of Justiciary must also notify the prison governor and the Secretary of State.[11] An applicant who is admitted to bail must, unless the High Court otherwise directs, appear personally in court on the day or days fixed for the hearing of the appeal, whether or not he is legally represented. If he does not do so the court will usually decline to consider the appeal and may dismiss it, though it may choose to determine it.[12] The court is slow to excuse a failure to be present when the case is called[13] because the failure is a breach of condition of bail (punishable under section 3 of the Bail Etc (Scotland) Act 1980).

**1** s 238(1).
**2** s 26(1); but see *Welsh, Petitioner* 1990 SCCR 763.
**3** s 35.
**4** Cf *Milne v McNicol* 1944 JC 151.
**5** *Welsh, Petitioner* 1990 SCCR 763.
**6** s 238(3). *Smith v McC* 1982 SCCR 115 - the so-called bail 'guidelines' case.
**7** s 247.
**8** s 235.
**9** s 251(2).
**10** s 251(6).
**11** s 251.
**12** s 238(2).
**13** *McMahon v MacPhail* 1991 SCCR 470.

## 9.09 Interim liberation (summary procedure)

A convicted person who is in custody and appeals under section 444 can apply to the convicting court for bail (interim liberation).[1] An application for bail must be disposed of by that court within twenty-four hours after the application for bail has been made.[2] It is made by completing the appropriate section of the form, either Form 71 (stated case) or Form 76 (note of appeal against sentence). The court 'disposes' of the application by deciding whether to grant it or to refuse it; adjourning consideration of that issue is not a disposal: *Gibbons, Petitioner*,[3] a case under section 28(2).[4] The wording of section 446(2), 'An application for bail shall be disposed of by the court within 24 hours *after such an application has been made*' is different from sections 28(2) and 298(2) where the wording is 'Such application shall be disposed of within twenty-four hours *after its presentation to the sheriff/judge*, failing which the accused shall be forthwith liberated'. It has not yet been decided by the High Court whether the rule that applies in sections 28(2) and 298(2) cases — viz. that the twenty-four hour period starts to run from the time when the application is presented to the sheriff or judge[5]

— applies to section 446(2). *Renton and Brown* expresses the opinion that application to the court does not mean lodging with the clerk of court; and that accordingly the twenty-four hours start to run when the application is presented to the judge or sheriff.[6] This is probably correct, but in *HM Advocate v Keegan*[7] Lord Cameron drew attention to the long-standing distinction between 'presentation' and 'lodgement of written applications' with clerks of court, so there may still be room for argument. The better view, it is submitted, is that the application is not 'made' until it is put before the justice or sheriff. In any event, section 446(2) contains no provision to the effect that if the matter is not disposed of within the prescribed period the appellant is to be liberated forthwith, so the consequences of failure to dispose of the matter within the prescribed time are less clear. One consequence is that the appellant is effectively deprived either of his liberty or of his right of appeal against a refusal of bail; as the statute gives him no remedy for such failure or its consequences he must have a right to petition the *nobile officium* against the failure to dispose of the application.

It appears quite clear from the whole context, but especially from Form 71 and Form 76 themselves, that the application for bail has to be in writing — cf. heading (4) of Form 71 and (3) of Form 76. If, in disposing of the application, the court refuses bail or imposes conditions and the appellant wishes to appeal against the refusal, or against any condition, the appeal to the High Court is by a note of appeal written, within twenty-four hours, on the complaint and signed by the appellant or his solicitor. If such appeal is not taken in this way within twenty-four hours after the judgment of the court disposing of the application the right of appeal is lost,[8] subject to the statutory automatic extension of any period expiring on a Saturday, Sunday or court holiday prescribed for the relevant court.[9] Once such a bail appeal is lodged a certified copy of the complaint and proceedings are transmitted to the Clerk of Justiciary, and the High Court, or any judge thereof, (invariably, a single judge in chambers), after hearing parties, has power to review the decision of the inferior court and to grant bail on such conditions as the Court or single judge thinks fit, or to refuse bail.[10] No fees or expenses of any kind are exigible from or may be awarded against an appellant in custody in respect of such a bail appeal to the High Court.[11] The Crown has no right of appeal in respect of a grant of bail pending determination of an appeal.

If, having been granted bail by either court, the appellant does not thereafter proceed with his appeal, the inferior court has power to grant warrant to apprehend and imprison him for such period of his sentence as remained unexpired when he was released on bail, and the period of imprisonment runs from the date of his imprisonment under that warrant of the inferior court.[12] If an appellant who has been granted bail does not thereafter proceed with his appeal (against conviction or conviction and sentence) but, at the time of the abandonment of the appeal is serving a term of imprisonment imposed subsequently to the conviction appealed against, the inferior court has power to order that the sentence or any unexpired portion thereof relating to that conviction should run from such date as the court may think fit, not being a date later than the date on which the term or terms of imprisonment subsequently imposed expired.[13] The relevant subsection envisages the exercise of a discretion by the sheriff or justice; so where the inferior court is contemplating an order under section 446(5) intimation of this intention must be given to the appellant to allow him to make representations to the court and to put before that court any information to be advanced as relevant to and necessary for the proper exercise of that discretion: this was decided in *Proudfoot v Wither*[14] where the High Court intimated that the appropriate way of dealing with a case in which the lower court was contemplating such an order was to give intimation to that effect to the (former) appellant to allow written submissions to the inferior court to be made by him or his solicitor; it would then be for that court to decide if a hearing was necessary before determining how the discretion was to be exercised.

**1** s 446(1).
**2** s 446(2).
**3** 1988 SCCR 270.
**4** Cf s 298(2).
**5** *HM Advocate v Keegan* 1981 SLT (Notes) 35; *Lau, Petitioner* 1986 SCCR 140.
**6** *Renton and Brown* para 16–67.
**7** 1981 SLT (Notes) 35.
**8** *Fenton, Petitioner* 1981 SCCR 288.
**9** s 451.
**10** s 446(2).
**11** s 446(3).
**12** s 446(4).
**13** s 446(5).
**14** 1990 SCCR 96.

## INCIDENTAL PROCEDURES AND INTERIM REGULATION

### 9.10 Interim relief pending appeal

It is clear that if a person is to pursue an appeal against conviction or sentence or both he will normally want to suspend or delay the consequences of the court's decision on guilt and punishment until at least the final determination of the appeal on the merits. There exist procedures for achieving this purpose. It is important to take care to observe carefully the timetables and the detailed procedural requirements laid down by statute. Although it is hoped that in a text such as this it is possible to describe these procedures accurately, there is no substitute for going to the statute itself each time until one is totally familiar with the steps to be taken, and when and how to take them. It may also be necessary to make an application for *interim* relief in the course of proceedings by way of application by petition to the *nobile officium*.

### 9.11 Disqualification, forfeiture, loss of licence etc

If when he is convicted in solemn proceedings a person is disqualified or some forfeiture or disability attaches to him by reason of his conviction then (subject to section 264(3)), the disqualification, forfeiture or disability does not attach for the period of two weeks from the date of the verdict. If he proceeds with the appeal whether against sentence alone or against conviction or both, the disqualification, forfeiture or disability does not attach until the appeal is determined.[1] Similarly, if, upon conviction, any property, matter or things which are the subject of the prosecution or connected therewith are to be or may be ordered to be destroyed, the destruction or forfeiture or the operation of an order for destruction or forfeiture of such property etc is suspended for two weeks or, if the appeal proceeds, whether by intimation of intention to appeal or by note of appeal, until the appeal is determined.[2] These provisions do not apply, however, if the enactment which makes provision for disqualification, forfeiture, or such an order upon conviction itself contains express provision for the suspension of the disqualification, forfeiture etc pending determination of the appeal.[3] The particular express provision then governs the matter. Thus, sections 39(2) and 41(2) of the Road Traffic Offenders Act 1988 provide expressly for the situation of an appellant who on conviction has been disqualified from driving. The court by or before which a person was convicted may, if it thinks fit, upon the application of the appellant suspend the disqualification pending an appeal against the disqualifying order.[4] The High Court has a similar power, to suspend the disqualification if, and on such terms, as it thinks fit.[5] Whichever court suspends the disqualification must send notice of the suspension to the Secretary of State.[6]

1 s 264(1).
2 s 264(2).
3 s 264(3).
4 Road Traffic Offenders Act 1988, s 39(2).
5 1988 Act, s 41(2).
6 1988 Act, ss 39(3) and 41(3).

## 9.12 Suspension of disqualification from driving pending appeal

There are special procedural rules as to suspension of disqualification from driving where an appeal is pending in solemn proceedings: they are contained in the 1988 Act of Adjournal.[1] If the sentencing court was the sheriff the appellant applies to the sheriff using Form 44A,[2] attaching a copy of the note of appeal which must be endorsed as having been received by the Clerk of Justiciary. If the sentencing court was the High Court, or if an application to the sheriff using Form 44A has been refused, the application is made by petition to the High Court, using Form 44,[2] which must be lodged with the Clerk of Justiciary. It will be observed that in either event the note of appeal must have been lodged before the petition is submitted. An intimation of intention to appeal is not enough. The petitioner or his solicitor must, on lodging the petition, send a copy of it to (1) the Crown Agent, and (2), if the sentencing court was the sheriff, the clerk of that court. The court may order further intimation and may dispose of the application in open court or in chambers. The application will be dealt with by a single judge whose decision is not subject to review or appeal. On an order being made on the petition the Clerk of Justiciary has to intimate as required by Rule 86(8) and (9). Rule 86(10) determines what the Clerk of Justiciary has to do on determination of the appeal. Rule 86 should to be referred for details of all incidental aspects of these applications.

1 Rule 86.
2 As amended.

## 9.13 Other applications pending appeal in solemn proceedings

(1) To obtain an extension of time under section 236B(2) using Form 39; see 'Extension of Time limits' — chapter 2, paras 2.31 et seq.

(2) To allow the appellant to be present at any proceedings in cases where he is not entitled to be present without leave. Section 240 provides that he is entitled to be present if he desires it, on the hearing of his appeal, except where the appeal is on some ground involving a question of law alone. In practice, the applicant is always allowed to be present at his appeal hearing. In all other instances he needs leave from the High Court to be present; but in practice all appellants are allowed to be present and there is no set procedure for applying for leave to be present (except in the case of Form 43 (below)); in effect the granting of leave is automatic.

(3) To appeal against a refusal of an application by a single judge exercising powers under section 247. Notification of the decision is given by the Clerk of Justiciary[1] on Form 42. The application to have the matter considered and determined by the High Court of Justiciary (ie by a quorum of three judges) is made on Form 43.

(4) To present the argument in writing: cf 2.10 above.[2] The application is presented by lodging three copies of the appellant's written argument with the Clerk of Justiciary along with a statement that he wants his case to be presented in writing, instead of orally. He must send the Crown Agent a copy of his written submissions and any accompanying papers.

(5) To suspend a disqualification for holding or obtaining a driving licence: see 9.11 and 9.12.

The powers of the High Court in relation to the matters referred to in paragraphs (1), (2) and (5) may be, and almost invariably are, exercised by a single judge, in chambers.[3] In all such applications and in all preliminary and interlocutory[4] proceedings and applications, other than those heard by a full court of three or more judges, the parties to the proceedings may be represented and appear by a solicitor alone.[5]

**1** s 251.
**2** s 234.
**3** ss 248 to 251.
**4** Cf *Perrie, Petitioner* 1991 SCCR 475 at 480.
**5** s 250.

## 9.14 Other interim regulation (summary), including suspension of disqualification

In summary proceedings, the court before which a person has been convicted has a discretionary power, pending determination of any appeal against conviction or sentence, to grant a sist of execution and to make any other interim order.[1] It may also suspend any disqualification, forfeiture or disability attaching to the appellant by reason of the conviction, or any order for the destruction or forfeiture of any property, matter or things.[2] This general power does not apply in respect of any disqualification, forfeiture or destruction or order under or by virtue of any enactment which contains express provision for interim suspension pending determination of the appeal.[3] Form 71 (application for stated case) and Form 76 (note of appeal against sentence) contain provision for applying for such suspension. Rule 132 of the Act of Adjournal (Consolidation) 1988 governs the procedure for suspension of disqualification from driving where a person who has been disqualified appeals against that disqualification by stated case under section 442.[4] An appeal against conviction is, of course, also an appeal against disqualification. The application for suspension of disqualification is made on the appropriate form of appeal. The court from which the appeal is being taken must grant or refuse that application within seven days of the making of the application, ie within seven days of the application being in the hands of the clerk of the inferior court. If the inferior court refuses to suspend the disqualification the appellant may apply to the High Court to suspend it; if he does so he must do so by note in the form of Form 80.[5] The note is lodged with the Clerk of Justiciary and the lodging has to be intimated to the respondent and to the clerk of the court which imposed the disqualification; that clerk must forthwith send to the Clerk of Justiciary (1) a certified copy of the complaint and (2) a certified copy of the minute of proceedings. The High Court may order such further intimation as it thinks fit and may dispose of the application in open court or in chambers as the court thinks fit. The order that the High Court makes on the note is intimated by the Clerk of Justiciary to the clerk of the inferior court by the sending to him of a certified copy of the order. If the order suspends disqualification the Clerk of Justiciary must send a certified copy of the order to the Secretary of State also, with such further information as the Secretary of State may require. In practice, such applications are rare and are always decided by a single judge of the High Court, whose order is not subject to review.

1 s 446(1): appellant in custody.
2 s 443A(1).
3 s 443A(2).
4 Rule 132(1).
5 As amended by the Act of Adjournal (Consolidation Amendment No 3) 1991, SI 1991/2676.

# Appendix

## I STYLES

| Style | Case |
|---|---|
| 1. BILL OF ADVOCATION, by ACCUSED: (against allowing amendments of complaint) | *Hoyers (UK) Ltd v Houston* (1991 SCCR 919) |
| 2. BILL OF ADVOCATION, by LORD ADVOCATE: (against a decision at a Preliminary Diet) | *HM Advocate v Mechan* (1991 SCCR 812) |
| 3. BILL OF ADVOCATION, by PROCURATOR FISCAL: (against precognition order by sheriff) | *Carmichael v J.B.* (1991 SCCR 715) |
| 4. BILL OF SUSPENSION, by CONVICTED PERSON: (against conviction and sentence) | *Wilson v Houston* (13 February 1990) |
| 5. BILL OF SUSPENSION, by CONVICTED COMPANY: (against conviction *et separatim* against sentence) | *Montgomery Transport Ltd v Wilkingshaw* (24 September 1991) |
| 6. BILL OF SUSPENSION, by CONVICTED PERSON: (against sentence) | *Cunningham v McGlennan* (20 August 1991) |
| 7. BILL OF SUSPENSION, by ACCUSED PERSON: (against sheriff's warrant to place accused on identification parade) | *Currie v McGlennan* (1989 SCCR 466) |
| 8. PETITION TO *NOBILE OFFICIUM*, by ACCUSED: (murder accused seeking bail) | *James McDonald Schiavone* (17 October 1991) |

## II LEGAL AID

Notice by Deputy Principal Clerk of Justiciary [19 June 1991]
Practice Note by Lord Justice General [4 December 1990]

# HIGH COURT OF JUSTICIARY

## I. BILL of ADVOCATION

Unto the Right Honourable
The Lord Justice General, The Lord Justice Clerk
and Lord Commissioners of Justiciary

1. BILL OF ADVOCATION

for

HOYERS (UK) LIMITED, a company incorporated under the Companies Acts and having its registered office at Leeds Road, Huddersfield, Yorkshire, — COMPLAINERS:

against

STEWART R HOUSTON, Procurator Fiscal, Lanark, RESPONDENT

HUMBLY SHEWETH

That the complainer is under the necessity of complaining to your Lordships of a pretended interlocutor pronounced at Lanark on 3 May 1991 by Douglas Allan, Esquire, Sheriff of South Strathclyde, Dumfries and Galloway at Lanark upon a complaint at the instance of the respondent, charging 'Hoyer International Limited' and another as therein set forth with a contravention of the Control of Pollution Act 1974, section 31(1), whereby the Sheriff granted the motion of the respondent to allow the complaint to be amended incompetently, erroneously and contrary to law, as will appear to your Lordships from the annexed statement of fact and note of the pleas in law.

WHEREFORE the complainer prays your Lordships for letters of advocation in the premises at his instance in common form; and in the meantime to grant warrant to the Clerk of the Sheriff Court at Lanark, or other custodier of the proceedings at the instance of the respondent against the complainer and another, and interlocutors following thereon, to transmit the same to the Clerk of Justiciary; and on consideration of the said proceedings to advocate the same, to recall the interlocutor complained of, to remit to the Sheriff of South Strathclyde, Dumfries and Galloway at Lanark to proceed with the complaint as accords and to find the complainer entitled to expenses; or to do further, or otherwise in the premises as to your Lordships shall seem proper.

ACCORDING TO JUSTICE, Etc,

## 2. STATEMENT of FACTS for COMPLAINER.

STAT. I. The complainer is Hoyers (UK) Limited, a company incorporated under the Companies Acts and having its registered office at Leeds Road, Huddersfield, Yorkshire.

STAT. II. On 20 November 1990 a complaint at the instance of the respondent charging 'Hoyer International Limited', Leeds Road, Huddersfield, Yorkshire and another was sent by recorded delivery post to Hoyer International Limited, Leeds Road, Huddersfield, Yorkshire. A copy of the complaint is annexed hereto. The said 'Hoyer International Limited' was cited to answer said complaint in the Sheriff Court at Lanark on 12 December 1990.

STAT. III. There is no company in existence registered under the name of Hoyer International Limited, nor did one exist at the relevant time.

STAT. IV. On 10 December 1990, Messrs Ford & Warren, Solicitors, Leeds wrote to the respondent purporting to intimate a plea of not guilty on behalf of 'Hoyer International Limited'. On 12 December 1990 said plea of not guilty was recorded by the court and a trial diet was fixed for 18 February 1991. On 6 February 1991 the complaint called again, when a solicitor purported to appear on behalf of Hoyer International Limited and there was presented to the court a joint minute of acceleration purporting to be signed on behalf of the Hoyer International Limited accelerating the diet from 18 February, 1991 until 6 February 1991. On 6 February 1991, the trial diet was adjourned until 23 April 1991.

STAT. V. On 23 April 1991 the respondent moved the Sheriff in terms of Section 335 of the Criminal Procedure (Scotland) Act 1975 as amended to amend the complaint by amending the name of the first accused from 'Hoyer International Limited' to that of the complainers namely 'Hoyers (UK) Limited'. The motion was opposed by the complainer. After hearing argument for the respondent and on behalf of the complainer, the Sheriff reserved judgment and adjourned the trial diet until 3 May 1991.

STAT. VI. On 3 May 1991 the Sheriff issued his judgment, granted the motion for the respondent by amending the name of the first accused in the said complaint by deleting 'Hoyer

International Limited' and substituting therefor 'Hoyers (UK) Limited' and adjourned the trial diet to a date to be fixed.

### 3. PLEAS-IN-LAW for COMPLAINER

1. The motion for the respondent being incompetent, and the Sheriff's interlocutor being incompetent, erroneous and contrary to law, the interlocutor should be set aside.

2. *Separatim, esto* the motion for the respondent and the Sheriff's interlocutor were competent (which is denied), the Sheriff erred in the exercise of his discretion by granting the motion.

3. *Separatim, esto* the Sheriff was correct to grant the motion for the respondent (which is denied), he erred in the exercise of his discretion by failing to dismiss the complaint.

ACCORDING TO JUSTICE,

### APPENDIX

1. Complaint
2. Copy Productions

# HIGH COURT OF JUSTICIARY

## 2. BILL OF ADVOCATION

Unto the Right Honourable
The Lord Justice General,
Lord Justice Clerk and
Lord Commissioners of Justiciary

## BILL OF ADVOCATION

for

The Right Honourable Lord Fraser of Carmyllie, Her Majesty's Advocate, COMPLAINER

against

DAVID MECHAN, Prisoner in the Prison of Barlinnie, Glasgow, RESPONDENT

HUMBLY SHEWETH

That the complainer is under the necessity of complaining to your Lordships against a decision of the Right Honourable Lord Morton of Shuna dated 28 June 1991 whereby the said Lord Morton of Shuna at a preliminary diet following upon the service on the respondent of an indictment at the instance of the complainer for trial in the High Court of Justiciary sitting at Glasgow on 8 July 1991 sustained a plea in bar of trial by the respondent on the ground that the respondent had suffered gross or grave prejudice due to undue delay in the complainer bringing proceedings against the respondent and dismissed the said indictment, and that unjustly, erroneously and contrary to law a will appear to your Lordships from the annexed statement of facts and note of plea-in-law;

WHEREFORE the complainer prays your Lordships for letters of advocation in the premises at his instance in common form; and on consideration of the proceedings at the instance of the complainer against the respondent to advocate the same; to recall the decision complained of and to do further or otherwise in the premises as to your Lordships may seem proper.

ACCORDING TO JUSTICE

## STATEMENT OF FACTS FOR THE COMPLAINER

1. The respondent has been indicted at the instance of the complainer on two charges of assault and robbery. The crime libelled in charge 1 is alleged to have been committed on 3 January 1990. The crime libelled in charge 2 is alleged to have been committed on 6 February 1990. The said indictment has been served upon the respondent for trial at the sitting of the High Court at Glasgow commencing on Monday 8 July 1991.

2. The respondent was arrested on 17 February 1990 and was cautioned and charged in respect of charge 1 upon the said indictment. On 21 February 1990 the respondent was placed on an identification parade and was identified by the complainer in charge 1. The respondent was also viewed by the complainer on charge 2 of the said indictment but was not identified by him.

3. On 28 December 1990 Crown Counsel, following upon receipt of a report from the Procurator Fiscal, instructed that the respondent be indicted with both the said crimes. An indictment was prepared for the sitting of the High Court of Justiciary at Glasgow on 4 February 1991 and a copy sent to the respondent's agents. The said indictment was not properly served upon the respondent and did not call at the said sitting of the High Court on 4 February 1991.

4. On 15 February 1991 a petition warrant was granted for the arrest of the respondent in respect of the two charges on the present indictment. The respondent appeared on the said petition at Glasgow Sheriff Court on 12 April 1991. This case was then continued for further examination and on 19 April 1991 he was fully committed on the said petition.

5. Following upon service of the indictment upon the respondent for trial at the sitting of the High Court of Justiciary at Glasgow commencing on Monday 8 July 1991 the respondent, by Minute of Notice under section 76(1) of the Criminal Procedure (Scotland) Act 1975, submitted a plea in bar of trial on the ground that he had been severely prejudiced due to the inexcusable delay of the complainer in taking proceedings. The said plea was argued before the Right Honourable Lord Morton of Shuna at Edinburgh High Court on Friday 28 June 1991 and at the conclusion of the hearing his Lordship sustained the plea in bar of trial and dismissed the indictment.

6. The complainer submits that the said decision of Lord Morton of Shuna was unjust, erroneous and contrary to law. There was

in the circumstances no undue delay on the part of the complainer and, further, if there was any undue delay the respondent failed to demonstrate that he had suffered gross or grave prejudice thereby such as to warrant dismissal of the indictment without the charges having been brought to trial.

## PLEA-IN-LAW FOR THE COMPLAINER

The said decision being unjust, erroneous and contrary to law, it should be recalled and the indictment remitted to an assize for trial.

ACCORDING TO JUSTICE

# HIGH COURT OF JUSTICIARY

## 3. BILL OF ADVOCATION

Unto the Right Honourable the
Lord Justice General, Lord Justice Clerk
and Lords Commissioners of Justiciary

BILL OF ADVOCATION

for

WILLIAM GEORGE CARMICHAEL
Procurator Fiscal, Hamilton, COMPLAINER

against

J................, RESPONDENT

HUMBLY SHEWETH:

That the complainer is under the necessity of complaining to Your Lordships against the decision of Sheriff Ian Christopher Simpson, Sheriff of South Strathclyde, Dumfries and Galloway at Hamilton, on 4 January 1991, whereby the said Sheriff Simpson, at a diet at the instance of the complainer for the precognition on oath of the tespondent, adjourned said diet until 8 February 1991, and ordered that the Respondent should, if she then wished, have a solicitor present to advise her during the course of her precognition on oath, and that erroneously and contrary to law as will appear to Your Lordships from the annexed statement of facts and note of plea in law;

WHEREFORE the complainer prays your Lordships for letters of advocation in the premises at his instance in common form; to grant warrant for serving a copy of this Bill and deliverance thereon upon J............, the respondent; and in the meantime to grant warrant ordaining the Sheriff Clerk at Hamilton or other custodier of the proceedings at the instance of the complainer to transmit the same to the Clerk of Justiciary; and on consideration of the said proceedings to advocate the same; to recall the order complained of or to do further or otherwise in the premises as to your Lordships may seem proper.

## STATEMENT OF FACTS FOR THE COMPLAINER

STAT 1. On 25 June 1990, the respondent made a statement to the police at Wishaw that George Jamieson, presently a prisoner in HM Prison, Shotts, had, on 21 June 1990, assaulted and raped her in her house at
Following investigation by the police, a report was submitted to the complainer.

STAT 2. The respondent was cited to attend on 19 July 1990 at the office of the complainer at 28 Clydesdale Street, Hamilton to be precognosced with regard to her allegations of assault and rape. She failed to appear for precognition, and was further cited to attend on 26 July 1990, and again on 7 August 1990. Each time she failed to appear. Accordingly, acting on the instructions of Crown Counsel, the complainer petitioned the Sheriff of South Strathclyde, Dumfries and Galloway at Hamilton for a warrant to cite the respondent for precognition on oath. On 14 September 1990 the Sheriff granted said warrant, and assigned 12 October 1990 at 10.00 am, within the Sheriff Courthouse at Hamilton as a diet therefor.

STAT 3. On 12 October 1990, the respondent failed to answer to her citation and a warrant for her apprehension was issued. Said warrant was executed, and she was brought before the Sheriff at Hamilton on 30 November 1990. On that date the diet was adjourned until 5 December 1990 to enable the precogniton on oath to be taken. The respondent was ordained then to appear.

STAT 4. On 5 December 1990, the respondent appeared before said Sheriff Simpson, at which time said Sheriff questioned the competency of the proceedings and adjourned the diet until later in the day to enable the complainer's depute to consider his position, and to allow the respondent to be interviewed by the then duty solicitor. When the court reconvened later that day, the respondent failed to appear, and the court accordingly adjourned the diet further until 6 December 1990, and again granted warrant for the apprehension of the respondent.

STAT 5. The Respondent was again arrested, and appeared on 6 December 1990 before said Sheriff Simpson, represented by said solicitor. She was found guilty of contempt of court in respect of her failure to appear on the preceding day, and the diet was continued for sentence until 4 January 1991. Said Sheriff further adjourned the diet for the precognition on oath of the respondent until 4 January 1991; and, despite an objection from the Complainer's depute, decided that the respondent should be allowed to be represented by a solicitor at that diet.

STAT 6. On 4 January 1991, the respondent again appeared before said Sheriff Simpson for precognition on oath. On that date, the complainer's depute attempted to renew the Crown's said objection, but was then confronted for the first time with a copy of a written judgment of said Sheriff on matters arising before him on 6 December 1990 which *inter alia* ruled that the respondent should be allowed to have a solicitor present to offer her advice during the course of her precognition on oath. Accordingly, said depute moved for a further continuation, the diet was adjourned until 8 February 1991 and the respondent was ordained to appear. On 8 February 1991, the respondent again failed to appear and a further warrant for her apprehension was issued. As at 12 February 1991, said warrant had not been executed.

## PLEA IN LAW FOR COMPLAINER

The Sheriff's decision to permit a solicitor acting on behalf of the respondent to be present, and to offer her advice during the course of her precognition on oath by the complainer being unjust, erroneous and contrary to law should be recalled and the said Sheriff should be ordained to proceed with said precognition on oath without a solicitor on behalf of the Respondent being present.

ACCORDING TO JUSTICE

ADVOCATE DEPUTE

HIGH COURT OF JUSTICIARY

Unto the Right Honourable The
Lord Justice Clerk and Lord
Commissioners of Justiciary

BILL OF SUSPENSION

for

RICHARD WILSON, or Broomberry Farm, Ayr,
COMPLAINER

against

S R HOUSTON, PROCURATOR FISCAL,
County Buildings, Lanark, RESPONDENT

HUMBLY MEANS AND SHEWS YOUR SERVITOR RICHARD WILSON

that the complainer in under necessity of applying to your Lordships for suspension of a pretended conviction and sentence dated 3 June 1987 whereby the Sheriff at Lanark found the complainer guilty of a charge of contravention of sections 81 and 89 of the Road Traffic Regulation Act 1984 most wrongously and unjustly as they appear to your Lordships prior to the annexed Statement of Fact and Note of Pleas-In-Law.

THEREFORE the complainer prays your Lordships to grant warrant for service copy of this bill and deliverance thereon on the said Procurator Fiscal, Lanark, the respondent; further to grant warrant ordaining the Clerk of the Sheriff Court at Lanark to transmit whole proceedings complained of to the Clerk Justiciary; to suspend the said pretended conviction and sentence simpliciter and to find the complainer entitled to expenses; or to do further or otherwise in the premises as to your Lordships may seem proper according to Justice etc.

## STATEMENT OF FACTS FOR THE COMPLAINER

1. That the complainer was served with a summary complaint at the instance of the respondent charging him *inter alia* that on 26 January 1987 on Ayr Road, Rigside, District of Clydeside, being a restricted road in terms on section 82 of the Road Traffic Regulation Act 1984 he did drive a motor vehicle, namely motor lorry registered

number SSG 958S at a speed exceeding thirty miles per hour, namely at a speed of 44 miles per hour, contrary to the Road Traffic Regulation Act 1984, sections 81 and 89. A copy of said summary complaint is appended hereto.

2. On 3 June 1987 the complainer answered the complaint at Lanark Sheriff Court and pled guilty to said charge. The Sheriff at Lanark imposed a fine on the complainer of £25 and ordered his driving licence to be endorsed with three penalty points.

3. It has subsequently come to the attention of the Crown that the said stretch of road was not a restricted road in terms of section 82 of the Road Traffic Regulation Act 1984 at the time of the alleged offence. The Crown have drawn this to the attention of the complainer and have indicated they will not oppose this bill.

4. The complainer is under necessity of applying, to your Lordships for suspension of said pretended conviction and sentence.

PLEAS-IN-LAW

1. The said plea of guilty having been tendered in error, the conviction should be quashed.

2. That in the whole circumstances complained of the said conviction and sentence following thereon should be quashed.

IN RESPECT WHEREOF

# HIGH COURT OF JUSTICIARY

## BILL OF SUSPENSION

Unto The Right Honourable the Lord Justice General, Lord Justice Clerk and Lords Commissioners of Justiciary

for

MONTGOMERY TRANSPORT LIMITED, 607 Antrim Road, Newtonabbey, Glengormley, County Antrim, Northern Ireland, COMPLAINERS

against

FRANCIS WALKINGSHAW, Procurator Fiscal, Sheriff Court House, Stranraer, RESPONDENT

HUMBLY SHEWETH AND SHOWS YOUR SERVITORS MONTGOMERY TRANSPORT LIMITED

that the complainers are under the necessity of applying to your Lordships for suspension of a pretended conviction and sentence dated 10 December 1990, whereby Ramsay R Dalgety, Queen's Counsel, Temporary Sheriff of South Strathclyde, Dumfries and Galloway at Stranraer found the complainers guilty on their own plea of a purported contravention of section 41 of the Road Traffic Act 1988 along with Michael Spence therein named and designed and therefor fined the complainers in the sum of ONE THOUSAND POUNDS (£1,000) most wrongeously and unjustly as will appear to your Lordships from the annexed statement of facts and note of plea-in-law. THEREFOR the complainers pray your Lordships to grant: warrant for serving a copy of this bill and deliverance thereon on the said Francis Walkingshaw, Procurator Fiscal at Stranraer, the respondent, AND FURTHER to grant warrant ordaining the Clerk of the Sheriff Court at Stranraer to transmit the whole proceedings complained of to the Clerk of Justiciary; to suspend the said pretended conviction and sentence simpliciter and to find the complainers entitled to the expense or to do further or otherwise in the premises as to your Lordships may seem proper.

ACCORDING TO JUSTICE Etc

## STATEMENT OF FACTS FOR THE COMPLAINERS

1. The complainers are Montgomery Transport Limited, a company incorporated under the Companies Acts and having a place of business at 607 Antrim Road, Newtonabbey, Glengormley, County Antrim, Northern Ireland.

2. That the complainers were charged at the instance of the respondent along with Michael Spence that they, being the owners of a vehicle, namely an articulated motor lorry registered number YIA 3288 did by the hands of their servant and employee, the said Michael Spence, use the said vehicle when the train weight of the vehicle exceeded the maximum train weight in Great Britain as shown in the plate affixed to the said vehicle, in terms of regulation 66 of the Road Vehicles (Construction and Use) regulations 1986 and regulation 80(1)(a) and the Road Traffic Act 1988, section 41, all as more fully set out in the said summary complaint, a copy of which is appended hereto.

3. That the said complaint called in the Sheriff Court at Stranraer on 19 November 1990, and was continued without plea until 10 December 1990. That the said complaint was determined by a plea of guilty being tendered and minuted on 10 December 1990. That the preceding Sheriff, Ramsay Dalgety, Queen's Counsel, Temporary Sheriff at Stranraer fined the complainers in the sum of ONE THOUSAND POUNDS (£1,000).

4. That section 41 of the Road Traffic Act 1988 provides *inter alia* that the Secretary of State may make regulations generally as to the use of motor vehicles. That the said Regulations, namely the Vehicle (Construction and Use Regulations) 1986 are Regulations to which the said section applies. That section 41 of the Road Traffic Act 1988 does not specify any offence. That the Road Traffic Offenders Act 1988, Schedule 2 provides *inter alia* the maximum sentences which can be imposed in respect of offences under the Road Traffic Act 1988. That the said schedule does not provide any penalty for any purported contravention of Section 41 of the Road Traffic Act 1988.

5. The complainers believe and aver that the said complaint at the instance of the respondent is a fundamental nullity. That the proceedings at the instance of the respondent were determined on 10 December 1990, that in the whole circumstances the complainers are under the necessity of seeking suspension of the said pretended conviction and sentence following thereon as incompetent.

6. *Esto*, the said conviction and sentence were competent which is denied, the sentence imposed was in any event in the whole circumstances excessive. The complainers are a company incorporated under the Companies Acts. They have no previous convictions libelled. The complainers are carrying on a business as haulage contractors. On the date of the said offence, the said Michael Spence was instructed to collect a trailer, pre-loaded, from the premises of Abbey Meat Packers Limited at Newtonabbey, County Antrim. That the said Spence collected the said trailer together with a delivery note showing the net weight of the load at 18,941 kilogrammes. Said weight purported to be within the maximum weight permissible being so overall gross train weight of 38,000 kilogrammes. The said Montgomery Transport Limited had regularly transported loads from the said Abbey Meat Packers Limited for a period of about ten years. The said premises were in the course of being closed down, as a result of which there was no weighbridge available to enable the said Spence to check the alleged weight shown on the delivery note.

7. That the said vehicle was weighed at Larne prior to being boarded on the Larne to Stranraer Ferry. On being weighed, it was found the maximum gross train weight of 38,000 kilogrammes wag exceeded by 1,370 kilogrammes being a 3.6% overweight. Notwithstanding that the said vehicle was found to be overweight it was permitted to proceed to the ferry for transportation to Stranraer. On arrival at Stranraer, the vehicle was again checked and found again to be overweight as a result of which it was impounded but subsequently released to the complainers premises in Stranraer.

8. The complainers believe and aver that the imposition of a fine of £1,000 was in the whole circumstances excessive. The complainers are a company operating about 200 heavy goods vehicles and 700 trailers. They employ reliable drivers, including the said Spence, who had 13 years experience. They relied, in the absence of a weighbridge, to check the weight at the premises of the said Abbey Meat Packers Limited on the delivery note supplied by the said Abbey Meat Packers Limited. That the weight exceeded was only 3.6% above the maximum weight permitted and the said Regulations were breached by the complainers in reliance upon a delivery note over which they and their employees had no control and in particular in respect of a trailer which had been loaded by the employees of the said Abbey Meat Packers Limited. The complainers believe that *esto* the said complaint was incompetent. The said sentence was in any event in the whole circumstances

excessive. They accordingly seek suspension of the said pretended sentence.

## PLEAS-IN-LAW

1. The said complaint disclosing no relevant offence the bill should be passed simpliciter.

2. *Esto* the said Complaint contains a relevant charge, the sentence imposed was in any event excessive and the bill should be passed suspending the sentence simpliciter.

IN RESPECT WHEREOF

## HIGH COURT OF JUSTICIARY

Unto the Right Honourable the
Lord Justice General, Lord
Justice Clerk and the Lords
Commissioners of Justiciary

## BILL of SUSPENSION

for

MARTIN CUNNINGHAM, COMPLAINER

against

JOHN GREGORY McGLENNAN, Procurator Fiscal,
Kilmarnock, RESPONDENT

HUMBLY MEANS AND SHEWS YOUR SERVITOR, MARTIN CUNNINGHAM, COMPLAINER:

That the complainer is under the necessity of applying to your Lordships for suspension of a pretended sentence dated on or about 22 May 1991 whereby Sheriff Croan at Kilmarnock sentenced the complainer to a period of imprisonment in respect of charges 1, 2, 3, 4, 5 and 6 contained in the complaint, more particularly described in Schedule I, most wrongously and unjustly as will appear to your Lordships from the annexed statement-of-facts and note of plea-in-law; Therefore the complainer prays your Lordships to grant warrant for serving a copy of this bill and deliverance thereon on the said JOHN GREGORY McGLELLAN, respondent; AND FURTHER to grant warrant ordaining the Clerk of the Sheriff Court at Kilmarnock to transmit the whole of the said proceedings complained of to the Clerk of Justiciary; to suspend the said pretended sentence *simpliciter*; and to suspend the said purported sentence *ad interim* and grant Interim Liberation and to find the complainer entitled to expenses; in the meantime, to grant interim suspension as craved; or to do otherwise or further in the premises as to your Lordships may seem proper.

ACCORDING TO JUSTICE, etc.

## STATEMENT-of-FACTS for COMPLAINER

1. That the complainer is Martin Cunningham, who was convicted in the Sheriff Court at Kilmarnock in relation to the charges

set out in Schedule I on the 4 December, 1990. The complainer was placed on Probation for a period of two years in relation to said charges with the condition that he undergo the alternative project scheme.

2. On 27 December 1990, the complainer appeared at Kilmarnock Sheriff Court on complaint in respect of one charge. The complainer was remanded in custody until 3 January 1991. The complainer was charged with charges more particularly described in Schedule II. The trial diet was fixed for 25 January 1991 and the complainer was remanded in custody until said date. On 25 January 1991 the complainer pled guilty to charges 2, 3, 4 and 6 on said complaint and sentence was deferred until 12 February 1991, in order that a social enquiry report be prepared. On 12 February on which date the social enquiry report was before the Court, the social work department put forward all the papers in relation to the breach of probation. Sheriff Russell indicated that he was not prepared to deal with the sentence in relation to the first complaint where probation had been granted in terms of section 388 of the Criminal Procedure (Scotland) Act 1975. The said Sheriff sentenced the complainer to four months' imprisonment from 12 February in relation to the charges 2, 3, 4 and 6 of the second complaint. The said Sheriff did not deal with the sentence in relation to the first complaint. The complainer's local agent asked Sheriff Russell to defer matters so as Sheriff Croan could deal with the matters together on the following Monday. This was refused. The complainer's agent repeatedly requested that the matter be dealt with at an early date.

3. On 22 May 1991, two days before the complainer's release on 24 May 1991 the complainer appeared to be sentenced in relation to the charges 1, 3, 4 and 6 contained in the first complaint (see Schedule I). The complainer was sentenced to three months in relation to the above charges and in relation to charges 2 and 5, the complainer was sentenced to thirty days.

4. The complainer should have had both complaints dealt with by the same Sheriff rather than delaying the sentence in relation to the first Complaint for three months before sentencing the complainer. The complainer has been in custody from 27 December 1990 and is due to remain in custody until August 1991. The complainer is 17 years old.

5. The complainer is under the necessity of applying to your Lordships for suspension of the sentences of the Sheriff on 22 May 1991. The said Sheriff acted harshly and oppressively in not sentencing the complainer in February 1991. That in the

circumstances it was harsh and oppressive to sentence the complainer on 22 May 1991 to a further period of imprisonment. In these circumstances the said sentence imposed in respect of the charges in complaint one should be suspended *simpliciter*.

## PLEA-IN-LAW

1. The imposition of a period of imprisonment on 22 May 1991 being excessive, the said sentence should be suspended and the Bill passed *simpliciter*.

IN RESPECT WHEREOF,

## SCHEDULE I — FIRST COMPLAINT
## SCHEDULE II — SECOND COMPLAINT

# HIGH COURT OF JUSTICIARY

## BILL OF SUSPENSION

Unto the Right Honourable the
Lord Justice General, Lord
Justice Clerk and Lords
Commissioners of Justiciary

## BILL OF SUSPENSION

for

THOMAS ANTHONY CURRIE, presently a Prisoner in the Prison of Barlinnie, Glasgow, COMPLAINER

against

JOHN G. McGLENNAN, Procurator Fiscal, Kilmarnock, RESPONDENT

HUMBLY MEANS AND SHOWS your Servitor, THOMAS ANTHONY CURRIE — Complainer.

THAT the complainer under the necessity of applying to your Lordships for suspension of a pretended warrant dated on or about the 10 day of July 1989 whereby Sheriff Croan Esquire, Sheriff of North Strathclyde at Kilmarnock granted warrant to the respondent, following upon a Petition at the instance of the respondent dated 6 July 1989, to compel the complainer to take part in an identification parade, most wrongously and unjustly as will appear to your Lordships from the annexed statements of facts and note of pleas in law.

THEREFORE the complainer prays your Lordships to grant warrant for serving a copy of this bill and deliverance thereon on the said John G McGlennan the respondent, and further to grant warrant ordaining the Clerk of the Sheriff Court at Kilmarnock to transmit the whole proceedings complained of to the Clerk of Justiciary; to suspend the said pretended warrant simpliciter and to find the complainer entitled to expenses; or to do otherwise or further in the premises as to your Lordships may seem proper.

ACCORDING TO JUSTICE

## STATEMENT OF FACTS FOR THE COMPLAINER

1. That on 5 June 1989 the complainer, the said Thomas Anthony Currie and others appeared at Kilmarnock Sheriff Court on a petition at the instance of the respondent, charged with murder and were committed for further examination in custody.

2. That on 13 June 1989 the complainer and others appeared at Kilmarnock Sheriff Court on a second petition at the instance of the respondent charged with murder and contravention of the Misuse of Drugs Act 1971, section 4(3) and were committed until liberated in due course of law.

3. That on 10 July 1989 the respondent presented a petition in Kilmarnock Sheriff Court, craving warrant for Officers of Strathclyde Police to take said Thomas Anthony Currie and others from Barlinnie Prison, Glasgow to 'D' Division, Police Headquarters, Baird Street, Glasgow for the purpose of taking part in an identification parade to be viewed by two named witnesses.

4. That by interlocutor dated 10 July 1989 the learned Sheriff granted a warrant in the terms sought by the respondent.

5. That the complainer respectfully submits that the learned Sheriff erred in the granting of said warrant and that he failed to give proper weight to the interests of the complainer and that in the whole circumstances of the case said warrant is unlawful and oppressive.

## PLEA-IN-LAW FOR THE COMPLAINER

The learned Sheriff's said decision to grant said warrant as craved being unjust, erroneous and contrary to Law should be recalled.

IN RESPECT WHEREOF

# PETITION
of
# JAMES McDONALD SCHIAVONE
to the NOBILE OFFICIUM
of the
# HIGH COURT OF JUSTICIARY

HUMBLY SHEWETH:

1. That the Petitioner appeared on Petition at Stirling Sheriff Court on 15 August 1991 charged with murder. He was judicially examined before Sheriff William Henderson and thereafter committed for further examination in custody, no plea or declaration having been made and a motion for bail being incompetent.

2. That he appeared again on the same petition and charge before Sheriff Henderson on 22 August 1991 and was fully committed until liberated in due course of law. Again, because of the nature of the charge no motion for bail was made.

3. That the petitioner is seventeen years of age, his date of birth being 30 September 1974. He is presently remanded in HM Institution at Longriggend. He has one previous conviction for breach of the peace for which he was sentenced at Stirling Sheriff Court on 3 April 1991 to be on good behaviour. He was due to appear again in respect of that sentence on 23 September 1991. The petitioner was not present in court for the deferred sentence and the court's disposal on 23 September 1991 is not known. The petitioner has no other convictions nor are there any other matters outstanding apart from the present case. At the time of his arrest he was in full time employment and resided with his parents at a fixed address to which he is welcome to return.

4. That following upon instructions given by the petitioner on 19 September 1991 to his legal representatives a section 102 letter indicating the petitioner's wish to plead guilty to a charge of culpable homicide was tendered to the Procurator Fiscal at Stirling. The petitioner was thereafter advised that a letter had been received by his legal representative, Mr Imrie, Solicitor, Falkirk advising him that the reduced plea of culpable homicide was acceptable to the Crown. The section 102 diet is to be held in Edinburgh on 30 October 1991.

5. That the petitioner wishes to make an application for bail pending the holding of the section 102 diet. Since the charge in respect of which he is now to be indicted is no longer murder but culpable homicide a motion for bail is competent. An application for bail was made to Sheriff Henderson at Stirling on 7 October 1991 but was held to be incompetent on the basis that it was made in respect of the original petition, which libelled the charge of murder. In those circumstances the petitioner's legal representative, Mr Imrie, withdrew the said bail application.

6. That the petitioner has no other means of applying for bail. He is accordingly under the necessity of making this application to the Nobile Officium of the High Court of Justiciary.

THE PETITIONER THEREFORE PRAYS THE COURT: To hold that the offence with which he is now charged is bailable, that there are no substantial grounds for refusing bail, that because of his age and personal history it is in the interests of justice that bail be granted and accordingly to admit him to bail pending the holding of said Section 102 diet; and to decern; or to do further or otherwise in the premises as to your Lordships shall seem proper.

ACCORDING TO JUSTICE

# II LEGAL AID

## NOTICE BY DEPUTY PRINCIPAL CLERK OF JUSTICIARY [19 JUNE 1991]

## CRIMINAL AND JUSTICIARY APPEALS: ADJOURNMENT FOR LEGAL AID

In December 1990, the attached Practice Note was issued to all Appeal Court Chairmen and Appeal Court clerks . . . However, following upon a statement made by the Minister (Lord James Douglas-Hamilton) in the House of Commons on 16 April 1991 . . . the Scottish Legal Aid Board have suggested that the contents of the Practice Note should now be brought to the attention of the profession at large. The Lord Justice General . . . has instructed me to advise all Justiciary clerks who undertake responsibility for Criminal and Justiciary Appeals, that, under reference to the aforementioned Practice Note, *adjournments, however, shall only be granted where the criteria set forth in the Practice Note have been satisfied, and they should not be granted as a matter of course merely because an appellant who has been refused legal aid wishes to have the refusal reconsidered.*

J ROBERTSON
Deputy Principal Clerk of Justiciary
19 June 1991

# PRACTICE NOTE

## TO ALL APPEAL COURT CHAIRMEN AND CLERKS

## CRIMINAL AND JUSTICIARY APPEALS: ADJOURNMENTS FOR LEGAL AID

In any appeal where legal aid has been refused and the court considers that, *prima facie*, an appellant may have substantial grounds for taking the appeal and it is in the interests of justice that the appellant should have legal representation in arguing these grounds, the court shall forthwith adjourn the hearing and make a recommendation that the decision to refuse legal aid should be reviewed.

LORD JUSTICE GENERAL
4 December 1990

# Index

When using this index, it should be remembered that appeals in *solemn* cases are dealt with in chapter 2, and appeals in *summary* cases are dealt with in chapter 3. Accordingly the index itself does not always indicate whether the entries relate to a *solemn* or to a *summary* appeal, other than by showing the chapter number as '2' or '3'. Similarly, the powers of the court in *solemn* cases are dealt with in paragraphs 6.01 to 6.13 and the powers of the court in *summary* cases are dealt with in paragraphs 6.14 to 6.20.